TO RAISE MYSELF A LITTLE

TO
RAISE MYSELF
A LITTLE

THE DIARIES AND LETTERS OF JENNIE,
A GEORGIA TEACHER,
1851–1886

AMELIA AKEHURST LINES
EDITED BY THOMAS DYER

THE UNIVERSITY OF GEORGIA PRESS ATHENS

Designed by Sandra Strother
Set in 10 on 12 point Century Schoolbook
PRINTED IN THE UNITED STATES OF AMERICA

Library of Congress Cataloging in Publication Data

Lines, Amelia Akehurst.
To raise myself a little.

Includes bibliographical references and index.
1. Lines, Amelia Akehurst.   2. Teachers—United States—
Biography.   3. Education—Southern states—History—19th
century.   4. Education—Georgia—History—19th century.
I. Dyer, Thomas.   II. Title.
LA2317.L67A37   370'.975   81-301
ISBN 0-8203-0562-6   AACR1

For Anna

Contents

Preface

The diaries and letters of Amelia Akehurst Lines provide a full and rich account of the life of a New York teacher transplanted to Georgia in the middle of the nineteenth century and shed light on a variety of social history topics. Rare and informative descriptions of education in both North and South from the teacher's point of view give special meaning to the documents, and they abound with commentary on internal and external family relationships, childrearing, and lifestyles among the middle class in the South immediately before and after the Civil War. Students of the South will find much to consider with respect to the development of racial ideas in a migrant from the North, the attitudes of northerners toward secession and civil war, and the relationships among southern social classes during the late antebellum period. The documents also reveal the middle-class white yearning for upward social and economic mobility.

These diaries and letters first came to my attention shortly after they were acquired by the University of Georgia Libraries. As a first-quarter graduate student in Kenneth Coleman's historical methodology course at the University of Georgia, I was advised that aspiring historians should early immerse themselves in manuscript collections. A visit to the Special Collections Division of the University of Georgia Libraries brought an introduction to Susan Barrow Tate, who recognized the unique qualities of the Akehurst-Lines Collection and recommended it to me for study. I am indebted to Professor Coleman and to Mrs. Tate for pointing me toward a fascinating and instructive project in historical editing.

During the five years that I have worked actively on this volume, I have accumulated debts to a large number of people. Besides Mrs. Tate, other staff members of the Special Collections Division have been extremely helpful. I am especially obliged to Robert M. Willingham, Jr., J. Larry Gulley, and Anthony Dees, now director of the Georgia Historical Society, dedicated professionals who repeatedly facilitated the often tedious task of transcribing and editing the manuscript.

I am especially indebted to several members of the staff of the Institute of Higher Education, the University of Georgia, who also aided in the project. Nancy Szypulski transcribed substantial portions of the diaries, and my research assistant, Diane Smathers, read and criticized the Introduction. Cindy Burt and Bridget Tester expertly typed the manuscript, and Mary Snyder helped in many ways. As always, Cameron L. Fincher, director of the Institute, exemplifies the best in department chairmen in his strong support of faculty research efforts.

I am also obliged to several friends and colleagues who encouraged the completion of the project. Clarence L. Mohr of the Frederick Douglass Papers, Yale University, used the collection in his own research and confirmed my belief in the need for its publication. James C. Cobb of the University of Northern Iowa lent strong moral support. Lester D. Stephens of the University of Georgia offered frequent and valuable counsel on a variety of matters. Numan V. Bartley of the University of Georgia pointed to the necessity of completing one major research project before undertaking another. I rejected his advice, but we remain friends. Charles Crowe, also of the University of Georgia, continued his strong support of a former student.

Finally, my gratitude goes to Anna Burns Dyer, whose good humor persists and whose tolerance for the idiosyncrasies of historians knows few bounds. In the end, however, it is her facilitation of the adjustment of another northerner to a contented life in the South that brings me to dedicate this book to her.

T.D.

Methodological Note

The transcription of the diaries and letters contained in the Akehurst-Lines Collection at the University of Georgia yielded nearly one thousand typewritten pages. Diaries exist for the years 1855–65 and for 1871, but the diary for 1856 is badly faded and almost completely illegible. The collection also contains a brief journal kept by Anna Maria Lines Akehurst. There are over three hundred letters and letter fragments. The collection was a gift to the University of Georgia from Mrs. Katy Calhoun of Atlanta, Georgia. Mrs. Calhoun, a stepniece of Anna Maria Lines Akehurst, was also a correspondent of Daisy Lines.

Spelling and punctuation have been altered only where indicated. A series of three asterisks within the body of a diary entry or letter indicates that material has been eliminated. Asterisks after an entry or letter indicate that one or more diary entries have been deleted.

Editorial intrusions have been kept to a minimum. Those individuals crucial to the narrative have been identified where possible.

To aid the reader, I have constructed a chronology of Jennie's life. Where there are doubts about the accuracy of dates, I have so indicated with question marks.

T.D.

AMELIA JANE AKEHURST LINES
CHRONOLOGY

1827?	Born, England
1829	Arrived in America
1841–43	In the West
1843–57	New York; began teaching as early as 1850
February 17, 1857	Arrived in Georgia
February 19, 1857– October 14, 1857	Euharlee, Bartow County, Georgia
October 14, 1857– January ?, 1858	Atlanta
January 18?, 1858– April 5, 1858	Stilesboro, Bartow County, Georgia [date of arrival uncertain; that given is first letter from Stilesboro]
April 15, 1858– June 5, 1858	Atlanta; Oxford, Newton County, Georgia
June 5, 1858– September 2?, 1858	Sardis Church community, Walton County, Georgia
September 6, 1858– September 14, 1858	Oxford, Newton County, Georgia
September 15, 1858– July 2, 1859	Covington, Newton County, Georgia
July 10?, 1859– August ?, 1859	Oxford
August 11, 1859	Married to Sylvanus DeForrest Lines
August 12?, 1859– September 3, 1859	Fayetteville, Fayette County, Georgia
September 4, 1859– January 6, 1860	Fayetteville
January 6, 1860– May ?, 1860	Newnan
May ?, 1860– July 28, 1860	Atlanta

July 28, 1860–   Marietta
August 29, 1860

August 29, 1860–   Atlanta
January 9, 1861

January 11, 1861–   Greenville, Meriwether County, Georgia
March 1862

January 23, 1862   Birth of Forrest Lillie Lines

March 1862–   Atlanta
July ?, 1864

May 1, 1863–   Visiting in Columbus, Georgia
June 2, 1863

September 21, 1863   Death of Lillie

July ?, 1864–   Columbus, Georgia
September 1865

August 7, 1864   Birth of Forrest Daisy Lines

September 1865–1869   New Haven, Connecticut

1866   Birth of Herbert Lines

1869?   Death of Herbert Lines

1869?–86   Macon, Georgia [with three months in Con-
                        necticut and New York in 1871]

1875?   Death of Sylvanus Lines

May 14, 1886   Death of Amelia Akehurst Lines

A NINETEENTH-CENTURY MAP
OF GEORGIA

Right: Amelia Jane Akehurst Lines
Left: Sylvanus DeForrest Lines
Center: Herbert Lines and Forrest Daisy Lines
Courtesy of University of Georgia Libraries,
Special Collections

PRINCIPALS

Amelia Jane Akehurst Lines, 1827?–86

Sylvanus DeForrest Lines, 1830–75?

Forrest Lillie Lines, 1862–63

Forrest Daisy Lines, 1864–1912

Herbert Lines, 1866–69?

Anna Maria Lines Akehurst
Cady Barham, 1822–96?

Introduction

"I have felt very ambitious to raise myself a little and to be something in the world," Amelia Jane Akehurst, New York schoolteacher in her mid-twenties, wrote to her sister-in-law in 1852. An aspiring member of the middle class, "Jennie" Akehurst wrote numerous letters during the period 1851 through 1886 and for much of the same time kept a series of journals. Together, the journals and the letters comprise a rare and extraordinarily rich record of the attitudes, values, and ambition of a white, middle-class American woman of the mid-nineteenth century.

Born in England, brought by her parents to the United States at age two, educated in New York, and transplanted to the South four years before the Civil War, Jennie Akehurst is representative of a large number of young women who relied upon themselves for support and worked hard toward the fulfillment of personal versions of the American dream. Despite the many social and economic constraints imposed on women by a male-dominated society, Jennie Akehurst had a powerful conviction that social and economic achievement would come to those who were diligent and worked hard. And, like many of her contemporaries in Jacksonian America, the ambitious Jennie never realized her dream. In that sense, her life is testimony to the mythical quality of the conventional wisdom that hard work, piety, and personal commitment were all that were needed to reap the promise of American life in the mid-nineteenth century.

Jennie's journals and letters, however, are a great deal more than an account of imperfectly realized ambition. They constitute a full chronicle of the life of a schoolteacher in a variety of school settings in both North and South and present an unusually candid picture of the competitiveness and the tedium of teaching during that time. The journal and letters also reveal much about the social relations and attitudes of the "genteel poor" and about Jennie's intense efforts to come to terms with her own religious values. In equal detail, Jennie's writings illuminate the broader political, economic, and social values of middle-class

American women and yield a great deal of information concerning family life, childrearing, and other facets of everyday life. Most significant, perhaps, these documents collectively supply an autobiography of a middle-class, white woman of the mid-nineteenth century.

Jennie Akehurst grew up in the Clinton, New York, area in a family that lived in a spartan atmosphere of Protestant piety. Her father, James, a tanner, brought his wife and young family to New York from England when Jennie was two. Early childhood was a happy time, "free from care and trouble," but the halcyon days ended in 1838 when her mother contracted consumption. Knowing that she would not survive, Mrs. Akehurst and her husband concluded that he would be unable to care for the children alone and that they must disperse their offspring into the care of "kind friends" who would provide good homes. Eleven-year-old Jennie found a place in the home of "a couple of her mother's choosing" and three years later joined her new family on a sojourn in the West.

In 1843 Jennie returned to her newly remarried father's home. The family now included Jennie, sisters Emma and Sarah, and brothers Joseph, Henry, and Charles. Nineteen-year-old Emma soon died from consumption and within a year the dreaded disease killed Sarah. Six weeks later, an infant half-sister died and shortly thereafter, Joseph, who had recently married, also died. These deaths, that of her mother, and other deaths in her family circle gradually darkened Jennie's views of life and deepened her religiosity.[1]

As a young woman, however, Jennie Akehurst had a zest for living to accompany her strong ambition. Probably educated in the common schools in New Hartford and Clinton, she seems to have obtained her professional credentials in teacher-training institutes.[2] After her schooling she began a search for a suitable position in the pleasant environs of the neat villages of upstate New York, near her home in New Hartford. Like many young women who entered teaching in the days before widespread public schools, Jennie had to develop clientele willing to pay her to educate their children in the rudiments of reading, writing, and ciphering. In addition, her role as teacher demanded that she serve the community in several other ways, as nursemaid, chaperone, and cultural arbiter. Her life in the villages in which she taught before she reached her mid-twenties was not unpleasant; she particularly enjoyed the wintertime rounds of skating and sleighing, springtime debates and commencements at a nearby college, and opportunities for conversing with educated men and women about literary, religious, political, and social topics.

Jennie had a good mind and used it to probe a number of topics of special interest. She explored religious subjects with special fervor and speculated imaginatively upon metaphysical matters. She was also capable of deep introspection and frequently embarked on excursions into self-criticism, peering closely at aspects of her own character that she thought deficient. Her reading ranged widely. She was especially fond of Martin Tupper's inspirational poetry and enjoyed an occasional romantic novel. While in her twenties she also read Milton's *Paradise Lost*, a professional journal, theological discourses, and religious tracts. A book on demonology and witchcraft, the complete works of Byron, a biography of Oliver Cromwell, Sir Walter Scott's *Ivanhoe*, Petrarch's *Lives*, various Shakespearean works, and Alexander Pope's poetry were part of one year's reading.

Most of her personal values took shape before she moved to the South. Like many antebellum Americans, she idealized male-female roles and romantic love. And, though she imbibed some of the conventional notions of the "cult of true womanhood,"[3] her reading, her diary entries, and her behavior showed that she rejected the notion that women had little to contribute outside the home. She displayed a remarkable piety that conformed with the "true womanhood" beliefs, and she tended to view women as special guardians of virtue. Although this did not mean that she felt that men had a lesser duty to behave according to scriptural standards, she did concede that men played more active roles in society, and she occasionally envied their greater freedom. Yet the diaries and letters disclose in great detail the actual circumstances of Jennie's life, circumstances that were infinitely more complex than those contained in the simplistic behavioral models constructed for nineteenth-century women in the prescriptive literature of the day.[4]

Jennie's views of society showed in her attitudes toward the various social groups with which she had contact. She disliked aristocrats and aristocratic pretension, had a similar distaste for the lower classes of the rural areas, and gradually acquired a strong animus toward blacks. Her views on social relations were conventionally genteel; protocol governed even casual contacts between people, and an elaborate code of behavior ruled the courtship ritual, a fact amply demonstrated in the graceful letters she exchanged with her husband prior to their marriage. Complex standards also ruled behavior on the Sabbath, but a weary Jennie occasionally violated these. Jennie had strong ideas about the value of work and occupational status. Above all, she approved the "active" life and had a concomitant disdain for sloth. She held physicians and the educated ministry in high esteem and thought highly of educators but fretted about the low prestige of her own calling. She admired musical, artistic, and literary accomplishment and published a few brief essays of her own.

In physical appearance, Jennie was small and perhaps frail. She described herself as "plain" and envied more attractive women. Perhaps this self-image accounted in part for her extreme shyness and her frequently expressed fear of meeting strangers.

Throughout her life, she experienced a succession of often unnamed illnesses that left her in frequent pain.[5] And, like most Americans in the days before aspirin and antibiotics, she had a number of painful "minor" complaints, suffering particularly from toothache in an era when dentistry was little more advanced than blacksmithing.

As early as 1851, Jennie showed signs of dissatisfaction with her life. Teaching grew tedious, pupils were unruly, and parents ungrateful. The hopeless quest for a secure, well-paying position in an area where teachers were neither well esteemed nor well paid prompted occasional thoughts of leaving New York for the opportunities of the West or perhaps the South, where her brother Joseph's widow lived. Although an occasional trip to a teacher-training institute brought some relief, Jennie increasingly felt a restlessness common to mid-nineteenth-century Americans. Like many other men and women, she rebelled at the lack of opportunity she perceived in the older part of the country in which she lived.

In 1852, prospects for change appeared with a letter from her widowed sister-in-law, Anna Maria Lines Akehurst, milliner, orphanage matron, and sometime teacher. Maria had grown close to Jennie after she married Joseph Akehurst, Jennie's oldest brother. After Joseph's death, the two women became fast friends and through the years developed a relationship in which Maria seems to have served not only as a confidant and friend, but also as a source of occasional financial aid and advice.[6] A surplus of teachers in New York had made it more difficult than usual for Jennie to find a school, and now she considered the possibility of migrating to Georgia. Perhaps she could come for the winter, she thought, and suggested to her sister-in-law that they rent two rooms, one for a hat shop, the other for a schoolroom.

Indecision and reluctance to leave her family prevented her going to Georgia, but she kept the idea alive in complaints to Maria of the oppressive New York social climate and in expressions of concern about her status. The social structure of town life in upstate New York seemed inflexible and thwarted not only professional ambitions but also foreclosed opportunity for upward mobility. She told her sister-in-law, "here I have no society for those with whom I would associate with look down upon me and those with whom I suppose I am classed *I cannot and will not* have anything to say to." "All I ask," she wrote, "is to be respected" and "have a place in respectable society."

For the next four years, Jennie stayed in New York, moving from school to school and engaging in the constant search for students that made teaching in mid-nineteenth-century America an entrepreneurial activity. In 1857, however, she finally resolved to leave for Georgia and seek opportunity in the South.

For Jennie the trip was an odyssey. Arriving in New York City at the end of the first leg of her journey, she peered down from her room on the fourth floor of the St. Nicholas ("the largest hotel in New York") and excitedly noted that the men and women below looked like little children. In Philadelphia, she tripped nimbly across the frozen Schuylkill River on planks laid from one cake of ice to another. "Many of the gentlemen expressed a great deal of fear and anxiety," but she "heard not a word from the ladies" and thought that "they displayed more courage than the gentlemen." From Philadelphia she journeyed to Washington, where she witnessed preparations for the inauguration of James Buchanan. The White House, she supposed, would soon be "Mr. Buchannan's home." She thought it "quite to bad to have an old bachelor live there all alone" and mused that perhaps the new president would "prevail upon some lady to share the house with him."

A visit to the Senate found "the senators . . . in their seats disputing and disagreeing about an appropriation for a railroad through Iowa." Jennie seemed less interested, however, in the politics of sectionalism than in the famous men who sat in that body during the late 1850s. Charles Sumner of Massachusetts held a special fascination. "Saw Mr. Sumner's seat where he was so shamefully abused by Brooks," she wrote in her diary. "Mr. S. is a very tall man and his desk is raised a little higher than the others."

The remainder of the trip through the Virginia and Carolina countryside passed quickly, and when Jennie arrived in the old Georgia city of Augusta she was captivated by its early springtime beauty and by the pleasant surroundings at the Planters Hotel, where she stayed before proceeding by rail to Atlanta. By comparison, Atlanta seemed backward and dirty, and Jennie began to worry about what awaited her to the north at her destination, the crossroads settlement of Euharlee, where her sister-in-law had found her a teaching position. On the bumpy stage ride to Cartersville, her uneasiness increased, and as she rode the hack from Cartersville still farther into the Georgia interior, she gradually realized that she would be living on the edge of the frontier. "I must say I am disappointed in the appearance of the place," she later wrote in her diary. "They told me it was a new place and I did not expect to see a village but I thought at least to see *one* street and a few pretty dwellings. I did not think I was to find a home among the trees." Bouts with homesickness compounded the difficulties of adjustment. But four days after her arrival, the school term began and Jennie plunged into the business of teaching in an effort to make a success of her new situation.

The diaries and letters are not only rich in detail about teaching in various settings but also offer numerous observations about such persistent educational concerns as optimum class size, the assessment of student performance, and maintenance of student interest. Jennie conceived of education broadly. She emphasized the acquisition of fundamentals in the various divisions of knowledge, but also believed that she had a strong obligation to instruct her charges in morality and proper behavior. Scriptural readings and prayer in the classroom (a controversial requirement in at least one school in which she taught) pointed toward the implantation of Christian beliefs, while detailed instruction in etiquette was intended to introduce her students to the refining influences of mid-nineteenth-century gentility.

The frustration Jennie encountered as a teacher and the daily tedium of the job gradually robbed her of any deep satisfaction the calling might have provided.[7] At Euharlee, she conducted a contract school where parents paid a fee each twenty-week term and contributed to the maintenance of the building. Although the setting for her "woodsy and lonely" school contrasted sharply with the village schools she had known in New York, her initial dismay at the remoteness of the location turned into a professional observation that the quietness of the forest made a very good environment for a school. Jennie thought the children better behaved but less inquisitive than her New York pupils, and she watched with pride as their academic proficiency improved over the course of the term. Relations with her patrons were good except for an occasional parental comment that the school day should be lengthened, a suggestion that met a firm rejection from Jennie, who commented in her diary that "neither law nor custom requires me to teach more than *six hours*."

Jennie's job remained pleasant enough through the spring and summer, but the arrival of autumn and cotton-picking time found her totally unprepared for the depletion in enrollment that accompanied the annual harvest. As picking progressed, the number of students in the schoolroom declined drastically and so did Jennie's income. When a neighbor told her that schools always closed during cotton picking, Jennie confided in her diary that if she had possessed that bit of information she would have been "loth" to take charge of the school in the first place. A town girl's dislike for the rural environment and her irritation over the enforced harvest vacation prompted her to leave Euharlee to seek steadier and more lucrative teaching in Atlanta.

When she discovered the keen competition among teachers in the city, Jennie regretted the decision to leave Euharlee. Although country life had been primitive, the cost of living had been low, and she had saved most of her earnings. In Atlanta, respectable lodgings were expensive, and competition for students made prospects for a satisfactory income uncertain. Nonetheless, within a few days after her arrival, she rented a schoolroom and made calls upon parents. Despite her best efforts, enrollment remained low, and she began to worry about balancing income and expenses. After long days in the classroom, she called upon prospective patrons, stressing her years of experience and the salutary aspects of education. The young teacher decided to advertise and composed a notice for a local newspaper:

A SCHOOL FOR GIRLS UNDER FIFTEEN, BOYS UNDER EIGHT
AT THE FOLLOWING TERMS
Twelve weeks in a term, four terms in a year
Primary studies per term $5;
Common English branches $7;
Higher English branches $9.

Unfulfilled promises to send children to her school made Jennie lose "all confidence" in the people of Atlanta, and she reluctantly decided to return to a rural location.

In her new position, Jennie tutored the children of a plantation owner and his wife who lived near Stilesboro, a few miles from Euharlee in Bartow County. The job seemed to promise security and a comfortable life, but Jennie was unprepared for the additional duties of caring for the children that occupied what had formerly been spare time. This unpleasant discovery led to confrontations with the mistress of the house, whose style of life the young teacher despised. Jennie wrote to a friend of her profound frustration at being the "governess in the family of a Georgia planter whose wife through a *false* education is not capable of giving one word of advice or making one wise suggestion in regard to the training of her own children." Resentful at being treated as a servant, she began the familiar search for another job, and when a replacement appeared, Jennie hurriedly accepted a position in a rural area of Walton County, fifty miles east of Atlanta.

Her new school, located near Sardis Church community not far from Monroe, had been organized in much the same manner as the one near Euharlee, but Jennie found the school and the surrounding area even more primitive. The Euharlee students had been courteous and bright, but Walton County pupils differed in both ability and demeanor from their northwest Georgia cousins. They were "so ignorant and so little acquainted with the improvements of the day" that Jennie doubted whether she would be able to please her patrons and gloomily forecast that she would be expected to teach from sunrise to sunset. Jennie felt a special obligation to introduce the girls to the rudiments of courtesy and proper behavior, but in spite of her efforts, she saw little improvement and often despaired of teaching students who had "so little refinement of feeling and cultivation of mind." She longed for a school in town, but memories of the anxiety that had accompanied the Atlanta experience stayed thoughts of an early return to the more competitive urban environment.

In the Walton County school, a strong sense of professionalism and a disposition that recoiled at parental interference led to occasional confrontations. Perhaps the most unusual of these occurred when a woman complained about Jennie's habit of beginning each day's classes with a prayer. When the young teacher heard of the complaint, she wrote at length in her diary about the problem and decided that her antagonist was a "meddlesome mischief making woman . . . ignorant, ill-bred and conceited."

Such unpleasant incidents convinced her to search for yet another job. Her strong desire to find work out of "the woods," where she might have opportunities for social contact with "polite" society, led her to deemphasize salary. In fact, pay for teachers in Georgia was considerably better than in New York and, while working only about three-fourths of the time during her first year, she had amassed nearly eight hundred dollars despite the difficulties of collecting from some patrons. Thus, when letter writing and personal contacts brought an offer for a different kind of teaching position, Jennie left Walton County with few regrets.

Her new position was as an instructor in the preparatory division of the Southern Female Masonic College in Covington, Georgia. Like most of the forty-odd female "colleges" in the state, this institution offered secondary instruction that placed strong emphasis on ornamental education—the acquisition of the social graces and skills prized by the antebellum elite. Friends resided in Covington, and Jennie looked forward to socializing and hoped for occasional trips to nearby Emory College to attend the college debates and disquisitions she had enjoyed in New York. Upon arrival in Covington, however, she found that she was expected to live with "college girls" aged twelve to fourteen. Gracefully written journal entries now became terse and choppy as Jennie tried to write while her young roommates chatted and cavorted nearby. "Dear journal," she wrote in one moment of acute frustration, "I cannot get one moment alone with you. Can not even be alone long enough to read my bible unmolested. I can not endure long to be thus obliged to be continually in the company of those with whom I have no congeniality." Evenings formerly spent in reading and writing were now given over to anxious concern that the absence of "inteligent [sic] substantial society" would cause her to lose "ground in regard to *mental culture*."

The frequent moves from one area of the state to another gave Jennie ample opportunity to observe Georgia society. Although she was aware of the complexity of the southern social structure, her interpretations of Georgia society reflected her staunch middle-class values. Early observations of Georgians convinced her that they "dress talk and eat and do everything different from the northern people," but as she adjusted to new surroundings the differences seemed less pronounced. At Euharlee and again in Covington she quickly made friends with "substantial" citizens and discovered few boundaries to social acceptance. On the whole, she thought the farmers, merchants, ministers, and doctors with whom she came in contact to be congenial society with values little different from hers, and it was in the company of those who belonged to or aspired to membership in this broad segment of southern society that she felt most at home. Her marriage to Maria's cousin, Sylvanus Lines, an amiable Connecticut-born printer, in August 1859, further solidified her attachment to the middle class.

Although her reaction to middling Georgians was positive, she had a strong and persistent dislike for the upper and lower classes of white society. Her disdain for the plantation elite showed plainly in her scathing condemnation of the "butterfly existence" of the Bartow County plantation mistress for whom she had tutored. Jennie's observation of the planter's wife led to the generalization that "one reared in the halls of fashion and wealth is but poorly fitted for the stern realities of life." She was thankful that she had avoided the "folly and sin" of such an existence and that her life had "of necessity been a *practical* one." A broader condemnation of privilege appeared in her reaction to residents of Augusta whom she encountered while staying at a Marietta hotel. "We have a crowd here from Augusta," she wrote, "they seem oblivious to every thing but their own comfort and amusement." This "promiscuous crowd" slept "half the day and then are prepared to sit up until midnight, singing opera music, dancing, talking and laughing in the highest key . . . wealth can-not and *does* not make them, either intelligent or agreeable."

If she found the aristocracy dissolute, she found lower-class whites scarcely less palatable. Her harshest condemnation fell on northeast Georgia residents, whom she regarded as shiftless, irresponsible "common crackers." Their "customs and manners were so different" that Jennie "shrank from intercourse with them, preferring solitude to society." Upon leaving the area she wished it might "never be my lot to live in *Crackerdom* again."

Although full acceptance of Georgia as her home would take some time, Jennie quickly adopted political and racial views that brought her within the southern consensus. Upon her arrival in the state four years before the outbreak of war, Jennie had condemned slavery and had reflected sardonically that she would have to refer to slaves as servants, after the southern usage. This linguistic concession, however, did not prevent her from forthrightly confronting the slavery issue.

Jennie's dislike for slavery was most clearly demonstrated when she first encountered the physical abuse that accompanied the "peculiar institution." A black overseer's savage beating of another slave prompted her to express sympathy for the victim, in spite of disapproval by the slaveowner's wife. Jennie confided to her diary that although "Mrs. G. saw my excitement . . . I did not care; indeed I should consider myself void of all humane feelings could I composedly look upon such barbarous treatment of a beast much more a fellow creature." Slavery, Jennie went on, was a "bitter curse" and a "dark stain upon our country."

On other occasions she wrote accounts of the heroism of slaves, and as late as 1860, she incurred the displeasure of her slaveowning landlady when she dispensed camphor to a black who suffered from a cold. The landlady warned against expressing sympathy, but Jennie persisted and commented that to do otherwise would be "acting against my nature and violating the most common law of humanity."

Despite these sentiments, Jennie developed negative feelings about blacks that seem closely related to her strong hope that the Union would not be destroyed in a contest over slavery. Blacks were a "necessary evil," and she decided that if the abolitionists knew them as she did, "they would not wish to abolish slavery, & give them liberty to roam at large through the country." As the sectional crisis deepened, her abhorrence of slavery diminished and she began to place blame for the nation's torment squarely upon slaves and abolitionists. She came to accept the notion that "*abolitionism* is the *prime cause*" for the impending disaster and that such "fanatics" should "mind their own affairs and let the South enjoy her rights in peace." For Jennie, Abraham Lincoln was an irresponsible demagogue whose election would ensure civil war.

Like many southerners, however, she thought fire-eating secessionists equally deplorable, and she expressed surprise that Georgians should regard disunion so lightly. "I do not know how people can anticipate such an event with so much calmness and unconcern," she wrote. When Georgians voted to secede, Jennie warned that they would regret secession, and she forecast accurately the ruin and ravage that would accompany civil war.

Jennie's wartime diaries and letters are less complete than those of the prewar years. She wrote occasionally of the cataclysmic events that surrounded her, but her primary concern was establishing a home for her family and escaping from the boardinghouse routine she had known for many years. During the war, her husband, Sylvanus, found well-paying work in the Atlanta area and received an occupational draft deferment. The improvement in finances enabled the two to rent a small cottage and, as Jennie put it, "go to housekeeping," leaving behind the confining boardinghouse existence.

The death of her first child in 1863 profoundly altered Jennie's attitude toward life. Always inclined to moroseness, she now fell at times into deep depression and ceased her diary entries. At war's end, she resumed the diary and once again began to preserve her letters, but the entries and letters became increasingly less frequent. During Reconstruction, the economic woes that had plagued Jennie and Sylvanus recurred and forced the family (which now included a new daughter, Daisy) to go to Sylvanus's home in Connecticut. Unable to maintain a steady income in New Haven, Sylvanus returned to Georgia, seeking once more the steady, substantial income that had evaded him most of his life. Money problems brought frequent separations during the late 1860s as Jennie, Daisy, and a new son, Herbert, remained in Connecticut while Sylvanus worked in Macon, Georgia, trying to accumulate sufficient savings to permit his family to join him. The family was reduced to three with the death of Herbert in 1869, but Daisy and Jennie were eventually reunited with Sylvanus in Macon, where they settled. Although Sylvanus continued to have business difficulties, he was able to furnish the family with some of the trappings of genteel living which he and Jennie had always wanted. His death in 1875 left Jennie with little money and forced her to return to the schoolroom to support herself and her ten-year-old daughter.

Mother and daughter continued to live in Macon. Jennie's aspirations for Daisy were strong, and she continually sacrificed so that there might be opportunities for education and socializing. When Daisy decided, after graduating from Wesleyan College in Macon, to become a teacher, Jennie must have had mixed emotions, recalling her own ambivalence about teaching and realizing that Daisy would likely leave home to pursue her career. Nevertheless, it is abundantly clear that Jennie took enormous pride in a loving and active daughter and equally certain that Jennie also enjoyed vicariously the variety of her daughter's social experiences.

Jennie died in near poverty in May 1886. The immediate circumstances of her death were carefully recorded in a letter from Daisy to the ubiquitous (and long-lived) cousin and sister-in-law Anna Maria Lines Akehurst Cady Barham. Daisy, who never married, remained a teacher until her death in 1912.

PART ONE

TEACHER IN NEW YORK

1851–1856

JENNIE TO MARIA[1]

New Hartford[2] Oct 16th 1851

Dear sister Maria

We received your letters last Saturday. I also received a circular from Sherburne[3] the trustees wish me to attend the institute which meets at Norwich[4] commencing next monday and continuing two weeks   it will be attended with some expense but I am going and I expect to leave home to morrow morning   while there I will keep a journal and send it   I have not time to write any more now as I am very busy prepareing to go   We are all well   17th   Left home yesterday at 12 arrived at Sherburne at half past eight in the evening. I expected Mr Kennedy would be at the hotell, waiting for me but was disappointed. I asked the landlord to bring me here, he did so and charged me three shillings quite an expensive ride for a short one, only ¾ of a mile. I expect to leave here on Monday for Norwich

Monday 20th   Mr Kennedy is going to Norwich to morrow & I am going to defer going until then so as to save the expense of going in the stage. O you do not know how I dread attending the institute it really seems as if I never shall live through it. how shall I ever get along among the many strangers.

Tuesday 21st   Have finally arrived at Norwich & have found a boarding place where are six of the young ladies from the institute. therefore I shall have company enough. I pay twelve shillings a week for board, shall commence going to school to morrow. Wednesday evening. The Exercises at the Institute. 1st   The students all assembled in the Bar (for we are in the Court House) a portion of scripture was read   then as many as could united in singing a hymn   a prayer was then offered by Mr Niles   The school is divided into four classes called A., B., C., & D   Each class were then sent to different rooms with a teacher to instruct them   Our 1st exercise was in grammar   next recess   then we again assembled in the court room & had a general ex-

15

ercise in reading   O! O! how my poor heart did beat at the thought of getting up & reading before so many teachers both old & young but when my turn came I succeeded much better than I expected   A lesson in Arithmetic was our next and last exercise for the forenoon   At one oclock we met together again   Our 1st recitation was in Orthography   Mr Niles instructed so we have a different room and different teacher for every branch   2nd exercise a lesson in Geography & history   3d recess   4th a general exercise in spelling   5th & last mental arithmetic Mr Pringle teacher   Evening exercise commenced at six oclock   I can hardly tell what they were   a little of almost everything   we had no lecture but all the teachers had something to say at nine we were dismissed   thus closes my 1st day at the institute   I am now in my room at my boarding place   my room mate has already retired & I must follow her example so good night   Thursday 29   The proceedings to day were much the same that they were yester day & I have nothing particular to write   Friday 24   I am enjoying myself right well & already feel well acquainted with nearly all the members of the institute, we had a fine lecture this morning from Prof. Padock   he exaltted our occupation to the highest degree which was quite flattering you know   Saturday 25   The exercises to day were general   we did not separate for class drills as usual but all assembled in the bar & together reviewed the studies we have been looking over the past week at noon the exercises were adjourned until monday so we have a play spell this afternoon & a merry time we have had since dinner but it is nearly 3 oclock and I must begin to do something   Our teachers wish us to write a letter or composition to be read next week I do not mind writing one but never can read it   Miss Stor wishes me to go out walking so good bye   Sunday 26th   I must confess that I have not spent this sabbath very well   have attended church twice to be sure but at home have laughed & talked with the girls all the time this morning a young Gentleman belonging to the Institute called Miss Smith & myself were dressed for church   he remained all the morning but we did not stay at home for him so I am not guilty of that   I am glad that I am not going to spend every sabbath here among so many young people

Wednesday 29th   have not written anything for two days & I believe I shall not write any more until I am settled at Sherburne   the proceedings are the same that they have been therefore I have nothing to write

Wed Nov 12   Dear sister I will now finish this letter for it is already dated enough   the Institute days are now over & I am settled in school again   I enjoyed myself at Norwich very much   a happier two week I never spent   I commenced school one week ago two day have 40 schollars in my department can not tell yet how I shall like it nor how I am going to like living at Sherburne as I have not yet formed any acquaintances except Miss Beebe the Preceptress she is my room mate   We board at Dr Owen's   pay 12 shilling per week   we have a room to our selves with a fire which is very pleasant but how I do wish you were my room mate should we not take comfort   I want to write a great deal more but have not room please write imediately good bye from

Jenny

I have no monney now to pay the postage on this but shall have by the time you answer it therefore you need not pay the postage on your next

JENNIE TO MARIA

New Hartford April 7th 1852

My Sister Dear

I have just been reading your last letter and can hardly make myself believe that it is two months since it was received, but such is the fact and I will not try to excuse myself for not answering it before as I cannot reasonably do so. I came home last week and am not going to return to Sherburne as there is going to be bu[t] three teachers employed this summer but I am not out of business. I have engaged the Manchester school for twelve shillings a week and my board. It will be doing better than I have ever done before but I do not anticipate much enjoyment   it is not such a situation as I should choose if I could have my choice but you know I have got to support myself and cannot do as I will but as I can   it will be near home that is one comfort and I shall have the privilege of seeing our friends often that is another and also save the expenses of traveling that is some consolation you know

*   *   *

from your affectionate sister
Amelia

JENNIE TO MARIA

New Hartford Sept 25 1852

To my Sister

Dear Maria,

Father and Mother[5] received your letter two weeks since, I have been waiting very impatiently for an answer to my last   I think you might have written and it has probably miscarried   My school closed three weeks since, I have no school engaged for the winter and am afraid shall not get on[e] here. I have been thinking a good deal of your proposition in your last and it is now my principal object in writing   I should like verry much to come and spend the winter with you if I could earn enough while there to pay my board and defray my traveling expenses and if you were still in the [?] shop I think I might but I am told that hat triming is very hard business and you know that I am not verry good at the needle and I should be afraid to come depending only on that, but I will tell you what I have been thinking of an[d] you can take it into consideration and let me know what you think of it   I thought we might rent two rooms and one I might have for a school room if I could get a few schollars it would be better than nothing   I might earn something at trimming hats too and perhaps get up a writing class and altogether make a live of it   now I do no[t] know as it would be possible to do as I have suggested but you know I do not know what kind of a place Ashland is   therefore do not laugh at my idea of it but write to me immediately and let me know what kind of a place Ashland[6] is and whether you think I had better come and if you do tell me how to come and how much it costs and do not fail to write instantly for I shall not do anything until I hear from you   I have made known my business and you must excuse me from writing any more for I cannot find a pen in the house to write legible with   Mother is gone to Utica and I am keeping house   I do hope I can come to Ashland   I want to see you very much   you must tell me what to do and I will abide by your decision   Please commit this to the flames as soon as you read it that is if you can read it

remember I shall be waiting for an answer
and I know you will be punctual?
from Amelia A

JENNIE TO MARIA

New Hartford Dec 23, 1852

My Dear Sister Sister

*   *   *

January 8th   Two weeks have elapsed since I commenced this epistle and here it lies unfinished. Procrastination the thief "has been with me or you would have received it before now but he shall interfere no longer." Father has been very ill with [?] in his face and head for some day's   the Dr regarded him quite dangerous and we were all alarmed but our hopes have triumphed over our fears and he is now recovering although very feeble. I have got no school yet. and no prospect of any. I have regreted it that I did not go to Ashland and have half a mind to start now   was I sure I could succeed as well as you do I would not hessitate, I dislike to give up teaching but it is so hard to secure a school and I have no one to assist me at all. Maria I do feel discouraged for I have felt very ambitious to raise myself a little and to be something in the world and not remain all my days a mere blank in society. and it seems as if I had tried hard to gratify my ambition which *I do not consider wrong* but what have I gained only the name of being proud and feeling above associating with those who are my equals, and looking to high in the world but how do I look too high all I ask is to be respected to have a place in respectable society and when away from New Hartford I have it but here I have no society for those with whom I would associate with look down upon me and those with whom I suppose I am classed *I cannot and I will not* have anything to say to.

for I have acquaintances at other places if not that are just suited to my taste. and with those I enjoy myself but with all my proud ambition I do not expect to reach the goal of my earthly hopes. perhaps I do look to high for a penyless unattractive girl like myself tell me if I do.

*   *   *

from your sister Amelia Akehurst

JENNIE TO AN UNIDENTIFIED FRIEND

Clinton Aug 1854

My Dear Friend,

It seems a very long time since I have written to you for the last letter you know was only an apologi and perhaps this will only be the same; for I do not feel much in the mood for letter writing but if you were here I would tell you my whole soul   it would be a relief as you say to have one confident friend; one to whom we could tell every thought and feeling of our heart without the fear of being laughed at, How pleasant to find one congenial spirit in this cold world; one whose sympathies are in common with our own; human beings need human sympathi and do you not think it is especially true with our sex? I have often thought that it was more natural for woman to yearn for a sympathising friend, to feel the need of one in whom she might always confide one on whom she might always lean, and one to whom she might always look for sympathy in an hour of trial, than for man; his mind is occupied and filled, with the sterner realities of life; there seems to be no void in his heart which affection and sympathy alone can fill, and yet they seem to possess the power of giving that affection and sympathy which can fill the void in our hearts; Now is that not quite a confession for one to make who knows nothing by experience of that

blissful state which is termed *being in love?* but you know I can im-
magine something about it, for I love my friends ardently and do not
suppose it is very different. truly all the satisfaction we find of an
worldly nature is in loving and being loved;
I think however I have said enough upon this subject. Now dont be so
cruel as to say I am *love sick* for of all desires of the [?] that to me appears the most horrible, the most degrading, it shows such weakness of
our mental faculties   why I could not respect myself nor expect others
to respect me if I was afflected with this mallady. not that I am incapable of loving or think it a weakness to love when our affection are
sought by one to whom we can yield them, but to love without being
loved first is awful to think of   my affections must be sought before
they are found.

DIARY

Clinton, Jan 7th [1855]   Have attended church twice today, did not go
out this evening on account of the storm. This morning Mr. Vermilye
preached an excellent sermon from Hebrews 13-8. "Jesus Christ the
same yesterday to day and forever." I like his preaching more and
more. If I do not proffit by it surely it will be my own fault.
This afternoon the Lord's supper was administered, as it was the first
sabbath in the year. It seemed more than usually solemn and interesting. There were quite a number united with the church   Five young
people by confession of faith—and several by letter. I feel that I have
lost much since I have been an Christian by not steadily attending the
church to which I belong. I thought I had good reason for not doing so
but do not think so now and have resolved to do differently. Have written to brother Ezra[7] this evening. Do not practice writing letters on the
sabbath but did not feel that I was doing wrong in writing to him. Poor
boy. He is away from us all and a letter seems like cold water to the
thirsty.

Wednesday 10th   Yesterday was a lazy day with me   Rose at seven in
the morning   After breakfast and prayers went immediately to my
school room and commenced the labors of the day. As it was the last
day of the term the children took the liberty to make a great deal of
noise and ask a great many questions   Intended to close school earlier
than usual, but kept half an hour. Later, after closing school made several calls and reached home at five oclock. Chatted with my chum
Mary until tea. Mr. and Mrs. Tuttle went out to spend the evening.

Mary is alone up stairs but I had the pleasure of Eliza's society as I was working in the kitchen. Mr. and Mrs. Tuttle came home just as I had finished. Mary and I retired at eleven. This morning the first bell rang a[t] seven, but we were so sleepy did not rise immediately—were ready for breakfast however. I did not feel very hungry at first but Mrs. Tuttle's Coffee and Johnny Cake were so good I ate a hearty breakfast. It is a delightful morning notwithstanding a keen north wind. I have been down street; it seemed strange to pass my school room as it was nine oclock. Some of the children said yesterday they were not coming next term. Feel rather discouraged   Fear I shall not have many scholars. Brother Charley called on me yesterday. He has grown so I hardly knew him. Expect to enjoy a good visit with him and brother Henry at home.

January 13th   This has been a very cold stormy day. This evening the snow is falling fast. Father says there is a prospect of sleighing. Hope to have a sleigh ride on my return to Clinton. I have been sewing all day. We had a call from Mr. Carr this evening. Poor man. He is becoming blind, father thinks he will lose his sight entirely; his wife is also quite feeble. They are sorely afflicted. How little we know of the suffering of many of our fellow creatures. Could we but witness only a small portion of it surely we should feel more grateful for our own happy lot. Mother and I have been talking over our own circumstances today and came to the conclusion that we were not as rich as we might be and did not enjoy quite as many luxuries as would sometimes be agreeable, but we finally decided that our condition was far preferable to that of many others and that we ought and would try to feel very thankful.

Friday 19th   Commenced school on Wednesday January 17th under rather unfavorable circumstances   Only nineteen scholars and as yet no additions. Hope to have more next week. Shall be completely discouraged if I do not. It is hard to teach and I know I sometimes feel it to be a hardship and complain more than I ought but I know by experience that it is harder still to have no school to teach. At such times I have resolved that I would never [?] because my duties were wearisome if the Lord would give me a field for labor and usefulness   I have chosen the ocupation of a teacher and do not feel willing to resign this office for any other, but sometimes I feel almost persuaded that it is my duty to do so thinking I am unfit for a teacher   Do not feel the responsibility which rests upon me as I ought. Do not feel that anxiety to instil right principles in the hearts of my pupils which a teacher ought to feel. How often might a word dropped from the lips of an instructor prove in the youthful heart like good seed sown in good ground bringing forth fruit to the honor and glory of God. O that all who are engaged in training the young mind might feel that we are not only preparing them for future life in this world but may we remember that there resides under our care an immortal part and while striving to to [sic] cultivate the intellect may we not forget the more important part but may strive to scatter crumbs upon which the soul may feed when time shall have robbed them of youth and tarnished their literary attainments

Last evening I received a letter from sister Maria the best letter I have received from her in a long time   She thinks of coming here in the spring and will remain if she finds business to keep her here. How pleasant it would be for me to have her with me if I remain here but almost fear I shall be obliged to leave as my school is so small.

* * *

Between four and five the wind rose very high the rain fell in torrents accompanied with peals of thunder and flashes of lightning, strange to say I slept through it all and did not rise until nearly eight, just in time to attend prayers. Had two more scholars to day. I hope that I may have a sufficient number to defray my expenses than I can remain until spring. Like being in Clinton very much. Have found many warm friends here. Consequently I feel very much at home and should regret leaving. Have felt very dull and [?] all intend to retire early hoping to feel better tomorrow.

* * *

Wednesday 24th   Another days labor is ended. school has passed off very pleasantly as it generally does when I feel right myself, Have just finished reading Shady side of life in a country parsonage.[8] Can hardly believe many ministers are subjected to as much trouble and affliction as was poor Mr. [?.]. Have always thought if I were a man it would be my greatest ambition to be an ambassador of the [?.] Have always thought a minister possessed more opportunities of doing good than persons in any other calling. It seems too as if they were better christians and could lead a more devoted life, although they are under no more obligation to do so than other christians.

* * *

Febuary 2nd   Dear book, one whole week have I neglected thee; but it is because nothing of sufficient importance has occured, to not[e] upon thy pages. I feel sad to night, and fly to thee for sympathy. I know of no particular cause for this depression of spirits, it is a feeling which will sometimes steal over me, in spite of my efforts to feel cheerful, and I can not always throw it of immediately, it often remains an uninvited, and unwelcome, guest in my heart for many days. Sometimes I find myself amid the clouds of despair which for a time hide the bright star of hope from my view, but she soon smiles upon me again and I arise shake off my sadness and plod onward with renewed courage.

*   *   *

Feb. 8th   The weather has been intensely cold, for a few days past. Thermometer thirty degrees below zero. Never suffered more from the cold than I have this past week, in going to my school room, and building fires. Have thought much about the poor; who are destitute of comfortable clothing, and food, during this inclement season. Doubtless many have perished, within the past week. O! how can I feel thankful enough that unworthy I, am numbered with those who continually [have] all the common blessings of life. To day it is quite mild.

*   *   *

Friend Mary and I anticipated spending the day alone in our own dear room, intending to have a good long chat mingled with pleasant recollections of the past and sorrowful feelings that we were so soon to part perchance never to meet again. Ere another week has rolled away she will be far from us.

Feb. 11th   At ten oclock Mr. Tuttle proposed that Mrs. Tuttle Mary & I should take a ride to Utica. As the day was mild and the sleighing good. Mary & I gladly accepted the invitation. We started at one. Our happiness would have been complete could Mrs. Tuttle have accompanied us, but domestic cares prevented and we were obliged to enjoy ourselves as well as possible without her. We had proceeded about two miles when the horse became frightened, whirled around, and acted very much as if he intended to throw us out of sleigh. Mary and I thought we would save him that trouble, as we preferred geting out ourselves to being thrown out in the snow or being crushed by the horse. Mary sat with uplifted hands, her face vieing with the snow for whiteness and her eyes threatening to leave their sockets. I waited not for a second thought and in my [haste?] to jump from the sleigh went head long into the snow, where I lay trying to collect my thoughts, until M. had followed my example. We then started on a run toward Utica. I know not how far we should have gone had not Mr. Tuttle called after us, assureing us the danger was over. In a few moments we were on our way again, And a hearty laugh we had at the ridiculous appearance we must have presented

* * *

Sabbath day the weather was mild and pleasant. Attended church all day. O! that I could feel a deeper interest in spiritual things. Why am I so groveling; so fond of earthly joys; Do I not realize every day that earthly pleasures are fleeting and unsatisfying, Its bright hopes are delusive. *All* happiness of a *worldly* nature is bought with the price of pain. Every thrill of pleasure is followed by a pang.

* * *

February 28th Went from school last night to Mr. Dillon's. remained all night. had a pleasant visit. Called on Mrs. Bangs in the evening and returned Williams Paradise lost which I have just read with interest. This is the last day of the winter months. Farewell Old winter, thy days are at last numbered; and who will mourn thy departure.

* * *

Friday 2nd. Found Mr. & Mrs. Tuttle gone when I came home from school. Asked Eliza if I might wash and having her permission commenced immediately finished just at dark, was going to dress for tea when Mr. Cambell called. Arranged my toilette hastily and went down   As there was no one to entertain him but myself was obliged to play the agreeable as best I would. Was detained from tea until eight o'clock then ate wit[h] a very good appetite.

Saturday 3d Mild and pleasant to day. Mrs. Tuttle invited me to attend the baptist covenant meeting but felt rather delicate about accepting the invitation fearing I should [be] looked upon as an intruder. Mr. Gregory a young minister accompanied them home to tea. I was pleased with his appearance and was quite amused with a little incident which occured. At the table he made some remarks rather disparaging to the presbyterians. after tea he asked me if I was a member of the baptist church here   I replied no but was of the presbyterian church. He appeared rather confused and apologised but said he could take nothing back. He is expected to night again presume he will be more cautious.

Sunday 4th The weather still remains pleasant This morning listened to an excellent discourse from the words "He was numbered with transgressors." This afternoon the Lords supper was administered. O what an unparalleled privilege with the disciples of Christ to gather around the table of our common Lord to commemorate his dying love.

*   *   *

Friday 16th   *   *   *   Have had another discouraging week in school hardly earned enough to [pay] my board and rent. But I have not been idle there is some consolation in that thought. I have at least earned my bread; and perhaps done a *little* good.

*   *   *

Monday eve April *2nd*   Have not had as tedious a storm this winter as has raged to day. I think we shall all appreciate pleasant weather when we are favored again. Had only fifteen schollars but they were very troublesome and kept me talking. Mrs. Tuttle has just had application for board   The applicants are law students[9]   Suppose we shall have three of them here soon.

Tuesday 3d   Much pleasanter than yesterday. My usual number of schollars were present, and have made so much noise that I am very tired. Tis evening attended sewing society at Miss Bairds. Mrs. Tuttle's cousin Mr. Brockett is here to spend a day or two.

Wednesday 4th   Attended Junior exhibition this evening   Was not very highly entertained. The music however was good.

*   *   *

Monday 9th   Felt very little like going into school this morning but the thought that two days would free me for the present nerved me for my task   After school received a call from Ellen Dillon. Spent much of the evening talking with Mr. & Mrs. Tuttle on the mode of baptism Neither of us were converted to the belief of the other.

Tuesday 10th   After school   Well my friend journal. The labors perplexities and vexations of another twelve weeks are over   I have again said good bye to my pupils and school room for a few days. I shall visit home and friends and again take my place in our own family circle and be cheered by intercourse with those whose society separation has learned me to prize. I shall travel about in the fresh air and thereby [recoup?] my strength both of body and mind; which is now well nigh exhausted   If my life and health is spared shall hope to return with renewed zeal and energy

Wed 11th   Am at home once more. Found father Mother and Eddy[10] alone brothers Henry & Charley have gone west. We do not know when we shall see them again. Eddie says he is glad sister has come home

*   *   *

Sunday 16th   The pleasantest sabbath we have had this spring. Father went to Utica. It is a long walk for him; but he does not feel interested in the preaching we have here. Mother Eddy and I attended the presbyterian church in the morning and the baptist in the after part of the day. We were all weary and retired early to rest.

Monday ev 17th   We have been cheered with one of the most delightful days with which spring can favor us. The birds have warbled, their song of praise from the rising until the going down of the sun: our hearts in unison with theirs have seemed to breathe forth the spirit of rejoiceing and adoration. Little brother Eddy like the birds has spent the day running about in the open air. Mother and I have contented ourselves with listening to the feathered muscians [sic] and enjoying the bracing air from an open window. This morning our humble friend Eliza called again before leaving town. This afternoon received calls from Mrs. & Miss Patterson. Father has gone down street this evening. Mother is reading in the good book. Eddy is making a writing book as he is resolved to keep a journal like sister.

*   *   *

Friday 21st   Feel to much fatigued to converse even with you my journal. Have had a rainy day which was unfortunate for Mother and I as we were washing. Probably before we have another chat dear book we should have taken a short journey   I may then have some news to tell you. Left home Saturday 22nd. Spent the 23d 24th & 25th with my friends at Manchester[11]   Found all well except Mrs. Cook who is very feeble. Returned to my home in Clinton Tuesday evening. This morning entered upon my school room duties again. Have commenced with sixteen schollars but hope to have as many more. Found my room at Mrs. Tuttle all ready for me: and a pleasant little room it is. expect to spend many pleasant hours in it with you my silent friend: and probably now then a feeling of loneliness will steal over me as I shall be alone when out of school. Mrs. Tuttle has now ten boarders eight of them gents. Mrs. Kellogg and I shall have to depend upon each other for society. It has been rather a dull day quite cooll and rainy to night. I feel some-what low spirited   Some sad feelings have taken up their abode in my heart notwithstanding my reluctance to receive them But I dare not pour out all my soul ever, in thy bosom, dear book; although I feel assured that thou art true. Full well I know that thou will not disclose to any one secrets confided to thee. But perchance the eye of a cold and careless heart might scan thy pages and for want of sympathy might sneer at and ridicule the inmost feeling and yearnings of the writer.

* * *

Monday 30th   Will devote a few moments to you, dear book. I feel quite cheerful to night although somewhat fatigued. Had six new schollars to day   My present prospects for a full school are quite encouraging. O! for patience and wisdom to fulfill my duties right   Since my return dear journal I have resolved not to be cut dow[n] by every trifling disappoint; but to make a greater effort to look on the sunny side of my life   For well I know that by indulging in these gloomy feelings I am unfited for the duties which devolve upon me   O! that I might ever feel contented with my lot feeling as Tupper[12] says "That it might and ought to have been worse"   It is nearly tea time I must arrange my toilette

* * *

Thursday 17th   O! my book what should I do were it not for thee. In thine ear I pour all my complaints. And thou art ever ready to receive them. Never hast thou given me a reproving look. I am lonely to night although I hear voices and footsteps on every side yet there is not one who has a thought or care for poor me. Not one with whom I can spend an hour in pleasant social intercourse. Verily one may feel alone in a crowd. I almost feel that it is wrong to indulge in sadness at this delightful season of the year. Nature is arrayed in freshness and beauty. Every blade of grass leaf and bud bespeak the power and goodness of God   All the works of nature seem to combine in praiseing the all wise and all powerful being who has created this beautiful world

Man alone the last but noblest work of creation is sinful and ungrateful   When I look away from my own sinful self and gaze and meditate for a while upon this pleasant home which God has created for man, I feel assured that nearly all our unhappiness arises from our own evil natures.

* * *

June. I can not think what day of the month   Nearly two weeks have elapsed dear book since I have spoken to thee and thou hast not reproached me for this seeming negligence but have lain quietly on the stand as if patiently waiting until I felt in a mood to converse with thee. Spring has given place to summer: but we can hardly realize it as the weather is yet cool. Have spent all my leisure hours in reading for several days past. Have read Eckermans conversations with Goethe the german poet was much interested.[13] Am now reading Iola May which is painfully interesting. Miss Elizabeth Cook called on me a few days since   I fear that I am getting really tired of teaching my duties have dragged so heavily the past week   I do not seem at times to have any command over my pupils. If they are disposed to be quiet and orderly all goes on well, but on the contrary if inclined to make a great deal of noise and trouble I am obliged to endure it feeling incapable of preventing it. Was obliged to punish Charley Bangs which was harder for me than teaching a week when all goes right. O! my book I wish you could tell me just how to govern my school aright I am completely discouraged with myself do not believe I know how to train and guide the young. O! that I possessed even a small share of the wisdom of Soloman and the patience of Job

Sabbath day 11th   O! how I have spent this holy day. My conscience smites me for wasting its precious hours in frivilous conversation.

*   *   *

Friday 15th   O! how I weary of this sameness. For two weeks nothing has occured to relieve the monotony of eating sleeping and teaching. This week I have hardly spoken out of school   Mrs. Kellogg is gone and I even take my meals alone. It seems strange in a family of eighteen persons for me to feel alone but so it is with me.

Saturday 16th   A delightful day. This morning wrote a letter to Mr. & Mrs. Clark. Have writen several the past week. Shall hope to receive answers soon. Mrs. K returned to day. Was glad to see her   Have talked and laughed more this afternoon than I have all the week. After tea Mrs. K and I took our work and sit on the piazza. Had a pleasant chat with Mr. Cambell the southerner.

Sunday 17th   O! what a beautiful world is this the earthly home of man. Whereever we turn our eyes we behold something to please the eye and charm the soul. Love for the beautiful is an untaught innate principal of the soul   Beauty whereever, and in whatever form we behold it possesses the power of enraptureing the sences and compelling us to pay involuntary homage at her shrine.

Evening. Another holy day and its privileges had gone. Have attended the baptist church all day. After the morning service the congregation repaired to a stream of water where the ordinance of baptism was administered by Mr. Swift. It was a solemn and interesting scene. One of the persons is feeble and somewhat advanced in years   She can not probably have long to serve her master here below. The other was one in the morning of life. In early youth, she has concecrated herself to the service of her Savior   O! that she may be an honor to his cause; an instrument in his hand of doing much good in this life; and a star in his diadem in eternity. Just at dark went out on the piazza to enjoy the twilight. Mr. Cambell joined me and commenced a conversation on the subject of religion.

*   *   *

Tuesday 19th   School went off pleasantly. Have just commenced reading Macaulay's history of England[14] My sewing must now be laid aside, for I can not work unless necesity compels me when I have any thing interesting to read. This evening Emma and I asked Luke to give us a swing after enjoying that Had a game at ball with Mrs. Kellogg, and then a chat with Mrs. Tuttle in the nursery, retired to my room at ten ready for repose.

*   *   *

Monday 25th   O! how my heart sinks within me. I feel that perhaps I am more in fault than my schollars, but if the fault is entirely in myself then I am not and never was fit for a teacher. For I know that I have sometime at least exerted myself to the utmost to make the school room and interesting and profitable place. My feelings in school to day almost prompted me to resolve at the close of this term to resign my office as a teacher and seek some other employment; but I know that I could not bring my mind to that although I feel at times that teaching is fast wearing out both body and mind. Such were my feelings on my return from school to night but after the perusal of my letters and enjoying the retirement of my own room my spirits were somewhat lighter.

*   *   *

Thursday 28th   Have had another delightful evening. Thought in school to day that I would retire early to night but it is to pleasant and eleven oclock finds me up and with very little inclination to retire. Mr. Cambell Mrs. Kellogg and I have been talking upon the subject of religion   The variety of opinions in regard to it The free moral agency of man, fatalism as is. I think Mr. C. is talented and well informed. I like to converse with him, He is a person in whose society one may learn, I can not however quite agree with him in some of his religious views

Friday 29th   Came to my room about nine after a pleasant tete [à] tete with Mr. Potter. Have never conversed alone with him before. I think he is quite agreeable. We talked upon spirituolism.[15]   He is not a believer. Mrs. Kellogg called me into her room   I went thinking to remain but a few moments. two hours have elapsed and I have just left her   We had a good moonlight chat. To morrow is Saturday shall not have to teach, it is no matter if I am sleepy.

*   *   *

Wednesday July 4th   I do not remember to have ever spent independence day as quietly as I have this   Have hardly been out of my room except to take my meals. Was invited to attend a picnic party but did not feel like going. Mrs. Kellogg has gone again and I am left alone. Shall not go to the table and shall hardly dare to leave my room. It is very unpleasant to be the only lady boarder I have no society here at all, and I find I can not content myself alone at all times. I like to speak and be spoken to occasionly. I never felt so much alone as I have this summer   Did I not continually have something to occupy my time and attention should suffer much from ennui.

*   *   *

Thursday 5th   My schollars have not got over the excitement of yesterday; and were very noisy to day. They all wanted to tell me how they spent the fourth. The boys especially imagined they had been very patriotic in fireing crackers and makeing all the noise in their power. I sometimes wish I had nothing else to do in school but talk with the children. One can be amused and interrested and oftentimes instructed by listening to their innocent prattle.

*   *   *

Thursday 12th   ½ 7   I am enjoying a thunder shower would that I could describe it as I feel it in my soul but alas I can not find words to express my feelings when witnessing this awfully grand phenomenon. It would take an abler writer than myself to do it justice. Any words that I could utter would seem to weak & tame. O that I possessed a command of language Then could I sometimes clothe and give utterance to the thoughts which crowd upon my mind   What am I or what do I know, alas nothing

* * *

Tuesday July 24th   Farewell to school room and schollars for a season. I am glad to be *free* once again   I love my pupils; and think I feel
some desire to do them good. I usually feel my duties to them to be but
a pleasant task: but I grow weary of the *monotony* and *confinement* of
the school room, and sometimes foolishly wish that I were not obliged
to teach. It seems rather hard to labor day after day and week after
week just to procure the necessaries and comforts of life: but I trust
this is *not* my *only* objects for *then* poor indeed would be the compensation. I would do a little *good* in the world. I would leave my mark on
the sands of time. I ask not I desire not that *fame* shall speak of this
poor worm when it shall have run its race; and he's sleeping beneath
the cloak of the valley. Then shall I be forgotten by the *world* and it
matters not; but I would that my memory might live in the hearts of
those who love me. To die and be forgotten by *all*; to die with *none* to
mourn my loss *none* to shed a tear upon my grave *none* to speak my
name with tenderness. O! this would be worse than a *thousand* deaths.
I'll pray that *some* may be spared to mourn my beir. I desire not to live
until *all* the dear ones that make earth attractive to *me* have laid them
down to sleep. No! no, *then* indeed would earth be a *dreary dreary
home.* I would live while I can *give and recieve affection*; *then* would I
die, and be forgotten by *those who care not for me.* I attended the commencement exercises last evening   Had good music by the bank;
prayer by the Rev. Mr. Hall of Syracuse, an address by the Judge [?]
from [?]   His subject the character Lord Bacon. A poem was read by [?]
of [?]. There was a great concourse of pupils and yet no two looked or
appeared alike and could we have looked in upon the mind there too
should we have found the same variety of thoughts tastes and feelings.
No two minds are alike says Tupper. As I looked upon the young and
the gay assembled there and heard the frivolous conversation between
the flirt and the [?] I felt to reiterate the words of the preacher "*Vanity
of vanities all is vanity.*"

Thursday 26th   Commencement is over; and all is still and quiet this
morning. Most of our boarders have left; and lonely enough it seems.
We miss those who have roomed here much more than those who only
came to their meals. Mr. Potter bade us good bye last night. He expects
to return here and we shall probably see him again. Mr. Mason & Mr.
Campbell too have started for their homes   Mr. C. resides in Virginia,
and Mr. M. in New Hampshire. When they first came here I did not
expect to become acquainted and did not wish too. With Mr. M. and Mr.

P. I formed very little acquaintance; and shall hardly think of them as acquaintances. *Mr. Campbell* I shall remember as a *friend* with whom I have spent some *pleasant* hours; and held some *interesting* conversations; and I must confess that it was with some pain I bade him good bye expecting to see him *no more*; and I can not help regreting that I shall enjoy his society *no more*.

*   *   *

Sabbath day 29th   This morning the presbyterian house of worship was rededicated this morning Dr. Vermilie preached an excellent discourse well adapted to the occasion. His text is found in the twentieth chapter of Exodus, part of the twenty fourth verse. Feeling that I had heard enough to meditate upon through the day and on account of the heat I intended to remain at home during the afternoon: but Miss Crassman & Miss Cody came in during intermission and I accompanied them to church. I am reading the life of Judson B———'s great missionary.[16] O! how small seem my endeavors to do good! how weak my desires for the advancement of religion how languid my piety how cold my love how wavering my faith   O! how I am filled with a sense of my own unworthiness when contemplating such characters as those of Judson & his wife

*   *   *

Hamilton[17]
Aug 10th   Left Clinton yesterday afternoon. Arrived here at eight oclock in the evening; after a tedious ride in the stage. It rained hard part of the way, the road was very rough, and my fellow passengers not very sociable: which all combined rendered the journey rather unpleasant. Was very cordially received by Mr and Mrs Beebe, and their youngest daughter. My friend Sophrania is in her school at Poolville[18] which is two miles from home. Matilda proposes that we ride down to Poolville; visit her sister's school; and at its close she will return with us. I shall like it much. We shall probably go after dinner unless the rain prevents. How very quiet it is here. The family consists of only three persons; and every thing seems to move on so still and orderly. This morning I was called from my room at seven to attend prayers, which occupied half an hour. Breakfast immediately followed. Since which Mrs. Beebe and Matilda have been occupied with domestic affairs; and I have been left to myself in the sitting room. Have been reading Taylor's out-door thinking.

*   *   *

12th Sunday   *   *   *   Mr Farmer called on the girls. I made my escape from the room just before he entered; and did not see him, although I was urged to do so. Perhaps he thought I was neigher polite or friendly. I am often called so on account of my foolish timidity. I wish I had not such a horror of meeting strangers.

*   *   *

Clinton Wed 15th   At Clinton again. Left Mr Beebe's accompanied by Sophronia & Matilda about nine this morning. Arrived at Hamilton just in time for the commencement exercises. On our arrival at the meeting house found Mr Parks at the door. He found a good seat for us. We were interrested in the speaking and charmed with the music. At noon Mr Parks and Mr Allen invited us to dine with them at the boarding hall. We felt rather delicate about accepting the invitation but finally did so and survived the agony of seeing more strange faces than I had time to count. During the day saw Ann VanDeusan and her Mother. Saw also a number of people from this place.

*   *   *

Found a letter and pamphlet for me from Governor Slade. It is too late for me to go west with his teachers this fall. I feel somewhat disappointed, but probably it is all for the best. Perhaps there will be a door opened for me nearer home.

*   *   *

Thursday 22d   Have been very busy with my school this week, that at night I have not felt like telling even you dear journal the occurrences of a single day. My school now numbers forty-eight. I am busy enough talking and walking all day.

*   *   *

Mon 27th   Was not able to attend church yesterday. Spent most the whole day upon my bed. Felt much better to day but not entirely well consequently my duties have dragged rather heavily. Had two new scholars. Do not care about taking any more. Fifty is as many as I can do justice to. I have several boys that I think it will require some firmness and descion [sic] to control. Have not had any serious trouble yet and hope I shall not have. Every teacher is subjected more or less to trials and perplexities; and I must expect to endure my share. O! that I may ever possess grace and patience to endure with meekness all the ills vexations and disappointments of life and may they serve to wean me from earth and teach me to look above for the happiness I desire to possess. Have just finished reading the Lamplighter.[19] It is a very interesting story which will not injure the mind of any one to read.

*   *   *

Wed 29th   Felt sad last night without knowing why. I do not feel well
this week. My lungs are very sore from coughing. My scholars cannot
realize but that I am always well and always feel like talking. I hardly
know how to arrange our afternoon exercises on Wednesday now that
my school is large. To have all of my two first classes read select pieces
takes up more time than we have to devote to reading. I decided to day
to have class reading as usual with the exception of a few older ones
who read well enough to interest the school. My boys had very little to
do not having sewing to busy like the girls. I was quite at a loss what
task to give them that would both please and instruct them. I finally
thought it would be a good idea to have them draw maps on their
slates, giving credits to those who merited them by perseverance. They
were quite pleased; and as the exercise comes but once a week perhaps
they will not tire of it. Since school have taken a long walk with Car-
rey. Went into a beautiful piece of woods where we found a nice swing;
but as there was no one with us stronger than ourselves we could not
enjoy it. Heard news from home to day. Mother has been sick a long
time. O! how I want to go and see them.

*   *   *

September 5th   Several days have elapsed since I have written in my
journal. Have had a good deal to ocupy my time and attention and have
hardly been alone. On Saturday the first day of autumn I made a picnic
party for my school. I engaged Mr Hill to take us to a piece of woods
about a mile distant. We assembled at the school room at eleven oclock.
Mr Hull came with his Cary All about twelve. There were between
sixty & seventy to ride beside all the refreshments were to be taken
there: which altogether made out three large loads. On our arrival the
children scattered in every direction makeing the woods ring with
their merriment, Nothing occured to damp their joy excepting a slight
shower; and; that seemed to dampen their clothes more than their feelings. We were beautifully supplied with eatables by the parents. The
time passed off very pleasantly and without any accidents. The last
load did not leave the woods until six oclock.

*   *   *

9th   Went to church this afternoon. Sit in Gen. [*Canostuck's* ?] slip.
Shall probably occupy a seat there for the present. Dr. Vermilie was
absent. His place was filled by the Rev. Mr Dwight. He preached from
the words Are they not all ministring spirits sent forth to minister for
those who shall be heirs of eternal life.[20] The subject is one upon which
I have dwelt much and in which I feel deeply interested. The idea of
pure disembodied spirits from the unseen world ministering to our

spiritual wants at one time warning us of approaching danger, at another urging us onward in the path of duty, cheering us in moments of despondency, and soothing our grief when called to drink from affliction's cup. O! it is to me a delightful thought a source of *pleasant* contemplation. And why may not these ministering *Angles* [*sic*] who men can not doubt are ever near us why may we not believe they are the departed spirits of *those who were once dearer to us than life*. I love to indulge in this belief, and if it be a *delusion* it is a *sweet*, a *happy* delusion to which I cannot refuse to cling. Often in years that have gone, when doubts and fears have arisen to perplex and discourage, when temptations has assailed, when grief has stricken my heart then I felt the presence of my *sainted mother, encourageing, warning, comforting* me. May it be the privilege of this spirit now [shaded?] with dust when it shall leave this clay tenement and attended by its guardian Angel visit the realms of bliss. May it then wing its flight back to earth and hover around the dear one that still linger there bearing on its wings and imparting to them peace & love.

*   *   *

13th   Received a pamphlet on baptism to day from a friend. I shall read it with interest but do not believe it will change my views on that subject. Since school have been calling on some of my patrons. Was received very kindly, and treated with politeness. Some of them have not yet paid their school bill for last term. To collect that was partly my object in calling. I was in hopes they would take the hint without my mentioning it but no, they seemed to have forgotten it; and as I dare not [?] came home with my purse as empty as when I went away. It worries me to think that I am oweing Mr. Tuttle and I can not pay him because I am not paid.

*   *   *

21st   I must complain of my school again   The schollars have been unusually troublesome to day   I have some days that cause me much anxiety and perplexity. What can I do to prevent their using profane language? Is it my duty to punish for every offence of the kind? Should I pursue that course I doubt whether I should succeed in breaking up that dreadful habit so firmly does it seem to be fixed in two of my scholars but discouraging as is the prospect of doing them any good it is certainly my duty to do what I can and leave the result with God. I can and will talk kindly with and pray earnestly for them. How much I feel the need of guidance from on high. I am so prone to do evil myself how can I direct others aright. Often do I feel that my patience are well nigh exhausted, but by divine grace and assistance I will endeavor to conceal such feelings from my pupils and ever present to them that spirit of patience and forbearance that becometh a christian.

22nd   Have been very busy all day but yet have accomplished very little. This evening attended a microscopic exhibition   was very well interested and amused.

*   *   *

October 19th   Went to the Post Office to night full of hope but came home disappointed again. What can this silence on the part of all my friends mean. Do they intend to punish me on account of my past negligence or indifference? If that is their object they have accomplished it. Another week of toil & care is over. The days and weeks are flying fast. Soon this term will close. I shall be glad of a rest; but perhaps it will be a longer one than I shall want. I am tired very tired of the school room and would like a long rest: but *poverty* forbids that indulgence. I almost feel at times that it would be a relief to throw off the burden of life and lay me down to die. Then should I be released from the cares anxieties and ills to which mankind is subject. Never did my prospects for the future appear darker to me than at present. Never did I feel myself so incapable of discharging the duties that devolve upon me   Never before did I morning after morning enter my school feeling that a heavy and unpleasant task awaited me   Am I always to lead the life of a teacher, am I to spend the strength and vigor of my days in the school room. Then the boon I crave is *wisdom, patience & meekness.*

*   *   *

PART TWO

TEACHER IN GEORGIA

1857-1858

DIARY

1857

Utica, February 9th. Monday evening, six o'clock. Away from home and friends, among entire strangers I commence my acquaintance with thee, new book. I filled the pages of my old book some weeks since and have neglected to purchase a new one until now, consequently the occurences of the past six weeks are noted down only upon my mind. I had quite given up the idea of going south this winter and was feeling quite contented and interested in my school when the news came that sister Maria had obtained a situation for me, and desiring me to start immediately. Although I had been feeling very anxious to go, and had been making some preparation yet the summons to go so soon excited me very much. The letters came Saturday evening and I decided to start one week from the following Monday as I could not very well arrange my affairs before. My teaching in Clinton has finished and weary as I had become of my school room duties the thought of leaving my pupils who had so long been under my care filled my heart with sadness. It was with a heavy heart that I entered my school room on Monday morning to meet the little ones once more. They had heard nothing about my leaving and supposed all was going on as usual. I dared not trust myself to tell them until I had discharged my morning's duties for I wanted to open my school as usual. I read a chapter and the children repeated their texts. I then requested them to sing all their hymns and as a favor to me sing as well as they could and they did so. We then knelt once more together around the throne of grace, but my feelings would not permit me to go through with *this* duty. I could control myself no longer, and instead of pleading in words for the dear little ones I could only give [?] to my desire for them by sobs; but the Lord saw my heart and knew what boon I would crave for them and I trust he will answer my prayers in their behalf and fit them all for his ser-

vice on earth and to adorn the Savior's crown in heaven. They all ran
home and brought me some little token of remembrance, which I shall
prize highly not for their value, but for the feeling of kind regard
which prompted the dear little ones to give them. Little Willie Lapham
brought me a sugar gum and there was really eloquence in his look
when he handed it to me. I remained with my pupils until noon and
then bid adieu to my school room in Clinton. The remainder of the
week I was very busy making preparations to leave. I tried to sell my
melodean but did not succeed and left it with Mrs. Tuttle [?] unless I
send for it. Sarah Cook came over on Friday and helped me about my
sewing. I took her home in the evening and bid adieu to my friends
there. O how heart breaking it is to leave friends when it seems so
doubtful whether we ever meet again. Ellen Dillon staid with me Friday night. Mrs. Tuttle invited us down to breakfast. I hardly dared to
go fearing my feelings would overcome me but I visitted and controlled
myself better then I expected to. Spent the morning in running about
the village and packing my trunk. Settled up all my business and was
ready to leave at two P.M. Now came the trial of leaving my own little
rooms of which I had so long been an occupant and saying good bye to
Mr. and Mrs. Tuttle who have been like a brother and sister to me and
their children to whom I have become so much attached. It seemed as if
I could not leave them and feel that their home was no longer my
home, but circumstances compelled to triumph over my reluctance and
hard as it was I must speak the parting word, shed the parting tear,
and leave perhaps the house which had been four years my home, and
the friends who had proven themselves kind and sincere. Mrs. Tuttle
accompanied me home. I found Mother unable to sit and father not in
one of his happier moods which made everything seem gloomy there.
On Sunday it was no more cheerful and I almost longed for although I
dreaded the hour of my departure. Poor mother, it seemed so hard for
her to be so sick just then for father is never himself if he is ill. Uncle
and Aunt Mary came up on Monday morning; uncle to go with father
and myself to Utica, auntie to stay with mother. I was ready to go
in the eleven o'clock stage. Mother felt very badly, I hope it did not
worsen her illness. I was fearful it would. I expected to take the six
o'clock train this evening but find I must wait until one in the morning. Father and uncle did all they could for me by three o'clock and
then bid me good bye about an hour later. I was sitting in the depot
beginning to feel lonely and friendless when to my surprise I saw Mr.
Tuttle enter. How glad I was to see him. He brought me some cakes
and apples and something still more valuable Mrs. Tuttle, Emma and
Little Meda's likeness. O how I shall love to look at them when I am far
far away. Mr. T. came with me to the parlor which is far pleasanter

than the depot sitting room and there bid me good bye and then I was left to myself among strangers. I thought then I had seen the last familiar face but Lydia Patterson came in a few moments and now she is gone and I do not expect to see any one I know until I arrive in Georgia if I ever do. There is a lady here waiting for the train from the east, due at ten it is almost time and she is going to the depot, I think I will go too and stay there until I start.

10th   Found a gentleman and his daughter at the depot last evening waiting for the same train that I was. Was of course very good to find company. The gentleman was very kind and his daughter very pleasant. We found it very tedious waiting; the cars were delayed and did not come in until four in the morning. Arrived in Albany at nine. Found that the Hudson river on account of the recent freshet could not be crossed, and there was no other way but to go to a hotel and wait until the water has subsided which we hoped would not be long as it was gradually decreasing. We went to a respectable and comfortable house, where we tried to make ourselves as contented as possible. Mr. Curtiss did not intend going any farther with his daughter and after seeing us settled for the day left us to the care of Mr. Ives a gentleman who was traveling in the same direction we were. He has been very kind and attentive to us through the day and we have enjoyed ourselves very well. Hope to get started again in the morning.

11.   Miss Curtiss and myself arose very early this morning hoping to get across the river in time for the seven o'clock train; at daylight went down to make inquiries; met Mr. Hughes in the parlor who informed us that the ferry-boat had frozen in the middle of the stream so there was no hope of crossing in that. The ice of course was not strong enough for a sleigh to cross as it was but a few hours since it had been crossed in a skiff. There was but one way that was to walk across which was considered a perilous undertaking. Although several had already come over, and we were so anxious to get started on our journey that we ventured to follow their example, and landed safely on this side. The first train had not yet gone, and Mr. Hughes was kind enough to hasten back after my baggage that I might start immediately. He brought it over himself and would take nothing for his trouble. He got checks for me and saw me aboard the cars and then left me to see to his own affairs. He was certainly very kind one could hardly expect so much from a stranger. I formed a good opinion of his character and shall not soon forget his kin[d] attentions to a stranger. Had been aboard the cars but

a few moments when I accidentally ascertained that there was a gentleman aboard traveling in the same direction as myself and going almost as far. He offered to protect me through my journey and see to my baggage if I chose to put myself under his care. I know it is not always safe to place confidence in a stranger, but I thought from the kind and dignified appearance of this gentleman I could trust him. He has been very kind to me through the day, and I do not know what I have done this evening when I arrived in this great city of New York had not I been under his protection. When we got off the cars he took a carriage for the St. Nicholas, the largest hotel in New York. I never saw so large a building before and it is magnificently furnished, too. I'm nearly almost frightened to find my *littleself* in such a large and splendid house. Went to supper but ate very little, could feel no appetite in such a large room surrounded with so many people. Have not yet learned the name of the gentleman I am with. I wish our people could see where I am tonight.

12.   Mr. Hendrick did not finish his business so here I am spending the day in this great city. I am in the fourth story, ladies and gentlemen in the street look like little children. Got along very well at breakfast this morn. Tried not to appear very awkward, did not feel very much embarrassed. Have been reading and writing all the morning. I dread going down to dinner but it will soon be over with.

13.   Left N.Y. last evening just at dark. Arrived in Philadelphia about ten; found we must spend the night here as there was no train for us to take until morning. Put up at the St. Pier[re] one of the best hotels. Found myself on board the cars again just at day-light. Walked across the Susquehannah [Schuylkill] today on planks laid from one cake of ice to another. There were several hundred passengers crossed in that way. I suppose it was a perilous undertaking as the ice was very broken up. Many of the gentlemen expressed a great deal of fear and anxiety. Heard not a word from the ladies, thought they displayed more courage than the gentlemen. All landed safely, however. Arrived in Washington City this evening where we are to spend the night.

14.   Mr. Hendrick told me this morning that there was no way for us to leave here until tomorrow morning. It seemed as if I could not content myself to remain here all day and another night too, but the day has passed very pleasantly. Mr. H. took me to the capitol this morning.

First went to the reception room where we saw some splendid pictures. Then into the senate chamber where the senators were all in their seats disputing and disagreeing about an appropriation for a railroad through Iowa. Saw Mr. Sumner's seat where he was so shamefully abused by Brooks.[1] Mr. S. is a very tall man and his desk is raised a little higher than the others. I saw Senator Seward,[2] Sen Butler[3] and several other of the great men of whom I have heard. From the senate chamber we went into the house of representatives where those honorable gentlemen were making a great deal of talk and noise about something. I could not understand what. We then went into several other rooms and saw all we could and then walked around the building on the outside. It is indeed magnificent. The grounds too are laid out very beautifully. What I saw there I shall never forget. After leaving the capitol we took an omnibus to the president's house which is really a pallace. I suppose it will soon be Mr. Buchannan's home.[4] He will have a large house all to himself. I think it is quite to bad to have an old bachelor live there all alone; perhaps he can prevail upon some lady to share the house with him. We saw the monument which is being erected in memory of Washington. Each state sends a block of marble. It will cost an immense sum, but will be a splendid monument when finished. I was very weary when I arrived at the hotel to much so to feel any appetite for dinner. I wish we could leave tonight—I dislike to sleep here again: Have had a pleasant chat with Mr. Hendrick. He invited me to go to the theatre this evening an invitation which of course I could not accept. He would not go without me so we spent the evening in talking said a good deal on the subject of religion he is not a professor. Tomorrow is the sabbath and I expect to proceed on my journey something I have never done before. I have thought it all over and it seems best that I should do so and I hope I am justifiable.

15.   At Richmond. Left Washington early this morning; rode in a steamer fifty four miles on the Potomac. The river was full of ice and it was cold; but I enjoyed it notwithstanding. It must be a delightful way of traveling in warm weather. After leaving the steamer we took the cars for this place. As we came into the city I was very much amused at the sight of so many colored people; as it was the sabbath the[y] had nothing to do but stand in the street and gaze at us. We took an omnibus for this hotel which seems to be a very good house. Have taken supper and Mr. Hendrick has gone out walking. I sat in the parlor a few moments but as there were many strangers thought I should feel better in my room. The weather is like summer here; the ladies in the street are dressed in summer clothing. It seems strange to me having

just come from such a cold region. I would like to know what the weather is at home today. I feel strangely at home here; this place seems familiar to me, and I know not why. It seems as if I had been here before. I cannot account for feeling thus. I like the appearance of this place much. Almost wish it was going to be my home. Mr. H. has returned much pleased with his walk. We have been having quite [a] chat, he has gone to his room. I must retire.

16   On our way again whirling swiftly along in the cars   Have rode all day and expect to ride all night; but I do not mind it. I am enjoying this journey so much that I shall feel almost sorry when I reach my destination. Mr. Henderick is very kind and thoughtful; my father could not do better for me. He relieves me from all care and anxiety. I wish our people knew how well I am protected, for undoubtedly they are anxious about me.

17   At Augusta—This is a beautiful place. I think I could make myself happy here if it was my home. We are at Planters hotel. Have had a good dinner and a pleasant room to rest myself in. I feel the effects of riding last night—my head aches badly. We start again in a few moments for Atlanta, shall reach there about three in the morning.

18   Atlanta. Have had a few hours rest this morning and a walk with Mr. H. before breakfast. I do not like the looks of this place much   It is too dirty. Expect to reach the end of my journey in a few hours. I cannot realize that I am so near sister Maria.

19   Reached Cartersville[5] yesterday at eleven o'clock. My kind friend and protector saw me safely landed, and then went on his journey after bidding me a fatherly good bye. How very very kind and pleasant he has been to me. How very fortunate I was to fall in his company. He has rendered my journey so pleasant. I cannot feel grateful enough. Yesterday he presented me a nice book "to remember me by" he said. He has certainly won my kind regard by his fatherly care and I shall think of him as a *friend*. He requested me to write after I get settled in my new home and I think I shall do so. Did not find sister waiting for me at the depot, so was obliged to hire a conveyance and driver at the livery stable. It was the most tedious part of my journey. Reached Mr. Shelman's after two hours ride. I will not attempt to describe the appearance by

sister as she came down the yard to meet me. She had worried herself almost sick about me as I did not come at the appointed time. She thought I was lost on the way. Instead of arriving on the fifth day as she expected it was the tenth. She certainly had cause for anxiety. It has cost me almost as much again as it would have done had I come directly though. I am not sorry however that I was detained on the way for I feel well paid for all the time and expense, O how I wish I could travel all summer instead of being shut up in school. Here I am at the south; is it possible! Oh! how different how very different do I find everything. I was prepared to see a change of climate and people but not so great a change as this! I see nothing that reminds me of my northern home but *sister*. I like the looks of Mr. Shelman's place and the appearance of himself and lady very much. The children interested me. They are very pretty. I don't wonder sister loves them. The slaves or servants as I must now call them are as comical as I expected. I went down to the quarter last night and was highly amused. They were all peeking and grinning at me each telling the other "dat am Miss Jennie" and bowing to me as soon as they had an opportunity. This morning Mr. Clayton came after me and here I am at *Euharlee*⁶ the field of my future labor I suppose. I must say I am disappointed in the appearance of the place. They told me it was a new place and I did not expect to see a village but I thought to see at least *one* street and a few pretty dwellings. I did not think I was to find my home among the trees. I tried to conceal my feelings but it was hard work when I was taken into my room which is neither *plastered* or *carpeted*. O! how bare it looked to me. I said to sister who accompanied me I *can not* stay here. It is something new to me to see people live in this way. At the north we should call it comfortless and indeed it seems so to me. This afternoon we called on Mrs. Clayton and she accompanied us to the academy where I am to teach. It is completely surrounded by trees and it seemed so woodsy and lonely that I could contain my feelings no longer and my tears were discovered in spite of my efforts to hide them. Sister laughed at me. I don't know what Mrs. Gleasoner and Mrs. Clayton thought of me. The people seem very kind. Mrs. Gleasoner does all she can to make me happy; but I cannot feel at home here although the kindness of the people will do much to reconcile me to such a way of living or *staying* rather. They dress talk and eat and do everything different from the northern people. Sister spent the day with me but has just gone back to Mr. Shelman's and I am alone with these strangers. Have unpacked my trunk and arranged my things.

20   Slept in this new place last night   Feel a little better in my room this morning bare as it is. O, how can people live so comfortless when

they are rich? What good does their wealth do them? Was invited to Mr. C. to dine   Expected to meet other company but did not, at dinner. Dr. Kirkpatrick came in before I came home. Had a pleasant talk with him. Like him much. Sister sent me word today that she would come for me tomorrow. It is really uncomfortably warm here; about such weather as we have in June at the north. Hope it will rain soon.

22   Sister came for me yesterday morning. Spent the day very pleasantly. I think I could content myself at Mr. Shelman's house   It seems quite like home. Went to church today right in the *woods* but if we went with the right motive we could worship the Lord as well there as in the most splendid church in New York city. But the house and people were such a novelty to me that I fear my feelings were anything but devotional. Came home with Mrs. C. and here I am in this plain room of mine again. Tis a little cooler today.

23d   Well my book have commenced my labors here with twelve pupils. Some of them appear interesting. I hope I shall succeed in winning their love, for I cannot feel paid for my labor unless I do. Mrs. Gleasoner has gone away. The servants have been cleaning my room. It looks much neater. If it was only papered, a carpet on the floor, and the bed a few *feet* lower it would seem quite like home. I am going to write to father and mother and must say no more to you my book.

24   Another day has passed just as yesterday did. Expect my life will be monotinoss here for there seems to be nothing to relieve monot[on]y. But I will make a great effort to feel happy. Have just commenced the book Mr. Hendrick gave me. Think I shall find it interesting.

25   A warm pleasant day. Sister called on me just before I started for school this morning. She came on horseback, as independent as could be. She says I must learn to ride. I would like it much. Have just sent a letter home. I did not expect to receive any yet awhile; but sister brought me one that was directed to Stilesboro.[7] I could not imagine who had written me so soon. Found it to be from Mr. H. my traveling companion. It contained but a few words, simply reminding me of my promise to inform him how I was pleased with my new home. Mrs. Gleasoner has been sitting with me this evening.

26   Am in my school-room. Tis the first time I have remained here alone after the scholars have left. It is certainly a very pleasant—airy room. Eleven windows looking in every direction of the compass. It is very quiet here too; a good place for a school. It is almost sundown. Mrs. G. will wonder where I am.

27   One week of school labor is ended. If every week could pass off as pleasantly my task would be a pleasant one. I must not expect all will move as smoothly; I have seen enough of life to know that one would be sorely disappointed in any such expectation. Mrs. Gleasoner has been out calling this afternoon. She has seen several of my patrons and says that they seem well pleased with my manner of teaching thus far. I do hope I shall gain their confidence and esteem as well as the love of their children. O how I want to see sister tonight; it seems so long to wait until Sunday.

*   *   *

March 2nd   I have suffered with the cold to day more than I ever did in the *North*. The weather is nothing as cold; but the houses are so open. The people do not prepare for winter here because it is so short; but I should [think?] [t]hey would like to be comfortable while it lasts.

*   *   *

4   Am shivering with the cold yet. I have 21 scholars. They behave well thus far.

*   *   *

March 16th   Have not written in my journal for nearly two weeks. I believe I will not neglect it so again although I have nothing very interesting to note down   yet if I have to return north it will be pleasant to read over incidents of my life at the south.

*   *   *

19th   I am really feeling quite homesick O! What would I not give to see one face from the north.

20th   The scholars have perplexied me to day. I fear I shall not have as much patience with them as I did with my Clinton scholars for I do not love them as well; but I still try to exercise as much patience as I ought; but shall not indulge them much   *Indulgence* is not patience however. Felt sad when I came home from school. O! If I could only go in my *own room* at *Clinton* how it would rest me; but were I once there I doubt whether I should have any inclination to return to this place   Went to the store with Mrs. G. after school, purchased a riding hat,—have just finished a long skirt—am now ready for a ride. O! How I want to see sister, how can I wait until Sunday.

21st   Mrs. G. and I went to Mrs. Leech's this afternoon   The ride was pleasant, the visit rather dull to me being an entire stranger. We were in hopes to hire Mrs. L.['s] Piano; but as it belonged to her deceased sister she is very unwilling to rent it; dont know what I shall do   it is too bad to forget all my music when it cost me so much time and money I ought to have been contented in Clinton where I had so many advantages; but I have sacrificed them all, and my melodean too, just to gratify my desire for a change, and an opportunity for seeing the country. After we returned from Mrs. Leech's I took a short ride on horse back. Think I can soon learn to ride.

Tuesday 24th   "Always darkest before daylight" is an old saying, and it is often a true one. Saturday I was feeling so very, very sad and lonely, and Sunday morning my heart was still heavier and I indulged in weeping freely. Went to church and saw *sister*. When I seated myself by *her*, the clouds seemed to scatter and I felt happy. She said her cousin Mr. Lines[8] was there; after church I had an introduction to him. Invited them both to go home with me. Mrs. Glasener joined me in the invitation which they accepted. We had a very pleasant visit. About four they spoke of returning to Mr. Shelman['s] proposing that I should get on a horse and go with them and remain all night. I liked that idea right well. Mr. *G* was going to use his horse but they got Mr. Clayton's for me. Had a very pleasant ride, reached Mrs. S. just at dark, spent the evening very pleasantly. Mr. and Mrs. S. seemed to exert themselves to render it [the visit] agreeable. Retired at ten, and was soon locked in the arms of slumber. Rose at six, breakfasted at seven then made myself ready to mount my horse for Euharlee. Just as I was to start, sister remarked she wished I would stay and go to Cartersville and to her surprise I replied I was quite willing to do so; but must see Mr. Clayton first, and ascertain if the horse could be spared. Mr. Lines said he should be happy to have our company. Mr. *G* said sister could have a horse, and Mrs. *G* wished her to go to do some trading. There seemed no obstacle in the way of our taking the ride provided I could have the horse. It was thought then that I should go immediately to Euharlee and decide the matter   Mr.   accompanied me. Found

Mr. Clayton at the mill. He said "take my horse and go;" went to the acd.y and informed the scholars, then turned our faces again in the direction of sister's. Galloped all the way there which I thought was pretty well for me. We dismounted and took a lunch, then turned our horses heads in the direction of Cartersville. Had to ride much too fast for me as it was such new business. I could hardly keep up with them. Mr. Lines wished to take the one oclock train for Atlanta and we were obliged to ride on the gallop most of the way to be in time; but I think we all enjoyed the ride, and was there half an hour before time. I like Mr. L. very much and hope he formed as good an opinion of me as I did of him. It seemed so good too to see a northener. Sister traded a good deal; some for herself, considerable for Mrs. Shelman. I made out to spend a few dollars too. Traded at Mr. Erwin's. Sister and I enjoyed our ride home much. Let our horses walk all the way, so we could have a good long time visit. Had the longest talk we have had at any one time since I came. Felt a little anxious when I left Sister at her home lest I should have some trouble in finding mine; but was happily disappointed for I reached Euharlee without the least trouble a little while after dark. I had rode twenty-seven miles on horseback and only my third attempt at riding in that way. No wonder I was so sore and lame that I could not walk without limping. Retired as soon as I had taken tea; but was to tired to sleep well for I was so lame that every time I moved it woke me. Did not feel much like going to school this morning; but made out to get there and have hardly got out of my chair to day. Two new scholars.

* * *

25   I have just returned from a walk with Mrs. G. by the crick side. I want to find a pleasant place to hide myself for meditation and reading. All things have gone of pleasantly to day. Am not quite so lame as yesterday. Received a note from sister this morning; she too is suffering from the effects of our long ride. I would like to know how Mr. Line[s] endured it. Have had a total eclipse of the sun to day; was visible in this state; but it occurred so near sundown and there are so many trees here that we could see but little of it. The tea bell tell[s] me to lay you down dear book.

26   Found Mrs. G gone when I came in from school. It always seems lonely to find her gone. Found my clean clothes had been brought to my room, and I have just finished mending some things that needed a few stitches. Have some sewing I intended to finish this week; but have just commenced a reading Georgia scences [sic],[9] and find it amazing al-

though neither instructive nor interesting. I believe I will finish it before I sew any. Some of the scholars have been rather troublesome to day, feel rather out of time to night.

* * *

28   Have been teaching to day to pay for my freedom on monday; had not my full number of pupils; dismissed early. I have just finished reading Georgia Scenes. I do not feel very much wiser than when I commenced it. Intend to read something more instructive next week.

29   I do not know why it is that I feel so sad and homesick every sabbath. I believe it makes me feel worse to see sister, and yet I could not live without seeing her. I had quite a cry in church to day. I suppose people thought me a foolish baby; but can't help it, no matter where I am. I am home feeling quite down-hearted. Sister sent my purchases at Cartersville to the Mill yesterday by a stranger and I had heard nothing of them, we were both fearful they were lost; but Mrs. Glassener sent Johney to look for them and he found them at the mill safe enough. That cheered me up a little and the arrival of sister soon after entirely dispelled the clouds. We have had a pleasant little chit chat. I wonder if we should ever get out of *talking time*. Have just read a sketch of sister's life which she was kind enough to prepare for my perusal. It interested me *very* much. Dear girl she has seen *many, many* sad hours, and undergone many heart-rending trials. How she has borne up so well is a mystery to me. I think she made too great a sacrifice of her own feelings and prospects for the good of others; but she done it from a feeling of sympathy and love, and a sense of duty, and *he* who could not appreciate and prize such feelings, was unworthy of the heart possessed of them. When she was sought by my dear brother Joseph, and ventured to let *him* take charge of her happiness, her wounded heart found a healing balm; and an object worthy of its *best affections*. O! I wish I could find a *Joseph*.

30   The first day of another week's labor is passed away   Has been a delightful day; the weather here is certainly much pleasanter that it is north. I like the climate here much better than at home; but nothing else as well. I wish I had my melodian here to practice on to night. Mrs. G. is gone to Mrs. Clayton's and I am lonesome. I believe I feel better in school than any where else. Harriet has just built me a rousing fire; they mean to keep me warm if nothing more.

* * *

April 5   Has been very warm to day   Mrs and Mr G. have gone to her brothers to spend the night and as I feel a little timid Hannah is going to sleep in my room. It is the first time in my life that a colored person ever slept in the same room with me   She has brought in her bed and put it in one corner and is now sitting on the floor looking at some pictures   I suppose she is sleepy and I will not keep her up any longer.

*   *   *

13   Yellow Harriet and Hannah have been in my room this evening. I read in the bible for them. Hannah is going to sleep in my room. My head aches badly, I must retire.

14   Mr. Glasener commenced planting *cotten* to day   Rcd no letters to day. Am feeling very homesick

*   *   *

May 1st   Commenced school at an early hour. Had but *ten* pupils. Did not think best to meet with them in the afternoon. Dismissed school for the week. Mrs G and [I] attended the discussion. Growth of grace was the subject which was one fraught with interest to every disciple of Jesus. No preaching this evening. I spent it in the sitting room as I wished to hear the ministers converse but none of them spoke to me, and did not converse upon any subject that was at all interesting to me. So the evening has passed without either pleasure or improvement. I made quite a mistake in date yesterday; called it the first of May when it was the last of April.

*   *   *

5   Have just returned from a walk in the garden. Vegetation is arrayed in beauty. I said mentally, as I walked and mused. This world is too beautiful to be destroyed. Were it destroyed and a new one created could it possess more to please the eye or charm the soul? Were it now peopled with fare and holy inhabitants surely it would prove the abode of unalloyed bliss. It is the opinion of some astronimers that the approaching comet will dash our earth to fragments. I do not know enough to have any opinion of my own; but that of others sends fear to my heart, and tremor to my nerves. If I were prepared to meet my Savior would it be thus? O! my book can you not answer me the question? Often do I ask my heart the question. Sometimes the reply is one of *trembling hope*; but at other times *hope* droops her pinions, and my soul is filled with *dread* and *uncertainty*. My mind and my soul are hungry; they crave I hardly know what. I have been reading a beauti-

ful poem of Moore's but it has only increased the craving. My soul pants for something out of my reach. The tea bell invites me to partake of the "meat which [perutheth?]" and I will do so to satisfy the cravings of animal nature which is necessary to existence.

*　*　*

7　Have felt as I used to in Clinton to day. Very dull and languid. School has passed off very pleasantly. My school duties are certainly less fatiguing than they were in C. and I am earning more here than I did there; but do not enjoy myself as well. I would like more society. Can not help suffering a good deal from *homesickness*. When shall I see my northern home and friends again? O! dear. O! dear. No letters yet! It seems as if I must fly home to night. Would that I could. Who could help wearing of this dull monotonous *existence*, for I can hardly call it *life*. One continuous routine of *toiling*, *eating*, and *sleeping*, will not satisfy me; nor do I think we ought to be satisfied with *bare existence*.

*　*　*

10　After sundown I took a lonely walk; but the loneliness was pleasant to me, for with nothing to disturb I could commune with the beauties of nature which surrounded me. I found a pleasant spot near the fall of water. There is a flat rock about two yards square and just above it a smaller one, upon which I seated myself. A tree on eitherside spread their branches around me, and at my feet was the rushing torrent of water. It is a wild and romantic spot, one that can not fail to arouse all the poetry in one's nature. When thus surrounded by nature, its beauty unmared by art, earnestly do desire the "pen of a ready writer" to relieve my soul of the burning thoughts which oppress it and to which this stammering tongue refuses to give utterance. But I have neither the gift of speech or writing; both are denied me doubtless for some wise reason, and I must be content to feel grandeur and sublimity, without *expressing* it.

*　*　*

12　I wish it would rain; a shower would be refreshing for it is very warm. My school room has been very quiet to day indeed   I have never yet had reason to complain of noise, for the pupils are very quiet; more so than my Clinton pupils ever were. Am feeling very lonely to night. Mrs Glassener is gone. Have been amusing myself looking at the negro children. There are five of them playing under my window. Poor little creatures; ignorance is bliss to them; for they could not be happy did they fully realize their condition.

*　*　*

22   Thirteen weeks have I spent in this little place. A quieter life I
never led; and it has not been *altogether unpleasant*. I have been very
much alone it is true, and have suffered in *spirit* for the want of *congenial* society. But I do not think it has injured me in any respect to be left
to myself for a few weeks. Have had nothing to excite me, and concequently have *eat* and *slept* more than I have for months, which has
had a beneficial effect upon my health. This seclusion also gives me
time and opportunity for reading and meditation which if rightly improved will benefit me vastly more than mingling in society. If I could
be with *sister* from now till monday morning should like it much. If she
had a home of her own I could; but as it is I must be content with visiting her occasionly. Has been a delightful day; is much warmer.

* * *

24th   Mrs Glassener has been quite ill to day. At breakfast she told me
she was unable to attend church; but I could be taken as I wished to see
sister; remarking that we had better stop whispering in church as people were making remarks about it. I felt hurt but did not reply fearing I
might say what I should afterward regret. I came to my room and cried.
I concluded I did not wish to go church; and ought not to go if I could
not behave with propriety when there. Mrs G has since told me it was
only some medlesome persons who spoke of it. I do not think sister and
myself have given any occasion for remark as we have been careful not
to whisper in time of service. But we shall be doubly on our guard now,
and shall not dare to sit together.

* * *

27   Have enjoyed myself very much since school. Mrs Glassener and I
had a delightful drive and a pleasant visit at Mr Shelmans Their
home is really a garden of roses, a rural and romantic spot. I almost
think I could be happy there for a short time at least. My eye could not
soon weary of the beautiful scenery upon which it could there rest; nor
the spell which the beautiful in nature ever throws over the soul be
readily broken. After feasting our eyes upon flowers and shrubery and
our palate's upon strawberries and other delicacies, we turned our
faces toward Euharlee, a direction I am always loth to take. I can not
like this place, or feel at home here; am always glad to turn my back to
it. I am tired of seeing nothing but trees and *wooden houses*. I am weary of the monotony of *eating, teaching*, and *sleeping*. I wonder if I shall
ever be more pleasantly situated. Perhaps I should not be happy if I
were. *Perfect happiness* is a stranger upon earth; and rarely *even* a
guest in the human heart. I will write no more for every thing looks so
dreary, dreary to night; my room so dull and unpleasant. O! if I had

wings I'd live above the habitations of mankind. I would join the feathered tribe; any thing would be preferable to this dull monotony. Good night.

28   Rose rather early for me this morning; but did not get to the table until breakfast was nearly over. Had the blues until I went to the schoolroom, then care and duty drove them away. Dr Williams was here to dinner. He is a young widower I would "set my cap" as they say, if I was in the habit of doing such things.

* * *

June 10   Well another day has passed away in the usual manner. Was very warm, until a heavy shower this afternoon cooled the heated atmosphere. Mr & Mrs Congers spent the day here. I have spent the last hour talking with Mr Wallace upon slavery, ventriloquism, spiritualism, woman's rights, etc. It is raining very hard; I will retire and let it lull me to sleep.

12   Well another five days work is done. As I walked home from school I was thinking if I am not very pleasantly situated. I have certainly a comfortable home and easy as well as pleasant school. One which gives me very little unnecessary trouble. The children seem to like me; and their parents seem pleased with me as a teacher. Thus I was flattering myself that all was going on so *smoothly*. But as usual something soon occured to interrupt this agreeable if not profitable train of thought. Mr Wallace told me some of my patrons would rather I would commence earlier in the morning and keep later at night thus giving them a very long intermission or confining them as well as myself in the school-room eight hours, which I shall *not* do. Neither law nor custom requires me to teach more than *six hours*. On my return from school made myself ready to go to Mr Shelmans, expecting sister would send for me but she has not. I presume she will send early in the morning.

14 * * * Came home on horseback accompanied by a servant; found it rather warm riding as he came rather fast. Have been very nervous to day, trembling at every sound. It is short [the time] according to the calculations of astronomer for a comet to make its appearance. A great deal has been said of it; and many have conjectured that our earth will be destroyed at its appearance. Like a good many others I have been

very much troubled about it. I know it is wrong to feel this, for a firm reliance & affectionate trust in God *ought* to disarm me of all fear.

* * *

17   Have been feeling very sorrowful to day   In spirit I have left this land of strangers and with the speed of thought have traveled to my northern home, visited the Lunatic Asylum and stood beside the couch of my suffering brother. Would that I were there in reality. My heart yearns to watch by the bedside of that dear brother and if possible do something to alleviate his distress.

* * *

22   Has been a very cool comfortable day. Did not have a full school. I understand the young people are getting up a cave party for next saturday. It is on my account as I am a stranger. Very kind and polite in them but my horror of promiscuous company makes me dread it.

* * *

July 1st   It is past the hour I usually retire; but I am very much excited to night and feel very little like going to sleep. Have to day witnessed cruelty for the first time at the south. *Dave* the negro driver beat Adam a young negro in the most brutal manner. It seemed to me that he would kill him. I felt and looked like fainting. Mrs G. saw my excitement but I did not care; indeed I should consider myself void of all humane feelings could I composedly look upon such barbarous treatment of a beast much more a fellow creature. Adam has gone off to night no one knows where. Perhaps the poor fellow has lain down to die some where in the woods. I am sorry for Mrs G. She is very much troubled. O! Slavery slaves what a bitter curse! What a dark stain upon our country! Mrs Spear and her mother spent today with Mrs. Glasener.

2   Nothing has yet been seen of Adam   I should think his mother would be frantic; but she seems to take it very cooly. Poor slaves are used to such things, and if they have natural feelings for each other they are hardly allowed to manifest it. Has been a cool day and is quite cool to night. Strange weather they say for this climate.

3   Am feeling rather lonely and sad to night. Did not receive any letters perhaps that is one cause. The cave party is given up for the present. Dr. Goldsmith called this morning and left it with me to decide,

and as I was not anxious to go at present for several reasons I proposed
having it postponed, which was readily agreed to. Sister will not send
for me to morrow, as she expects I will go to the cave. I shall have the
whole day to myself, and probably spend it alone too. Adam has come
home. He has been hiding out in the woods since his beating without
food. Poor fellow! I presume he suffered too much to feel any appetite. I
was fearful he would get whipped if he lived to return; but he has not
been very harshly reproved I believe. To morrow is independence day;
expect to spend it more quietly than I ever did before.

7   Several days have elapsed since I reported to you my bosom friend. I
spent Saturday the fourth of July alone in my own room, my fingers
busy with the needle and my thoughts far away amid the scenes and
friends of other days. I was not lonely or sad; but enjoyed myself better
than I have a day in a long time. Mrs G. went away early in the morning and did not return until late in the evening. She then came to my
room to see how I had passed the day. I told her I had felt unusually
happy without knowing why. She sat with me a few moments and we
were having a pleasant little chat when upon looking out of the window she exclaimed, here comes your sister and Mr Lines. *Then* I felt
happy and *knew why*. I can never look out of the window and see any
thing that pleases me as well as sister riding up to the gate. I had kept
on my morning dress all day not expecting to see anyone, consequently
I had to dress before I could meet them. Mr Lines shook hands like an
old friend although he is quite a *new one*; and sister gave me a kiss
that made me think that some few *love* me. We passed the evening very
pleasantly. Sabbath day all attended the presbyterian church in this
place, heard Mr Telford preach. Sister wished me to go home with her
which I did; but did not have any visit with her or her cousin. We all sat
in the parlor, and Dr. Stephens spent the afternoon with us. I wanted to
return home in the evening but they all thought best for me to remain
until morning which I did. Was then accompanied by Mr Lines. We had
a pleasant ride and talk. He dismounted at Mrs G. and stayed a few
moments, then bade us good morning. I presume I shall never see him
again. I thought his [?] was *rather cold*, never offered to shake hands. I
believe I never saw anyone yet but that they in some way or other
pointed an icecicle at my heart. Did not feel in the best [mood?] for
teaching yesterday, had but sixteen pupils, and got along very well.
There is a school opened in the baptist church by Mr Jarvis. He only
teaches Arithmetic. Wrote a long letter to Miss Beebe last night. Hope
the mail will bring me one or more to night. Mrs Phillips is at Cartersville visiting her friends   Mr Wallace is attending Mr Jarvis's

school. It is warmer to day. I think we are going to have *melting* weather again

* * *

10   Well I have taught one *long term* at the south. Twenty weeks. How long it seems to think of it; but how soon it has passed away. Such a quiet life as I have led too or would think time would have dragged; but it has not, no I have enjoyed this quiet   Have been [?] over the past, something which I indulge in perhaps too much. I feel well pleased with the way school has passed off. I am satisfied with the improvement the children have made, also with the manner they have conducted themselves. Have heard no complaints from my patrons; but on the contrary, some for kind remarks and warm commendation; which can not be otherwise than gratifying to a teacher's feelings. I trust I have gained the kind feelings of my pupils. They have certainly won my affection, by their good behavior.

* * *

12th   Have just returned from the methodist church. Mrs G. was not able to go, and Mrs Phillips had no inclination to go; so I was compelled to go alone with three gentlemen or remain at home; chose the former. Mr Wallace waited upon me to and from the carriage very politely. Mr Davies preached rather a scolding sermon. Evening; expected preaching at the baptist church but rain has prevented. Have been lieing down this afternoon, but not sleeping; have been reading a sketch of Dr Good's life. Dr Goldsmith has loaned me an interesting work of Dr. Good's which I expect to derive much instruction from. The wheat bugs flutter around the candle so much, I can not read, write or think, and will say good night.

* * *

Sunday 19th   Went to Mr Shelmans on friday morning remained until last night. Mr Wallace came for me; had a pleasant ride home. Wanted to bring sister home with me but she could not come. It makes me almost provoked to see her confined there so closely   The confinement and care of the children are wearing her out. Besides she has numberly things to try her exceedingly. To a casual observer it would seem that she had a quiet and pleasant home, and in some respects it is so. Well there are trials and difficulties in whatever situation in life one can place themselves; no path is exempt, but there are certainly some trials more difficult to bear than others. Sister has a portion of the *difficult ones.* * * *

Evening 9½ The tempter came off conquerer and I remained away from church to day. Have spent the most of the day at home on my bed reading; Just at sundown started for a walk; met Mr Wallace and he accompanied me. He is very pleasant and as an acquaintance I like him very well. I hope he does not think any more of me than I do of him. Am not flirt enough to desire any warmer feeling than I can return. He invited me to go to Cartersville to church next sabbath. I replied I would like to go which is true; but I do not like to go alone with him for it will cause remark. I hope something will occur to prevent my going without causing hard feelings.

Mon 20th Well I have commenced school again. Commenced with nineteen pupils. Has been excessively warm. I think I have suffered more with heat to day than I have before. this summer. Mrs Glassener's hand received a call from Dr Goldsmith this morning   I was benefited by the call for I had a very pleasant chat with him. Topic mental philosophy. He gave me some light on some points and some new ideas; but I could not see with him in some respects or adopt his views entirely.

*   *   *

27th Sabbath eve, have been to Cartersville with Mr Wallace to day. I really did not want to go but I saw no excuse to offer. The rid[e] was pleasant or rather it would have been if I had had pleasant company, for we had neither sun nor rain to encounter. Mr Telford preached an interesting and solemn discourse. The Lords supper was then administered which is ever to me an interesting scene. I did not partake with them although my spirit yearned to do so. Reached home in safety at three oclock. Was cheered by the arrival of sister soon of my return. She came with a sad countenance, for she had sad news for me to read, in a letter from mother also in a newspaper. My poor afflicted brother still lingers on the shores of time but in a suffering condition. His physician gives us but little encouragement to hope for his recovery. To add to our distress we have just read in the paper an account of the burning of the *Asylum*. Several were severely burned the paper states but no lives lost. I am fearful that my helpless brother was among those who suffered from burns; and the dreadful thought will force itself upon my mind that perhaps he perished amid the flames   Horrid thought I will try to drive it from me, for, it seems as if it would drive me frantic   It is time to retire and I will lay me down but I doubt if I sleep much to night.

28th Did not have one hours undisturbed sleep last night. My poor brother, and the Asylum in flames were constantly before my eyes. I am very nervous to day so much so that I can hardly guide me pen; but have written two letters, and must write t[w]o more after school to night. It seems to me I have a good deal to trouble me. My melodean has not been heard from. Must write to Mrs G. to see when it was started. What if I should lose that as I did my bonnet. Two oclock calls me to the school room.

Evening   Have just finished a letter to Mrs Tuttle   was going to write to Carrie but it is too late. Mrs G. has not returned from Cassville[10] expect I shall be disappointed about going to morrow although I have dismissed school on purpose. Well never mind.

29th   Have spent this day *very pleasantly*. Had given up going to Cassville as Mrs Glasener did not return last night; and I was trying to submit to the disappointment as cheerfully as possible, when Dr Goldsmith called and politely offered me a seat in his buggy saying he was going up and would be happy to have my company. *Of course* I accepted the invitation with pleasure, for what young lady could refuse accompanying such a handsome and interesting young gentleman. It is needless to say the ride was delightful; how could it be otherwise with such pleasant company. Reached Cassville in time to witness a part of the exercises at the female college.[11] At noon went with Mrs Glasener to Mr Cobbs to dine; found some very lively young ladies there; had singing and playing on the piano, which made me think of *home, home, home*. how sweet the word! At two oclock went back to the college remained until five then started for home   Our ride home was quite as pleasant as it was in the morning. It was pleasant to *me* at least for since I have been in Georgia, I have met with so few persons who seemed to have any feeling in common with me that my own thoughts have almost become *stagnant* for the want of *airing* them, [Young?] says thoughts shut up will *stagnate*. But mine have had a good airing to day. which is a relief. A feeling of sadness is creeping over me I know not why it is, unless the incidents of the day made me think of the *past*, which is *always painful*.

* * *

[August] 5   At school. A few moments to myself while my pupils enjoy their freedom in the open air. The weather is excessively warm notwithstanding the abundance of rain which has fallen every day for more than a week past. I am feeling very dull and languid this week which makes time seem very long. I want saturday to hasten in its approach, for I am so anxious to see sister. Am reading Popes Poetical Works[12] Find most of his pieces *intensely* interesting His Essay on Criticism and Temple of Fame interested me highly. Commenced his essay on man this morning. I suppose that is the *master piece*. Well in thinking of *Pope* I have forgotten my school and am giving them a long recess.

* * *

12th I think this has been the warmest day I ever experienced. It is very tedious to teach such weather. Had my full number of pupils to day consequently my duties were more interesting. Compositions and speaking this afternoon. I suggested keeping journals and writing letters to my older pupils. I could not tell from their appearance whether the idea struck them favorably or not. They are so very different from my Clinton pupils. I can not tell what pleases or interests them. O! how I would like to spend one hour with the little flock that have so often greeted me in my school room at Clinton. How much they would have to tell me! and how eagerly they would listen to me. The dear little ones I know I can never love pupils again as I loved them.

* * *

26th Mrs Eaton has lost another son. William died last night, was buried this afternoon. It was a solemn scene. The friends appeared to feel it deeply especially the poor mother The Lord sanctify the affliction to them all, and pour the oil of consolation into their wounded hearts. There are a number of persons very ill with typhoid fever in this neighborhood. My health is still granted me, but I know not how long it will be spared to me. I can not help feeling anxious. O! that I could deposit myself in the hands of the Lord and feel safe, for I know that whatever is his will concerning me will be right, for he can do nothing but right.

* * *

September 2nd Have not written for one week. There has been no more deaths from fever but several persons are still prostrate with it. A new case to day. O! that the Lord would stay its progress; but whatever is his will we have no right to complain for he doeth all things well I have been feeling very unwell for a week past. have taken a good deal of medicine which I think has helped me.

September 26th My poor journal how I have neglected you! and my only reason for doing so is that I have not felt like writing. Have just

had a weeks vacation in my school   Yesterday sister and I returned
from Atlanta where we have spent the most of this week   We enjoyed
our trip very much, and spent out time in Atlanta very pleasantly   Mr
Lines took us all over the city, and introduced us to acquaintances of
his who were from the north   We enjoyed our visit with them *so much*.
There is still a good deal of sickness and death in this vicinity; it makes
me home sick. I know I am as safe here as at home for the Lord is here
as well as there; and if it is his will so to do he can protect me from
disease and death as well when I am among strangers as when surrounded by all that are dear, and if it is not his will neither home nor
friends could shield me. One of Mrs Glaseners negroes have died and
now another one is very ill.

Sabbath day September 27th   Attended worship at Raccoon today.[13]
There was a greater multitude than the church could hold and services
were held in the grove. I should think there was over a thousand people
assembled together   It was such a novel scene to me that I must confess I could not hear much of the sermon   After the morning sermon
the grove was turned into a dining hall. So much provision I never saw
at one place before. In the afternoon there was preaching in the grove
and in the church. I could not endure the heat of the sun and sought
shade in the church. Saw sister and had a little talk with her. Poor little
Dave is not much better.

*   *   *

October 2nd   Here I am almost alone in the school room. Only *four*
pupils. The people here can not prize education very highly or they
would not take their children from school to put them in the cotton
field. Mrs. Glasener says the school always closes when the cotton
opens. Had I been aware of that fact; Should have been loth to have
taken charge of it. This week has seemed very long; especially the time
spent in the school-room: With so little to occupy ones time and attention, times drag rather heavily.

*   *   *

4   I saw Mr. Presly about the school. He thought Miss Fowler would
not return and said he thought there was a good opening for a school. I
do not think Cartersville a desirable place of residence; but still prefferable to *this place*.

*   *   *

5   Alone in my school-room. Have just dismissed my pupils, and shall
probably meet them no more. Have closed my labors here as a teacher;

and I can not say that I regret it, for I have never liked the situation   I begin to feel that perhaps I done wrong to leave Clinton. If the Lord does not see fit to prosper me here I shall certainly have reason to feel thus. Well old Academy I must bid thee adieu. I hope my labor within thy walls has not been in vain   I trust I have felt some little desire to do good to the children and youth who have been under my care; but now I must leave them to receive instruction from others   O! that I could feel the sweet assurance that I had made some good impression upon their young minds that should be like good seed sown upon good ground, and resulting in their eternal well being and in the honor of my God, with whom I will leave my little flock. Farewell old Academy farewell.

6th   How strangely it seems to remain at home all day. I do not feel right, had rather be in school. Tocoa came over this morning and afternoon to read and spell. I made out my bills this morning; their amount exceeded my expectations. Not a word yet from Atlanta, Maryetta or Cartersville. I am feeling very sad. The future seems veiled in gloom; but I trust this dark cloud has a silver lining, which will ere long be revealed to me. Let me rely firmly upon one that is stronger than I am, I *know* he will direct my ways aright. Good night my friend journal.

7th   Still another day has fled. Recieved a paper from Mary Van Deusen to day. How surprised I was to see a piece of *mine* in print   Mary has had my essay on *Life Changes* published. A note from sister to-night. I wish I was with her. Have spent the day practicing, reading, sewing, knitting, and talking.

*   *   *

10   Yesterday the mail brought me a note from Mr Lines giving me encouragement to go to Atlanta and open a select school. I hastened up to Mr Shelmans to consult sister. We concluded I had better go. I answered Mr Lines letter to that effect. Providence permitting shall probably leave Euharlee in a few days.

*   *   *

12   Can spend but a moment with you dear journal. My room is all in a confusion; have just commenced packing my trunks. Sister came down to day to my surprise. We went to [Mr.] Smith's, and I was quallified as to the accuracy of my report of county scholars;[14] so that is over

with. We had a most delightful ride   I can not realize that I am to leave Euharlee in the morning; the fact seems to pleasing to be *real*.

JENNIE TO MARIA

Atlanta Oct 15 / 57

My Dear Sister
    You will I know feel anxious to know every circumstance pertaining to my journey and my arrival here. I wanted to commence a letter yesterday but could not get to my writing materials. Well I bid adieu to Euharlee yesterday morning *without a tear*. Mrs Glasener, Mrs Clayton & Mrs Phillips accompanied me in the carriage to Cartersville. Called at Mr Brandons but he was not at home concequently did not settle with him   I told them to pay it to you or Mr Clayton. I called at Mr Erwin's store and told him that *you* would settle my bill with him. If you see Mr Brandon before coming by Atlanta, he can pay you & you can pay Mr Erwin   In case you do receive the money from Mr Brandon *be sure* to take *good* bills and then *be sure* to settle with Mr Erwin *while they are good*. We must not keep *paper money* on hand for there is a general suspension or failure of the banks.[15] Yesterday Georgia Rail Road bank was good; at five oclock it suspended; to day the bills will not pass. If you receive any mony for me you must pay some of my debts with it. I have but one bill that is $5 on [?] bank S.C. I am going to break it to get as much as possible. But now I will return to *minor* matters. Mr Presly saw me on board the stage and processed my checks. My melodean went in the express and cost [?] extra. Found Mr Lines, Mrs [?] and Miss Michell at the Depot. Mr Lines has changed his boarding place. Mrs [?] said I must come home with her for the present but she did not know whether Mrs Michell could take me permanently or not. But I shall not apply for board here. You would not ask why if you could look into the room I am occupying. Mrs [?] says she knows I would not like it. Mr & Mrs M. are very good people but they have a house full of children and but few servants and both do just as they please. This is a great bare empty room with four windows and you can hardly distinguish objects through them so thick is the dirt. The bed is simply a *straw* matress. They could not do my washing either. Now shall I pay $15, per month for such accomodations? I have to go round and see the people before opening school; and shall look for a boarding place. Called on Mrs Welton last night.[16] I shall try to get board in a private family for in all the boarding houses they charge *so high* and accom[modate] so miserably. I have not seen Mr Lines one moment

alone; and have told him nothing. I am afraid I shall not find a boarding place in time to write to your uncle but if I do I will surely write. It will make no difference if you do not know before you come for I will meet you at the cars. If you do not come you must write so that I can get it on *Tuesday*. Mrs Cartnell is going out with me this afternoon. I think I will run up to Mrs [?] this morning.

Thursday before breakfast. Good morning Miss Anna. Am I not smart already and waiting for breakfast. Had a pleasant call on Mrs [?] yesterday morning; returned here to dinner. Soon after a violent storm came up which prevented us from going out. So yesterday passed and nothing done about a school or boarding place. We are going directly after breakfast and hope to accomplish much before the day is gone. Mr Lines spent last eve, with us. I am going to make an article in regard to my school, and wish you were here to advise me. I think I will write it in this manner

A school for girls under fifteen, boys under eight at the following terms
Twelve weeks in a term, four terms in a year.
Primary studies per term $5;
Common English branches $7;
Higher English branches $9

A deduction will be made when the pupil is absent half the term. Have copied this article with some alteration   The breakfast bell so now good bye

After dinner. Mrs Cartnell and I have been calling all the morning but to purpose. I begin to feel a little anxious. Shall commence on monday however with those that are promised. O! how discouraging this scholar hunting! You told me to write *every particular*; but you need not tell others. I expected there were scholars enough engaged to commence with, did not you? But I was successful in finding a boarding place at the first place I applied. Am going to board at Mrs Floyd's   she is a widow lady with no children. She is *rich* and has a neat little home and plenty of servants. I like her appearance much. I did not see my room but presume it shall be neatly furnished. She is to board me and have my washing done, room taken care of for $15.00 per month. That seems high, but Mrs Cartnell says I could not get it cheaper, for comfortable accomodations. Now if I can only get up a school I shall feel satisfied. Be sure and come next week   I expect there are letters at Euharlee for me by [?] get them. Remember if you take any money for me pay it over to Mr Erwin *while it is good*. There is a great panic about money here. I am going to Mrs Floyd to morrow morning.

Shall write to your Uncle to morrow. Hid[e] this letter I dont want it seen   Tell [?] I will have my melodean up when she comes   Kiss the children for me

As ever yours,
Jennie

DIARY

18   Several days have elapsed since I came to Atlanta and I have noted nothing on thy pages dear book. I am yet unsettled and my prospects for a school are not very flattering   Shall commence to morrow however with the few that I have engaged. Have seen a great many people since I came here, for I have been making calls nearly all the time   Since I came in town have been boarding at Mr Michells; but on the morrow expect to take up my quarters at Mr Hanams. O! how much I am thrown [?] among strangers   Wonder if I shall ever find a permanent home before the graves claim this poor body? My expenses are going to be so great that I am fearful that I shall be involving myself in debt and not earning sufficient to pay. It is indeed a hard lot for a penniless girl to go forth alone in this wide world to seek maintainance. I wish I was a man   then I would not fear; but alas what can a poor timid woman do?
I think I shall like Atlanta if the Lord sees fit to prosper me. O! how anxious do I feel   If I do not succeed what can I do? the thought *frightens* me. I have seen several northern people in town which makes me feel at home. Evening. Just after tea Mr Lines called and asked me to go to church. Heard Mr Rogers preach at the Presbyterian church.[17]

19   Well I have opened my school under rather discouraging circumstances. Only five pupils to commence with. If I had even twenty I should feel contented for then I should feel that my income would defray my expenses. My school-room is pleasant; and I think my boarding place will prove to be a quiet pleasant home. Came here this noon to take my first meal. Mrs Hanam appears like a kind pleasant lady; Have hardly seen Mr Hanam. They expect other boarders I believe, so I shall not be alone. My room is one of the front parlors a large pleasant room and very neatly furnished. Have been unpacking my trunks to night   just one week since they were packed. I hope sister will be with me tomorrow night. It seems a long long time since we parted; just one week to night

20   Went to the depot after school found sister and Cleo there. Called on Mrs Welton then came to my new home. Sister liked the appearance of my room very much. Mr Lines has spent the eve with us, and helped to put up my melodean   Something is wrong about it, shall have to have a melodianist see it. Sister brought me a letter.

21st   Cleo and I went to school this morning   sister went to the dentist's. My little pupils told me they were going to the fair this afternoon, concequently I did not return to the school-room after dinner; but went with sister to Dr Campbell's office,[18] Sister took ether and had eight or ten teeth taken out. She did not take enough to make her insensible to pain however, and suffered intensely. I stood by and held her hands through the whole. I did not know that I possess so much courage. I examined my melodean to day and found that it was all right; but was not up right; soon rectified the mistake, and this eve gave Cleo her tenth lesson

*   *   *

23d   A cold dreary day. Am in my school-room and shivering with the cold. My stove is up and I have plenty of wood but it smokes badly. Have had a fire all the morning; but it has gone out, and I do not know as I shall have any pupils this afternoon they thought they were going to the fair again. Evening. Have been very busy sewing since school. Have spent the eve, entirely alone. Had a call from Mr Wallace of Euharlee to day   seemed rather pleasant to see him again. He took some pains to call upon me I thought he would if he came to Atlanta. Have felt quite unwell for several days, am now suffering from influenza which is at present quite prevalent here. Do not expect to sleep much to night; but I will retire and make the attempt.

*   *   *

25   My second sabbath in Atlanta has passed. Went to church this morning with Mrs Hanam. Heard a very good sermon from Dr Dubose,[19] and the *best* singing that I have heard in *Georgia* this afternoon. Mrs Hanam wished to call upon a friend who was to leave town in the four oclock train. She invited me to go with her, we went to the [post?] House, and then to the Depot where all was noise and bustle, I suppose sabbath stillness never reigns there. The sun has shone brightly to day and it would have been pleasant had it not been for a strong wind, which has already dried up the mud and almost made it dusty even since yesterday's rain. Mr Lines called this evening and I went to church with him. The services were nothing. We came home

before nine. Mr & Mrs Hanam had retired. Found Sarah the servant in the sitting room; and she seemed to think we could not dispense with her company for she remained in the room until Mr Lines left. I have coughed almost incessantly to day which has given me a violent headache, and I must lay it on the pillow as soon as possible.

26   In my school-room again but with very little to do. No additions to my school. I must go round to night and see what I can do   Really I begin to feel alarmed. My income is at present a mere trifle compared with my expenses   I do not like the idea of spending the earnings of the past year to pay my board here when I am earning nothing. O! dear a teachers life is truly a hard one. Gladly would I lay down the burden of a teacher could I have home and friends without it, even were it in a peasants cot; if loved ones gathered around its hearth it would be a home of happiness to me. O! I am so weary of being my own guardian in this *cold heartless* world.

27th   Made several calls last night; only the promise of one pupil at present, but a partial promise of three in a few weeks. I think it will be my best way to call around myself; but it [is] something I dislike to do it seems to much like begging for schollars. Ah I have too much *pride* and am too *sensitive* for a *poor teacher*. My five pupils are here to day. Am afraid one of them will give me some unnecessary trouble. She is not an agreeable child; but I will do what I can to make her so.* * *

28th * * * Expected a new scholar to day, but she has not come. What am I to do? This teaching school day after day with but five pupils is neither pleasant, interesting nor profitable.

* * *

31st   Spent the morning sewing; this afternoon have been [looking] about for scholars. I do not know whether I have gained any; had the promise of several; but I find it is not the *fashion* here for people to keep their word; concequently when they tell me they will send I can not feel sure they will. O! how I dislike scholar hunting. I would feel above it did not necessity compel me to do it. I am willing to ask for scholars until I am known as a teacher, then I hope to have them without; but I *will* not beg for them, no I would as soon beg for a morsel of bread. I can see nothing degrading or humiliating for one to gain their own support in any calling where God sees fit to place them; and if they discharge their duties faithfully no matter how humble the station it can not detract from their dignity or respectability but that person will dignify the office he holds. This was the sentiment of Epaminondas[20] the Theban general when discharging the duties of streetsweeper which task was imposed upon him by his ungrateful subjects, to degrade him and teach him humiliation. There are many Thebans in our day, but very few like their noble general.

I had my feelings sorely tried this afternoon. Called at a small house to make inquiries as to the children in that neighborhood, and of course made known my business. She looked at me with an eye of scrutiny and rudely said The fact is there are so many of these *half handed* school mistresses going about that the people are getting tired of them. I felt at first like sinking out of sight   then my prid[e] came to my help. I wanted to tell her not to apply that term to me, for I prided myself on being a *whole handed* "school mistress"   Indeed I would not stoop to do any thing in a *half* handed way. What I do I will try to do *well*. However I concealed my resentment and talked as politely as possible to her, and she finally treated me more like a lady   Well I am a stranger in a strange city and I suppose I must learn to be looked upon with the cold eye of criticism and suspicion

November 1st   Yes cold dreary November has come   At home I suppose they begin to feel the keen winds of winter; but here the weather is still mild. To day it is very warm and pleasant. I wanted to go to church this morning but Mrs Hanam was not well enough to go out, and I did not feel enough at home to go alone. Spent the morning reading, and the afternoon writing. After tea Mr Lines called and we went to church. Heard the most interesting and solemn sermon that I have listened to in a long time. Like Mr Roggers very much, he has a very, pleasant voice and an easy delivery. I do not know when there has been such a delightful moonlight evening as this. I enjoyed my walk highly. Mr Lines appeared rather sober to night. I hope he does not feel *obliged* to come & go with me to church.

2nd   Monday night again. How swiftly the days and weeks roll by! No new scholars to, how strange! Called on Mrs Cartnell to night enjoyed the call *so much*. She is certainly a *beautiful* as well as an interesting woman. Her husband has reason to be *proud* of her; undoubtedly he is of the same opinion. I wish I were not quite so *plain* looking; but why need I care my *true* friends will love me just as well as if I were a *beauty* yes they *love* me as well for my good qualities *if I have any*; but they can *never* feel *proud* of such a *plain little creature*; and I am really *vain* and *foolish* enough *sometimes* to desire to win admiration. Then again I feel satisfied with my personal appearance as *reconciled* to it rather; and only desire to be *loved* and *respected* not admired.

*   *   *

4th   Two or three showers to day; but pleasant notwithstanding. Two calls at my school-room. Mrs Cartnell & Mrs Welton. My school is so small that my duties are irksome. The school-room can not be made very interesting with but six pupils. My courage and ambition will soon fail me if my number does not increase. Mrs Henam had an early tea to night. Mrs Beman and I then repaired to the parlor. Mrs. Beman knit and I sewed, and *she* done the *talking* about half past seven Mr Lines called. Mrs. B. retired to her own room immediately   I suppose she thought he was a particular friend of mine, and she would leave us alone. She was mistaken however. he is a kind friend and pleasant acquaintance; but nothing more. But people will have their suspicions and make their remarks if a gentleman only calls upon a lady.

Had the most agreeable visit with Mr L. this eve that I ever had. He expects to leave next week for South Carolina where he will remain a few weeks then return to his northern home. I regret his departure for I shall then feel more lonely than ever. Well it is late I know by the watchman's cry, "All is well" surely it is time to retire.

*   *   *

9 * * * Mr. Lines was here this evening, brought me some reading: the evening as usual passed off pleasantly. Mr. L. asked my age, and when told appeared surprised as is always the case when I tell my age; for people always take me to be four and even six years younger than I am. Expect Mr L. will cut my acquaintance now he knows how *aged* I am

*   *   *

11th * * * Mr Lines called last eve and invited me to a panorama of a journey from Boston to Itally. Was highly interesting.

*   *   *

13th * * * Mr Lines spent last eve with me: I enjoyed myself finely, hope the rest of the company did. Mr L. said he was perfectly miserable, not withstanding my efforts to entertain him. Dont know that I shall see him again he leaves town to morrow   Shall miss his society *much*.

14   Has been a day of freedom from school-room duties. Spent the morning sewing this afternoon have been out calling shoping and seek-

ing a boarding place; but as yet have not found a desirable one, do not know but I shall have to take up with one that is *undesirable*, for the present at least. Called upon some people who had partly promised to send to school to me, but they had decided to keep their children at home until after christmas. Never saw people before, but had some *little regard* for their word. Am rapidly loosing all confidence in the people in *Atlanta*; and really I know not what course to pursue, there seems no other way but to remain here for the present, and I would feel comparitively satisfied to do so if I were only paying my way, but I am not half doing it and how can I feel otherwise than very anxious. Well my book I'll change the subject. Have spent this eve *very pleasantly*, and yet a sad and lonely feeling has been creeping over me   Mr Lines has been here. It is the eve of his departure from town. He said he had the *blues*, and indeed he seemed rather low spirited; but he will soon be among old acquaintances, and then Atlanta and its *attractions if it has any* will soon be forgotten. We have parted as *friends*, and I trust nothing will ever occur [to] sever the link of friendship. He asked to correspond, to which I assented. I never commenced or expected to commence a correspondence with a gentleman but what something happened to break it up. Wonder if it will be so now. Dear book I am confiding a good deal to you   I know you will not betray my confidence.

* * *

19   A very disagreeable day; has been raining a little. Had a strange dream last night. I dreamed I hired out to do *house work*. Well I don't know what I may come to yet; but that would *certainly be the last resort*. * * *

20 * * * But some how I do not feel as if I should have a good school in *Atlanta*. It does not seem as if I was going to remain here long. O! how I do wish there would a door open for me somewhere. Some how this place seems so *cold* and *dreary* to me. Suppose it is because I have met with such poor success.

* * *

30   Several days have elapsed since I chatted with thee dear book. Spent saturday in a very quiet manner. Mrs W was sick and on the bed until nearly night   then feeling a little better she took a short walk with me. Our business took us up White Hall St.; it was t[h]ronged with men. I never saw so many persons in [?] except on some *great* day. Atlanta is verily a business place. I went up to Mrs Landice early sabbath morning for the purpose of going to church with her. She had told

me that she would take me to the presbyterian church with her but she
had just learned that the minister at her own church was to speak his
farewell sermon and excused herself from going to my church and as I
could not go alone I accompanied her. After the services which were
lengthy she insisted on my returning home to dine with them. It
seemed to much like visiting on the sabbath to suit me but it seemed
impossible to politely refuse her invitation and I accepted.Soon after
dinner Mr Craig came in   I have before been introduced to him but
have had no acquaintance with him. He is a member of the presbyterian church and being told that I was also, and a stranger in the
place he seemed to interest himself a little for me. He said he would do
what he could to aid me in becoming acquainted with the members of
our church and he knew they would feel an interest in my welfare and
do all they could to help me in getting a situation as teacher. Tuesday
evening he is going to call with me [on] a Dr DuBose   I feel very delicate about calling; it does not seem the way to do   I am a stranger and
I would prefer to have people make the first call on me. The manners of
the people here are so different from the people in the north that I don't
know how to act. I almost hope something will occur to prevent my
going to Dr DuBose's for it does not seem right for me to make the first
call with no especial errand and with a young gentleman too   I came
to school in the rain this morning; found no pupils here. Mary and Augusta soon came but I can not spend all my time with them and am
devoting a portion of it to you my book. O! how hard it rains how
dreary and desolate it seems! I shall not remain in the school-room all
day with but two pupils. Will stay long enough to discharge my duty to
them and then go home

*   *   *

2nd * * * Took tea with Mrs Landice. Soon after which Mr Craig called
for me to accompany him to the house of our pastor. The walk was certainly pleasant; and once arrived at the Dr's house and introduced my
fear and uneasiness *took wings*. Found the family very social and
friendly, and I really enjoyed the call. The minister and his lady promised to use their influence for me in getting pupils. I like Mr Craig *very
much*; he is so easy and free in his manners, that it made me feel quite
at home with him. Hope we shall become better acquainted. Received a
letter this morning that showed I was not forgotten by one whose
friendship I prize. Well dear book I must not spend all this intermission with you, for there are other duties that claim my attention.

*   *   *

26   Nearly one week since I have written in my journal. This morning
found two letters in the office. One from sister which I hastily opened;

was glad to find enclosed $16; $15 of which I was oweing to Mr Hanam for one month's board. I did not know just where they lived, and knew it was a long walk, but feeling very anxious to have that debt off my mind, started in pursuit of their abode. Found it after a long fatiguing and mudy walk. Mrs Hanam appeared very glad of the money. Mr Hanam was not at home for which I was sorry as I wished him to give me a receipt, for I have not unbounded confidence in him. On my way home called at Dr DuBose's had a very pleasant call, which was partly on business, hope it will amount to something, shall know next week. Yesterday was my first Christmas at the south. They celebrate the day here as we do the fourth of July at the north. * * *

28   This morning while dressing for breakfast pondered in my mind whether it was not best to dismiss school for this week, to please the children, follow the fashion of other teachers, and give myself time to prepare for another term. Consulted Mrs Welton and by her advice decided to do so. Was preparing to go in the street, when I was very much surprised by a call from Mr Shelman. He soon made his business known, which was to try and engage me as a governess for his children. My sister is about [to] leave them, which they regret *exceedingly*. I could give him no decicive answer to day, am going to have until friday to think about it. Have been writing an essay on *self control* this evening; is now ten   I must retire

*   *   *

30   Another rainy day: have not been out of the house; have accomplished considerable sewing however. Two letters to day. Mrs Shelman wrote in great haste to urge me to come to them immediately as governess for their children. If I did not dislike country life so much I would not hesitate about going; but as I do, shall not make up my mind to go if I can get a situation in the college.[21] Mr & Mrs Shelman have been very kind to sister and myself, and I would like to show them that I appreciate their kindness by obliging them; but if I go there I shall loose my prospect of a school here, and I can not make up my mind to remain long in the country, for it has no [?] or advantages for me; if I go shall have to give up things musical and painting lessons. O! how wish I knew what it was best to do! A letter from S.C. today   Short but kind and friendly.

31st   The last day of 1857! in a few hours it will have gone with its record of good and evil; not one moment can linger with us, not a moment can recall. The last day of an old year is always a sad one, to day I have felt not only sad but troubled. Have not yet decided in regard to going to Mr Shelmans I find myself very reluctant to leave Atlanta and go into the country; but feel I shall be obliged to do so—well I have been praying the Lord to open a door or [?] and prosperity and perhaps that is in answer to my prayer If so Lord grant me a willing heart to obey the call, and grace to assist me in a faithful discharge of my duty.

SYLVANUS LINES TO AMELIA AKEHURST

New Haven, Ct., Jan 3d [1858]

Friend Jennie:

I dropt a few lines to you just before leaving Columbia; but they were hurried and I scarcely know what I wrote except that I promised to write to you on my arrival home, which I will now attempt to do.

My passage home was a short and pleasant one. I left Columbia on Monday afternoon and arrived in New York on Wednesday night; taking the cars on Thursday noon and at four o'clock I was at my Mothers door,—they appeared very glad to see me and to welcome me home, I found my mother brother and sisters all well.

On my passage homeward I did not stop in Washington, partly on account of weather and then I was anxious to get home by New Years. I took the steamer from Portsmouth to Baltimore and had a fine trip up the Bay.

While in Columbia I enjoyed myself tolerably well, but I missed the acquaintances which I had left in Atlanta. On Christmas night I attended a large party there and spent a few hours very pleasantly, but not as well as I should with the same number at the North, the ladies in the South, and especially in Columbia, as a general thing, lack that sociability which is so characteristic of the ladies at the North, and I could not feel that freedom which is requisite for enjoyment.

New Years day passed off very quiet and pleasantly; the old custom of making "calls" on that day was observed, but not to that extent which has characterized it in former times; I visited some of my old acquaintances, but many of them are gone: some have married and moved away, while others have gone to their last resting place, and by them I am reminded how frail is our existence here on earth. In looking about me, I miss a friend here and an acquaintance there, and on inquiry I am told that they are *dead*! and how strange the feelings that come over me when I look back into the past—perhaps the days when we were associates or schoolmates, when their prospects for a long and happy life were as good as mine and perhaps better, then am I reminded that my turn may come next; even now while I write is the bell tolling for one who attended the same school with me, and who but last Friday was in the bloom of health and to-day is being borne to the tomb; he was run over by an enjine and died within an hour;—but I would not weary you nor call to your mind painful reflections like these which have almost forced themselves upon me and I have penned them as it were involuntarily.

Jennie, let me hear from you often, for although many miles intervene between us, yet we may not be entirely separated, for by the impressive language of the pen can we converse together and perhaps to our mutual benefit.

You have very kindly granted me the privilege of writing to you and also promised to answer my letters, which I hope will not be too formal but an interchange of friendship and good feeling between us. Write me how your prospects are at present—have you obtained a better boarding place yet? If you should tell Mrs. M. and Mrs. C. that you have heard from me, please give them my regards I shall endeavor to write to all my acquaintances soon. I think I wrote to you to send me [Cousin] Anna['s] address but I am not certain please do so as I am indebted to her to the amount of at least one sheet of paper.

I am out of business at present and the prospects are somewhat unfavorable this winter, and should they continue so I think it very probable I may return to the South, perhaps to Atlanta.

I think I have already wearied your patience and I will stop writing for the present.

With the kindest regards I remain

Yours Respectfully,
Sylvanus

JENNIE TO SYLVANUS

Stilesboro Jan, 18th /58

Mr. Lines

Let me commence this sheet by congratulating you on finding yourself once more amid the home circle, and mingling again with those who are dear to you. I can imagine your feelings, and theirs, on your arrival home; for I know by experience what it is to meet loved ones after a long separation and I know too what it is to find many a vacant seat in the family circle; to miss a loving smile here and a kind word there. Of the many that once gathered around my fathers hearth, but few are left to welcome me, should I ever return   You are spared this trial; all to whom you bid adieu on your departure are spared to greet you now

You speak of the sadness which steals over you in learning that many with whom you were associated in other days have passed away from earth; also of the serious reflections which it calls to your mind. Mr Lines it is well to reflect thus for we too are *mortal*. Now let me leave this subject for minor matters.

Your letter [mailed] at Columbia was early received and although short was acceptable as a token of remembrance. Your last came to hand just as I was leaving Atlanta. I have bid goodbye to that place for the present; but it was with great reluctance that I did so, for really I had begun to feel quite at home there.

You doubtless feel quite surprised to see by my date that I am in the *woods* again. Well we can not mark out our own path-way; could I have done so, *never* would have I returned here. Probably the Lord has sent me back for some good purpose, and I must submit. As soon as Mr & Mrs Shelman learned that my sister was going to leave them, Mr S. started for Altanta, to see if I would not like her place in his family; or at least fill her place as a *teacher*. Did not feel prepared to consent immediately, as I was still hoping for success in Atlanta   concequently I took a week to decide. Mrs Shelman wrote since in that time, insisting upon my coming. There were several new schools starting in Atlanta at the time; Miss White had left the college and was going to open a school in the Davis house, near my school-room. I had too much pride to *beg* for pupils as others did, could not depend upon the promises of the people   found it difficult to obtain a pleasant boarding place without paying an exhorbitant price. In consideration of all these obstacles, finally concluded it was not best to baffle with such discouragements and uncertainties, for the sake of being in town, when I could have a quiet and comperatively *easy* if not a pleasant home in the country. Do you blame me? I do not regret going to Atlanta, for I enjoyed myself while there, and would like to have remained had it been best. I can not begin to tell you what a time Anna had getting away from here; will leave that for her to do. She is nicely settled at Col. Harrises. I do not mean settled for *life*, they have made no such arrangements yet to my knowledge. She has her birds   They do not appear to like the country very well, or at least it has not had a good effect upon their dispositions; for they quarrel so badly that sister has had to separate them. I do not expect to see her often as Mr & Mrs Shelman wish no communication between families. She will never come here. no one shall prevent my visiting her however. Direct to her at *Cartersville*. Mr & Mrs S——. are very anxious to have me engage to remain with them one year if no longer. I will do no such thing; they shall not consider me a *fixture* as they did Anna. My duties are much lighter than Anna's were, for I would not consent to *entirely* fill her place although I receive the same compensation. Before finishing this Mr Lines, permit me to thank you for your last frendly letter. It is *such* letters that I like to receive. In writing this I have tried to avoid formality, and fancy I have succeeded, for had I *felt* formal should not have wearied you with so long a letter. I beg you will excuse the scrawling appeerance of this sheet, as I have written it by candle light which is the only time I have for reading or writing as I am with the children all day. Good night;

Respectfully Yours
Jennie

SYLVANUS TO JENNIE

New Haven, Feb 4th

Friend Jennie:—

Somewhat surprised, and I may say, happily so, was I to receive your letter, *dated at Stilesboro*; for not until then was I aware of your removal or of your intention of leaving Atlanta, but since a week or two before I left I have had my doubts as to your success in securing a good school, and have of course felt interested on your account, and when I heard that you had got back, I knew that your mind would be freed from the anxieties *and* perplexities which you had to encounter while in the *hands of your friends* in Atlanta.

Perhaps if you had remained there long, enough you would have had a good school, and if their promises had amounted to any thing you would, but it taught me at least one thing, not to place too much dependence upon people's promises in future. I think you was fortunate to secure the place you have if it is your intention to remain South another season, for although you are very much confined, yet you have a quiet and, in many respects, a pleasant home, with none of those discouragements incident to keeping a school in the city. Fortunately, too, you have Anna's experience in the family to patern from, and can take advantage of your independence. I think you are wise in not engaging to stay a year as you can do that as well without an engagement as with.

I have had nothing to do since I came home, and time begins to hang heavily on my hands. I spent a few days in the country but the most of the time I have been home. Business is something that is obsolete,— even the *shape* of money is almost forgotten, and mechanics of all kinds throng the streets on every pleasant afternoon, but it has got to be so common that people do not complain as long as they can get enough to eat; prospects for better times are gloomy for the present. I intend to return South before long as I am getting tired of doing nothing, and there are a plenty out of work besides myself, who have the first right to situations.

The weather here is delightful, and I fear I shall be cheated out of my anticipated sleigh-ride, as so far there has not been snow enough for a sleigh to run. I have been about sick with a cold for the past two weeks, but I am much better now.

When I commenced this sheet I thought I would not weary you with more than two pages but I have filled up the third and I cannot stop without expressing to you the pleasure that your letter (which you chose to call a "long" one) afforded me and may their shadows never be less in future.

Hoping to hear from you again soon. I remain

Very respectfully Yours,—

Sylvanus

JENNIE TO SYLVANUS

Glen Pleasant²² Feb, 7/58

To Mr Lines

Once more has a little messenger arrived which I deem it a pleasure to answer; and the duties of another day over, I find myself quietly seated for that purpose. If the friend who penned the lines was here, I fancy I could spend the evening more pleasantly in conversation than in writing; but as that can not be, my pen and ink must serve as a substitute. What should I do in this quiet country home did not little tokens of remembrance laden with kind regards from distant friends often find their way to this lonely spot and, like sun beams shed light upon my pathway and gladden my heart?

Very rarely does any thing occur to relieve the monotony of my life at present; and yet time does not hang heavily, or pass wearily away as I imagined it would: every day cares and duties have given it wings. Through the day I am constantly with my pupils, either in the school room, in the nursery, at the piano or on the play ground. Never feel free from care until they are locked in the arms of slumber; then I "draw a long breath" and sit down to read or write. Many of my evenings are spent as I am spending this, in answering letters: when not thus employed, I must confess a feeling of loneliness steals over me: I find my spirit yearning for the companionship of friends. Why weary you with a catalogue of my duties and trials. *You* do not know what it is to be a governess in the family of a Georgia planter, whose wife through a *false* education is not capable of giving one word of advice or making one wise suggestion in regard to the training of her own children.

Ah! one reared in the halls of fashion and wealth is but poorly fitted for the stern realities of life. Sometimes I have murmured that it was not my lot to sip more freely from the cup of pleasure and gayety; I am learning the folly and sin of merely a "butterfly existence" and feel thankful that my life has of necessity been a *practical* one.

One year to day since first I stepped upon Georgia soil. Then one year seemed a long, long time to remain in "Darkiedom," but it has passed and perhaps another will pass before I return to my northern home. Really I am becoming quite resigned to this half civilized mode of living, or staying rather. My greatest fear is that I shall imitate the manners and language of the people, shall guard against it however, for you know I am not partial to the Georgian. Am glad I am not at the north, these "hard times" it is hard enough here; but it must be worse there if even the "shape of mony is forgotten".

I am glad to hear you are coming south again: hope you will return to Atlanta. Before leaving that place I heard several of your friends express a wish that you might return. I know you would be cordially welcomed should you do so. I have not heard from Atlanta since I left; wrote to Mrs Welton a few days since; shall expect a reply soon. I left my stove with her to be [?] I suppose you have written to Anna. I have visited her but once. enjoyed the visit much. Col. Harris is very social and friendly, and Miss Harris a pleasant young lady. They make one feel quite at home.

Have called upon my old friends at Euharlee. They expressed themselves "mighty" glad to see me. I had rather be here than there. Mr Clayton the gentleman who was to collect for me, has by negligence lost $30, Is not that too bad? We have had a few days of very disagreeable weather; it is warm and pleasant now. Flowers are in bloom. I will not call this a "*long*" letter; but fancy you will after reading through it. Please do not vex me with but "two pages" in reply.

Receive this as a token of regard
From Jennie

JENNIE TO MARIA

Glen Pleasant Feb 16

My Dear Sister

It is late; but I must pen a few words to you. The mail brought me no letter to night. I was so much disappointed on sabbath day that you did not come along. Mr. Anesworth the teacher at Stilesboro took dinner and spent the afternoon here. He is from Madison Co. N.Y. and is acquainted with many people that I am. Seemed pleasant to talk with him. Mrs Shelman has a lady interst as governess. She is in Philadelphia and has been South three years and liked so well that she is anxious to return. She has written two letters to Mrs Shelman, and I should judge it very desirous to secure this situation   Mrs Shelman is very much pleased,—says she shall send for her. She does not urge me to stay now; but she acts fair about it shows me the letters etc. Nothing is said about when she will come or I leave. They know I have no situation; and we can not expect that they will exert themselves much for me after all that has passed. I am *of* course feeling *very anxious.* In many respects this is not a desirable place but it is decidedly *comfortable* and easy; and sure. I had made up my mind to remain until I secured a pleasanter home or saved enough to take me home. To remain or not remain is not now *optional* with me. I must look else where. If I could only go to *Marietta* that would be delightful. My object in writing to night is to talk to you on this subject. Mrs S. has just paid me a visit expressing herself so much pleased with Miss McNamer's letter which came to night.

See if Col. Harris does not know some one in Maryetta whose influence I can obtain in getting a school. If not there see if he does not know some other place. Another thing for you to think about. I do not want to leave that $30, in Euharlee. Mrs S. says Mr Clayton aught to pay it also that I can easily make him do it and advises me to do so. Now what is your advice; speak to your *friend* if you please.

Has the Col gone to Alabama yet? If not when is he going? I had thought of writing you next saturday; but if he has not gone, and will be gone by next I will wait until then as I think you prefer me to come then as you will be lonely. Give my love to Miss S. Dont tell her all I write. I want to see you *so much*   Drop me a line if you can before saturday, that I may know whether to come or defer until next week. My pen refuses to write *legibly* so good night.

Your sister
Jennie

P.S. When you go to Cartersville please get me fifteen letter stamps and a pack of white envelops

Jennie

SYLVANUS TO JENNIE

New Haven[23] April 5th

Friend Jennie

It is now some five or six weeks since I received your well filled and heartily welcome letter and I have no doubt you have made up your mind that I had dropt you from my list of correspondents—not so, for you are among my most valued ones. I shall not make an apology, for my penmanship will do that for me. A short time after I arrived home, I took a very severe cold which so debilitated me that I was taken down with the lung fever which confined me to my bed for nearly four weeks; for the last week I have been able to walk a short distance each day, but am still very weak. This is my first attempt at writing and my nervousness and weakness almost forbids this, but to day I am left alone and my mind wanders back almost unconsciously to the past, and I think of the many pleasant hours that I have spent while in Georgia not the least of which were among my endeared acquaintances in your present vicinity, and I could not resist scratching a line or two; I might write a *sheet* or *two* would *my* strength and *your* patience endure it but I will try not to weary you.

For nearly two weeks of my sickness my physician was in doubt which way it would turn with, but with the comforts of a home, the attentions of an affectionate mother and loving Sisters I could want for nothing, and I am now enabled to dismiss my physician and are in hopes to be able to attend to my business in the course of two or three weeks. Fortunately for me we are having a very early spring and most delightful weather so that I enjoy my morning walk and are sometimes apt to go beyond my strength, for which I receive many a caution. While I was sick I received a letter from Mr. Delaney wishing me to come on as there was a situation in Nashville, Tenn., but I was not aware of its contents for two weeks afterwards although I was told that I attempted to read it when it came.

I intend to return to the South again during the coming season but my sickness will probably delay me some.

I suppose things move along in the same monotonous routine with you as ever, but I hope you will not get tired of it and return shortly before I visit Georgia again, as I am anticipating many agreable horseback rides and sociable chats together in the "sunny South."

I suppose, too, that Couz. Anna still occupies her new home, and enjoys herself well as any other Southern land-lady can   I shall expect to hear that she has got married in every letter that I receive. Please tell her that her letter was received and will be answered as soon as strength will admit.

I have fairly filled this sheet out after all and if you can make out to read I shall feel repaid for my ink and pen are miserable and my mind to disconnected to write, but I know you can read my account for that. Let me hear from you on the receipt of this, and I am in hopes that I shall not be obliged to render the same excuse for negligence again.

Very truly, Yours

DIARY

1858

Monroe [County] June 6th 1858   Truly "life is a checkered path, made up of changes." Such has been my experience for the past few weeks. When I filled the last page of my journal for 1857 I was at Mr Shelmans teaching. I left there on the 5th of April and in company with sister started for Oxford Newton Co, on a visit to her relatives. Stopped in Atlanta and spent a few hours very pleasantly with our friends. Reached Oxford safely and was cordially received by sister's *new found* relatives. We remained several days with them enjoying ourselves finely. As I had then no school and knew of no opening for one, thought best to remain in Oxford until I did. Found a very pleasant boarding place in the family of Mrs Jennings consisting of herself a daughter and two sons, also several boarders, students in Emory College.[24] The kindness and hospitality which I received in that family will ever be remembered with *gratitude*. I can but wonder at the interest they manifested in me when I was a perfect stranger to them; and as I became more acquainted, Mrs Jennings and her daughter seemed to bestow upon me the love of mother and sister, and *well* could it be appreciated by one whose heart often yearns for the *unparalelled* love of a *mother*—the sweet companionship of a sister. They completely won my heart, and made me feel that I was at *home* and with *friends*, and not a friendless, homeless stranger. Mrs Jennings did all she could to aid me in obtaining a situation to teach; but every door seemed closed against me; the anxiety and suspense I endured I hope it may never be my lot to suffer again. I could have been very happy had it not been for *mental* trouble, as it was I passed very many pleasant hours   Jennie Jennings is one of the lovelist girls with whom I have ever become acquainted. I never saw one more pure minded, innocent,—artless, generous, and self sacrificing than she is; to know her is to *love* her. We have become very *warm* friends; I trust nothing will ever occur to break the golden link of affection and friendship that binds our hearts. Remained in Oxford nearly two months. Made application for a situation in the college in Covington;[25] hope I have succeeded in obtaining one. The term does not commence until September, I did not like to be out of school until then, and hearing through Mr Doolittle sister's uncle that a teacher was wanted out here in the *woods*, I decided to come and teach for them for a few weeks. Yesterday Mr Paxson the gentleman in whose family I am to board came to Oxford for me. To day finds me among strangers again and still worse in the country.[26] Attended church to day and heard a very plain old gentleman preach; but the love of

Christ lit up his aged face and rendered musical the tones of his trem-
uloss voice. The audience consisted of the most rough looking people I
have yet seen. Have spent the afternoon talking with Mrs. Paxson. I
like her thus far very much.

Mon. 7th   Well her[e] I am in the schoolroom again; but with only
eight pupils. The pupils about here are so ignorant and so little acquainted with the improvements of the day that I shall find it hard to
please them   I suppose they will expect me to teach from sunrise to
sunset; but that is more than I shall do; if I teach an hour or two longer
for them than I ever did before that must suffice. Sardus church where
I am teaching is a large, airy, cool, room, being situated *right in the
woods*, the sun can not shine upon us well. I have answered one letter
to day to Mr. L. I shall be quite busy as I am answering letters.

JENNIE TO SYLVANUS

Monroe June 7th 1858

To Mr Lines
  My Friend
    To what have you attributed this long silence? Not to negligence or
forgetfulness I trust, neither of which have been the cause. Most certainly should I have given myself the pleasure of writing to you long
ere this, had your letter reached me in due times. With several other
letters it lay in the Post Office at Cartersville nearly *two months*, and
all that time I was feeling *so anxious*, for In Atlanta I learned that you
were very ill. At times the gloomy thought crossed my mind that perhaps you were in the *grave*. You may judge then how *well pleased* I was
to recognize your hand writing, among several letters which sister has
just forwarded to me at Oxford where I have spent the last two months
doing *nothing* which is decidedly the most fatiguing labor I ever performed. Left Cass Co, on the 5th of April in company with sister. Made
a short but pleasant visit in Atlanta; reached Oxford on Wednesday
evening, where we were cordially received by sister's *new found* relatives, and enjoyed our visit finely. I hoped to get a school in or near
Oxford, and the Doolittles promising to aid me, I remained for that
purpose while Anna left me for Winfield, Columbia Co, where she was
to remain several weeks with Col. Harris's family. She wrote to your
sister from that place making enquiries about you; but received no reply until her return to Cartersville.
    While in Oxford I boarded in a very pleasant family and was treated

with a great deal *of* kindness and hospitality. Mrs Jennings and her daughter endeavored to make me feel that I was at *home* and with *friends*, and not that I was a lonely friendless stranger. Their kindness will ever be remembered with heart-felt gratitude. Had it not been for *mental* anxiety, should have enjoyed myself well, as it was I passed many pleasant hours. Could see nor hear of no opening for a school, until a few days since   Mr Doolittle heard there was a teacher wanted in the country twelve miles from Oxford. As much as I dislike the country I gladly consented to accept the situation. To day finds me in the school room again. My prospects however are not at all flattering. There will be but few scholars and [?] on the county which will pay me but per day. I am in the woods again, with every thing *even more* uncongenial to my taste than it was in Euharlee; but if I have my health and defray my expenses I will not complain. The anxiety I have suffered the past few weeks have made me more willing to conform to circumstances. I have only taken the school for three months, which will soon pass away. I hope to teach in the college at Covington the next term which opens in September. The faculty has given me a good deal of encouragement, but not a decided answer. I *know* from the *past* that I am capable of doing better than I have done since I came South; concequently it wounds my pride and hurts my feelings to think that I have to take up with these poor country schools, with these common *crackers*. Perhaps it is wicked to feel thus, and I have tried to overcome the feeling, but have not yet succeeded. I want to tread willingly and with meekness the path wherein God would have me walk, be it ever so rough and tangled; but it is a weary task to school the heart into passive fortitude, to teach it to bear without a murmur the trials and ills to which we are subject while on earth. Do you not find it so? I suppose your illness interfered with and delayed your return South; but I hope it will not prevent your return entirely, if indeed you are not already here. I am at a loss where to direct this letter, not knowing your "whereabouts" believe I will send it to New Haven, if you are not there your friends will forward it to you. I am so glad you were at *home* when you were suffering, where loved and loving ones could minister to your wants, and do all that affection and sympathy could suggest to alleviate your anguish. With an *own dear mother* to watch beside ones couch, surely it must be *almost* pleasant to suffer. It seems to me the most bitter cup from my *own* mother's hand would be *sweet* to me, But I must not write of my *mother*   it is anguish to think of her. O that she could have been spared to me. Anna made me a short call on her return to Cartersville a few days since. I suppose Col, Harris will be married before many months but *not* to sister. She would not have him. She like me is not partial to the Southerners. She has an excellent home and can have as long as she lives if she chooses to remain.

You doubtless think I left Mr Shelmans very abruptly and wonder why I did so. Truly it was very unpleasant for me there, feeling as they did toward Anna. They would not allow the children to speak of or to her. Mrs Shelman was continually "yerning" over to me the circumstances of her leaving, throwing out insinuations against her, as if *she* could prejudice me against my *only* relative in Georgia. But unpleasant as it was I should have remained until I could do better; but as they *appeared* so anxious to keep me I thought it was optional with me to go or stay concequently I would not bind myself to remain any definite time. They took advantage of this, *pretending* to think they were in danger of loosing me any day, and before I knew anything about it a lady from Philadelphia was daily expected. She came and I left. Mr Lines I am ashamed of having written so long a letter. Please show me that you consider me [?] by writing as long a one in reply immediately

Yours Sincerely,
Jennie

DIARY

Wed 9th * * * Eight pupils to day and ten long hours have I spent with them. *Hope* I have discharged my duty to them; should think I might in that length of time. * * *

Thurs 10th * * * I am glad to lie down at night and dread to rise in the morning, then to spend so many hours in the school room busy all the time about *nothing* is really more fatiguing and enervating than more active labor; if my school was large and I was only expected to be with them a *reasonable* number of hours I should find my duties more interesting, but here I have to stay from 7½ in the morn until 6 at night teaching *eight* children.

Friday 11th   Well one week has passed here in the *woods*. Five days of school labor is performed. Hope my school will be larger and more interesting next week. I wish I could get to the Post Office to night for I think there must be letters there for me. Now were I in town I could go the office rainy as it is, but here I am in the country and while here must suffer all its disadvantages. Today has been very cool and pleasant, consequently I have suffered less from drowsiness and languor. Their was a violent storm of wind and rain this afternoon. The trees near the school room were prostrated, and the *many others* that surround it were swaying to and fro, trying to resist the power of the rude blast which threatened to sweep away everything in its path. I never saw such fierce storms at the North as I have witnessed in this warm climate. When the wind had *breathed* out its fury, and as if weary with its exertion, began to sigh heavily, then the rain drops fell to lay the dust with which the air was filled. I could but compare this storm of nature to the storm of passion which *too often* sweeps over the soul prostrating for a time the tree of reason scattering the *finer* and better feelings with which the soul is endowed. Like the wind it ceases not until exhausted. Then a sigh of shame and sorrow heaves the bosom. Tears *perhaps* of penitence shoot down the cheeks. O! shame! shame! that such a tumult of which should ever convulse the sort of man which was made in the image of God, endowed with *reason* and immortal[it]y.

* * *

Monday 14th   Tonight finds me both *sad* and *cheerful*. My school has increased to 19. Several young ladies came to day which would add interest to the school if they were more *refined intelligent* and fa[r]ther advanced in their studies. But I am resolved to do all in my power for there improvement both intellectually and morally. * * *

Tuesday 15th   Really I am *very weary* to night. My school is small; but it is not interesting, it is always more fatiguing for me to teach such a school than one replete with animation and interest. Most of the pupils the older girls especially have so little refinement of feeling and cultivation of mind that is a task to try and interest them. I feel discouraged to night and despair of ever leading them into *lady-like* deportment. I do *not* I *can* not like teaching in the country; *every* thing is uncongenial to my tastes. But let me remember the anxiety of the past few weeks and become [?] and *thankful*. Let me seek for happiness in a faithful discharge of duty and for peace of mind in something that is *not earth-born*; something that earth can neither give nor take away.

> "*O, for a closer walk with God,*
> A *calm* and *heavenly frame*;
> A *light* to *shine upon the road*
> *That leads me to the Lamb.*"
> * * *

Friday 18th * * * I begin to feel a little more courage in regard to the improvement of my pupils. They appear a little more civilized for the last few days. * * *

* * *

Sunday 20th   A bright pleasant morning; but it bids fair to be a very warm day. I have just left the breakfast table and seated in my room with you in my lap dear journal   I am prepared for a chat but it must be with an inanimate book for nothing else is near with which to hold converse. Millie the maid has just put her dark face in at the door and says "forever writing well, well," I replied yes in that consisted my greatest happiness. She looked at me with astonishment as if she could not comprehend how there could be any comfort in a pen and ink. I suppose a piece of *corn-bread* and *bacon* would possess more charms to her eye. There are services at Sardus Church to day; an old school baptist is to preach. They usually dwell so much upon their own doctrine and deny the truth of others that I do not like to hear them preach. I do not think I shall attend the meeting to day but remain at home and read and write.

Sunday evening. I finally concluded it was best to attend church to day as I have no *good* reason for remaining at home. I saw *decidedly* the roughest looking people that I have yet seen any where. Really I did not know that there were such *ancient*-looking people in existence. Their dress and manners made me almost fancy I was living in the day of the old patriarchs. I can not say that the sermon (if such it could be called) interested me, but the preacher although unlearned may be a devoted christian. I dare not judge him and will not criticize his preaching. I heard from Oxford today by way of Mr Jessee Doolittle who dined with us. No news from that place he told me. Old Mr Dickison was here to dinner also. Mrs Paxson tried to laugh at me as he is a widower but he is so *old* I did not feel at all *teased*. Mr Paxson's mother a very old lady came here to day; she is going to remain some time I believe.

Monday 21st   Two new scholars to day; one a young lady, the other a little boy. Have now 21 under my care, which keeps me quite busy. Almost every scholar has a different book which prevents my classing as I would like to do. Well never mind I will worry along with them and do them all the good I can. We have had a delightful shower to day which has cooled the air much. I taught school until after six tonight. It is now dark and close my journal and enjoy a twilight meditation.

*   *   *

Wednesday 23. * * * Mr. Stovall wrote to me respecting a school. Also inclosed one from a friend of his in Clarksville[27] in the northern part of this state. where there is an opening for a school. Mr. S. says it is a pleasant, healthy town; very good society, and what is not of little moment to me, mostly *Presbyterian*. Did I not expect a position in Covington college, should gladly accept the one at Clarksville. As it is I can not at present decide, not having yet received a decided answer from President Fulton.[28] * * * It is excessively warm to day. This morning the heat oppressed me so much that I hardly felt able to drag myself around the school room. About eleven oclock one of the little boys exclaimed, There is a snake! We all looked in the direction he pointed and behold there was a *black* snake up near the rafters. I told the older boys to try and kill it. One of them hit it with a long stick, it fell to the floor and before he could give it another blow it made its escape through a wide crack in the floor. I was very much frightened but no more so than I am every night. Although I have never yet seen a snake in my room I am continually expecting that I will and am foolish enough to lie awake at night watching for them. I wish I could trust myself in the hands of God, instead of trying to take care of myself. I wish I could *think less* of myself and feel less anxiety for my safety. I ought to feel perfectly safe, knowing that God will do his own will concerning me; and whatever that will is I ought to feel submissive, even if it is to die from the bite of a venomous snake. Have two letters ready for the maile, but no opportunity to send them to the office.

Thursday 24th　Dr. Barret passed the school-house this morning and by him I sent some letters to the office. Wish he might bring me one or two in return; but do not expect that pleasure to day. Retired about eight oclock last night and was soon in the "land of dreams." I was very weary in body and mind and "nature's sweet restorer" has made me forget my fatigue. But long as was the night I felt little inclination to rise when aroused from slumber a little after four. Early rising is very good as a *theory*; but to practice, takes more self-denial, ambition, and resolution than I can boast of possessing. I think I have a fair trial of becoming accustomed to it at present and of liking it if *custom* would make me like it. But I despair of ever practicing it only when obliged to do so. This morning the family sat down at breakfast just as the clock struck five! Now it seems to me *almost uncivilized* to eat so early in the morning. And as for making one feel bright and lively all day, it does not have that effect upon [*me*] but quite the contrary for I am sleepy and dull and languid *all day*.

After school. I *did* get a letter to night also a Harper's Magazine from some kind friend, I think from Mr Lines. [?], Mr Stovall wrote me again respecting the school at Clarksville. They have procured a teacher.

Friday 25th   Rested *well* last night, and feel refreshed this morning. There Millie has just come in to arrange my room, and it is impossible to write when she is in sight displaying her *ivory* at *her own wit* and *my* expense. So good bye book for this time.

After school. Am almost too weary to write, my book. The heat has been very oppressive, and the scholars *rather* troublesome, both combined have nearly prostrated me. The third week of school labor has passed, and nothing of importance has occurred to annoy or perplex me. My pupils behaved quite as well as I expected they would, and advance, *I think* in their studies. Teaching is a *wearing, enervating* business.

* * *

SYLVANUS TO JENNIE

New Haven, June 27/58

Friend Jennie:—

Long and anxiously had I looked for a line from you, nor could I devise the cause of its non-arrival, and I had about given up looking, when at last my eyes was greeted with another of those well known and much welcome messengers from my absent but not forgotten friend, and I assure you my heart was gladened while reading it, for I had imagined that I had offended you from something I had written, although I was unconscious of what it might be as I seldom remember minutely the contents of my letters. A week or two ago I received a letter from Mr. Delaney who wrote me that you had left Mr. Shelman's and had gone to Oxford, so that I made up mind that you had not received my last.

I am very sorry that you have had such poor encouragement since you have been in Georgia, for certainly your cup of vexation and disappointment has been full, but I hope your lot will not always be as hard as the past year has proved to be. I am in hopes that you will not get so discouraged as to return North this summer, for I am anticipating much enjoyment on my return should I find my friends there.

I have entirely recovered my health, although I was fearful that it would go hard with me, as my fever left me with a severe cough which almost baffled the skill of my physician, and so debilitated me that I was scarcely able to go about. I was unable to do anything for nearly five months so that I heartily appreciate the blessings of health now that I am again restored.

The weather here is very warm, thermometer ranging from 95° to 100° in the shade and I am almost melted and run down, and should I not fill this sheet you must not blame me as my disposition is good enough but want of animation and what is more, something to write about that would interest you is my excuse. Had you ever been to this place, I know you could not but be interested with and would like to hear of it. The city is now in the bloom of lovliness,—with her magestic shade trees, her splendid avenues and carriage roads leading into the suburbs and adjacent towns, and then again her beautiful harbor affording an opportunity for those who are fond of sailing to escape from the oppressive heat and tumult of the city and enjoy the delightful sea breeze as it wafts one o'er its waters. A few nights ago I accompanied a party of ladies and gentlemen on a sailing excursion and a joyful time we had of it,—the moon was shining bright, not a cloud to be seen, and with a fair wind we glided down the harbor, hailing one after another of the numerous sail-boats as we passed them freighted with cargoes of a similar nature as our own, and in the place of the cold formality, so common in every day life, could be heard the cheers of one party after another as they rung through the air, and now and then would their voices echo, in some familiar tune, back to the distant shore telling only of their enjoyment as they receded from view. After "cruising" about for some two or three hours, we "*came about*" and bent our sails for the shore, which we reached about twelve o'clock well pleased with our trip. Notwithstanding the enjoyment my mind would wander back among many distant friends who were deprived of such pleasures as these, and I would wish that they too could be with us.

Although my sickness prevented me from returning to the South as soon as I anticipated yet it is my intention to leave here as early as October and sooner if business should improve, as I learn that it is very dull at present.

In your last, you closed with an apology for writing so "long a letter" but that was needless for be assured nothing gives me more pleasure than to receive and peruse your letters, and would gladly reciprocate were it my power. Please write me again soon, as I am waiting to hear from you.

Yours as ever,
Sylvanus

Written hurriedly with a poor pen

DIARY

Monday 28th Yesterday was decidedly the longest and lonliest day I ever experienced. Perhaps the fault was in me but I think not *altogether*. Did not feel well this morning, and dreaded to go to the school-room, but when once there, my duties did not look so formidable. Had three new scholars. All behaved well to day. Am constantly anxious lest something should occur to disturb the peace and quiet which at present reigns in the school room. I will continually remember my weakness and look above for strength to enable me faithfully to discharge my duties and direct aright the little flock committed to my care. * * *

Tuesday 29th * * * Scholars have been a little more troublesome than necessary to day. I can bear with all *necessary* noise and perplexity, but any that is *intentional* or unnecessary troubles me *exceedingly*. Two pedlers have sought shelter from the rain. They came directly behind us from school, and as we quickened *our* pace *they* did the same. Frances and I thought they were after us, and we became considerably alarmed. I presume our fears were *groundless* however. I fear my pupils got very wet before they reached their homes. They have so long a distance to walk; but I should not think so warm a rain could hurt them. I feel that it would be refreshing to be out in it myself.

* * *

July 1st Thursday evening Have felt but little better than I did yesterday. I do not know why it is that at times a feeling of coming trouble oppresses me; when I know of no care whatever. When teaching it is a presentiment of trouble in my school. So strange is the feeling sometimes that I dread and almost *fear* to enter the school room. I think a person who has committed some great crime and is continually expecting to be taken can feel no worse than I do at times. Really such a feeling is painful beyond description. I can not account for it in any way only constitution weakness of my nerves. I think it is almost necessary, and certainly desirable that one of my temperament should be surrounded with an atmosphere of sympathy, pleasantry, and kindness. I suffered with this strange, agonizing feeling this morning; gloom like a heavy pall has hung over my spirit all day. This afternoon a heavy shower came up, Mr Paxton was near the school house culling grain; he came in until the rain ceased. I attempted to hear my pupils recite in concert, but my timidity got the upper hand of my courage, and I almost made a failure. How strange that I should be so timid after having taught school so long, and having been so much among strangers. I do feel so vexed with my self to think I can not have more control over my nerves and appear more at my ease. Mr Paxson came for us to night as the branch was to high to cross on foot. Just after we reached home Mr Dickison and Mr Baker from town called, and enquired for me. I was so wet and muddy I was obliged to dress before I was presentable. I was introduced to Mr Baker and had a very pleasant chat with him; like his appearance well, he appears so easy and gentlemanly. They tell me he is a very worthy young man, highly respectable, and what is much to his credit a *self-made* man. I think more of that class than I do of those who have never done anything for themselves; merely recieved from others. I like the *active* not the *passive* man or woman. * * *

* * *

Saturday 3d   Rose at an early hour feeling very miserably; but the feeling wore away after breakfast. Sewed until dinner. In the afternoon went to Monroe with Mr & Mrs Paxson. Was glad to find myself in town once more; wanted to remain there. Made a few purchases; had to go to every store, and then did not succeed in getting the articles I wished. Saw several very good looking *bachelors*, but thinking they were married men, I did not put on any *airs* at all. One of the gents was so *very* good looking had I known he was yet in a state of celibacy my *maiden heart might possibly* have fluttered a little. Looks however have very little effect on me and leave no impression on my heart. The manners and actions are what please or displease me. I thought to have received a letter to night from a friend of mine, but I was disappointed. I begin to think that friend wishes to drop me from his list of correspondents. Well if he is *anxious* I am *willing*. I have not a correspondent whose name I would erase from my list, until they requested it by word or action; then it would be done *cheerfully*.

* * *

[July 4] Evening. Filled two of thy pages this morning journal, but must note down a little more. Attended church this morning. Heard old Mr Baker preach. He made some very appropriate remarks on the liberty of our nation, and the bravery and suffering of those by whom it was obtained. I think I heard the most elegant prayer that I have listened to in Georgia. It was offered by Mr Bass and was very appropriate for the day. * * *

Monday 5th   Rose early and felt miserably this morning; ate very little breakfast and had the *blues* about going to the school room. Understood I was to have two new scholars who would be a great trouble to me. I do not feel like encountering trouble from rude and ill-bred children. I am willing to teach them and do all I can for their improvement but I do not want to take charge of children who have no training at home and I do not intend to have trouble in this school, for if their [are] any disposed to cause it, they will be expeled or I shall resign my office as teacher. I do not expect to teach the school long and I wish to get along pleasantly the few months I remain. * * *

* * *

Wednesday 7th   Well my book I *am cheerful* to night and must tell you why it is. For the first hour in school this morning I with difficulty refrained from weeping so heavy was my heart and so low my spirits. I had not heard from the faculty at Covington college and had almost given up hearing and was wondering what to do for the future. About nine oclock I heard a carriage approach, on going to the door [?] Mr Doolittle and his son Alonzo, his wife and little Willie, all from Oxford. Right glad was I to see them. Mr Doolittle said Prof. Jones, one of the faculty of Covington college had been to Oxford expecting to see me there, and had left a message with Mrs Jennings for me, the substance of which was that my services would be needed in the college at the opening of the next term on the 16th of September next. I can not describe the feelings which this little piece of news gave rise. Such a sudden transition sadness to joy, from anxiety to relief, from suspense to certainty, I never before experienced. It was almost too much for me, *nervous* as I am to hear; after the first excitement of feeling was over, I felt prostrated. It is well the news came to me in the morning; had it been near night I should have lost many hours sleep. I expect there is now a letter in the office for me from Miss Jennings. Hope to receive that and others soon. Twenty-three scholars to day, quite a respectable number. Have just finished a letter home.

* * *

Saturday 10th   Have been trying to sew to day, but have done very little. Mrs Paxson has been with me nearly all day; so I have *talked* more than sewed, for I can not do both unless my sewing is very plain; I have been fitting a crape dress which was no easy task unaccustomed as I am to sewing. Mrs P. told me something that vexed me to day. Mrs. McCrey a woman in the neighborhood has taken it upon herself to criticize my rules in school. She does not like it because I have prayers in school and because I give perfect and imperfect marks. I do not intend to ask Mrs McCrey how I shall proceed in my school-room duties or what rules I shall have. I consider myself competent to make and inforce my own rules. As regards opening a school with prayer I think no christian could object to that. I have not so much confidence in my own power to do right that I can engage in the responsible duties of a teacher without first asking the blessing and assisting grace of God. I dare not trust in my *own strength* to guide the young minds right. Besides I consider it a duty as an example to the children. I think it is a teacher's duty to train their pupils *religiously*, and *morally* as well intellectually. I shall proceed as I have commenced; if I do not please others, I shall satisfy my own conscience. I will not neglect a known duty to please any one. I fear I was *rather* hasty this morning in regard to Mrs McCray's interference; But really nothing makes me more indignant than to have any one trample upon my rights in the school room. I have made teaching my profession, my care and my study; and I have the *vanity* to think that I know more about it than those who have had no experience in the responsible and *thankless* calling of a teacher; but I think I have said enough on this subject for the present, and will drop it.

Mr Doolittle is here to spend the night. He brought me a letter which he to day took from the office. It was from Sister. She is feeling very sad, lonely and friendless about these days. And she has a good many things to make her feel so. I wish I was near her, that if possible I might sympathize with and comfort her. I do not know how to be thus deprived of social intercourse with my only relative in Georgia.

*   *   *

Tuesday 13th   Have done little else but weep since I came home tonight. Mrs Paxson saw Mrs McCray to day and she talked very unkindly about me as a teacher. She disapproves of my taking time to pray in the morning before commencing my duties; she does not think of the school-room as a proper place. I thought all places and all times and under all circumstances it was our duty and privilege to crave the blessing of our heavenly parent and ask his assisting grace, for without it *I* can do *nothing aright*. Mrs McCray also criticizes my mode of instruction very severely. What *can* she know about it? and if she did know all my proceedings in the school-room *she* is not competent to judge if they were right or wrong. If I am right she is a meddlesome mischief making woman, and judging from her conduct I should pronounce her ignorant, ill-bred and conceited. The way she has treated me is certainly impolite, unkind and unchristian. Such things trouble me so much I do not know but I had rather leave the school; and yet I should hardly be justifiable for leaving because one is dissatisfied (and without a cause too), when all others are so well pleased. Mrs Paxson showed so much feeling for me, and talked so kindly that it made me love her better than ever. She begged me to remember that Mr P. and herself were friends to me and also many others, and that Mrs. McC.

could not injure me, she was only hurting herself. I did not go to tea tonight: after it was over Mr P. came to my door and called out "Miss Amelia go to supper; don't let that old hard shell trouble you; the rest of your patrons have unbounded confidence in you." The speech amused and encouraged me. I went to tea, or coffee rather, and a cup of the stimulating beverage raised my drooping spirits somewhat. I think I will write a note to Mrs McCray tomorrow something as follows.

> Mrs. McCray
>   I regret to learn that you are not pleased with my mode of instruction. I like to satisfy my patrons, and thus secure their good will and kind regard. But from several years experience in teaching I have learned that it is impossible to please all and I have adopted this rule. I will do just as near right as lies in my power, and satisfy *my own conscience* as regards my duty. Then if those who patronize me are pleased I am thankful. If not I can not help it and would prefer to have them send elsewhere. Those only who have learned by experience know what the trials and perplexities of a teacher are; and when increased by *unnecessary* complaints, the burden is more than I can endure. As regards opening my school with prayer; *that* is a duty and privilege which nothing can tempt me to omit. I have not so much confidence in my own ability to do right that I can engage in the responsible duties of teaching the young without first asking the blessing, and assisting grace of God. I think you can not have been rightly informed in regard to Joel's behavior. He is a good boy in school. Out of school he is doubtless like all other children, at times, quite too rude. When I know of any of my pupils doing wrong on the play ground I shall certainly reform them; and if necessary use the rod, but I think as far as possible it is better to rule by *love* than *fear*. When I understand the disposition of my pupils and earn their love and confidence I have no fears but that I can manage them *successfully*. As I have not had the pleasure of forming your acquaintance I thought best to write you a few lines. Hoping that after you have read it you will think better of me,
>   I am Res. Yours
>   Jennie

There, I think there is nothing in the above that can wound or irritate her feelings. Shall copy this tomorrow and send it to her.

Wednesday 14th   A very delightful day; but I have not felt like enjoying it; Have felt very nervous, in consequence of what I heard last night. I sent Mrs McRea the letter by Joel.

Thursday 15th   Another fine day. My mind is in the same state as it was yesterday; unfit to enjoy anything unless surrounded by different influences. To be situated as I am at present, certainly has a very bad effect upon my mind. It is more than unpleasant, it is painful for me to feel obliged to remain even for a few months where every thing is un-congenial to their tastes and discordant to their feelings. Hours seem *days, days, weeks; weeks, months.* And now that their is an unpleasant association connected with this school, time and duties will drag more heavily than ever. Tis true I am not obliged to remain, and at times I think I will not force my inclination to yield to my judgment in this case. Then again I resolve to conquer my feelings, and if my life and health is spared teach on until the college opens in Covington. Mrs Mc-Cray has not sent Joel to day. I hope I shall never hear on the [?] of her.

Friday 16th   Have felt gloomy and troubled to day; and *not* without cause. My pupils have not behaved as well as usual either. This after-noon I was sick and had to leave them for a few moments. Did not reach home until near *seven oclock.* Rather a late hour to dismiss school I think. People around here seem to put *teaching* on a level with manual *labor*, and expect as many hours service from a teacher as they would from a day laborer. But it is ignorance and want of appreciation in them. I wish I could conform to their views of teaching with more pa-tience and amiability than I do. * * *

Saturday 17th   When I awoke this morning it was with a feeling of relief that I remembered that it was *Saturday.* I sewed very [?] all the morning on my dress. This afternoon went to Monroe; made a few pur-chases, and was examined as to my qualifications as a teacher by Mr Atkins and Mr McDonald two of the five gentlemen appointed to exam-ine teachers. It was not with a very good grace that I submitted to this ordeal, for I felt that so many years experience in teaching ought to be a sufficient proof of my ability to teach, at least in a school like *this.* I have been dreading this examination; but it passed off more pleasantly than I expected. The certificate of which I was pronounced worthy is to be left with the ordinary to whom I am to hand in my report and from whom I am to receive my money. Mr Atkins is a teacher in Monroe, and Mr McDonald a lawyer. Both of them *young* gentl[e]men. After the ex-amination was over they threw off the dignity of inspectors, and were very social and pleasant. I feel relieved and more cheerful to night.

* * *

Wednesday 21st   It is late my *only* friend, and I can not say much to thee. Have written to Mr Lines, and commenced a long letter to Sister. I am feeling very *unhappy.* Mrs Paxson is treating me very coldly almost unkindly. What I have done or said to merit such treatment is more than I can tell, but it crushes my heart. *Cold* looks and *cold* words do more than my sensitive nature can bear. O! dear I sometimes wish I was void of feeling and sensibility. To night I feel completely *lone* and *friendless.* A loving letter from mother this morning, brought the sweet assurance that I *have friends* those who love me well, but then they are so *far far* away in that *dear* northern town where every street yes every house is so familiar to me and around which clings all the joyous associations of childhood. I will retire and perchance I may dream that I am a child again in my own *home* with my own *loved friends.*

JENNIE TO SYLVANUS

Monroe July 21st 1858

To Mr Lines,
    My Friend:
        This evening finds me as usual alone in my room. I have been enjoying the twilight hour, which has now passed. The darker shades of night have taken the place of that calm gray light. The queen of night has risen radiant with light and glory. She looks down upon earth from her home in the sky, and her bright rays dispel the darkness with which night would shroud us. Her soft beams have soothed my spirit into a pensive mood, and I would sit and muse in her genial light; but her influence is saddening as well as soothing; she will talk to me of the scenes and friends of other days; I feel too much like an *exile* at present to enjoy such meditations   so I have lit a *home-made tallow* candle which stands in a very *unromantic* brass candle-stick. and romance can not linger in such a dull light, surrounded with so much common reality, and they have left me, to spirit with the moonbeams, and to bear some desponding soul aloft on their wings. It is pleasant at times to forget *uninteresting* reality and on the wings of fancy visit a world of ones own creation; yes it is *pleasant* but not *profitable* I suppose you *strong-minded* men never indulge in such folly as building *air castles;* and lest you should think the less of me for confessing myself guilty of such weakness, I will drop the subject, hoping you will excuse me for annoying you with such nonsense.

Speaking of a bright night recalls to my mind the description you gave me in your last of a sailing excursion which you had enjoyed so much. I should think you would often repeat such a pleasure as that must have been. I can not imagine any thing so delightful as a sail by moon light.

I am glad you think of returning South; but I think it must be something of a trial to tear yourself away from such a pleasant home, and I shall not feel sure that you will really do it until I know you are here. A Harpers Magazine came to me not long since, for which I suppose you are the one to whom my thanks are due. The perusal of its pages whiled away several hours very pleasantly. The history of New Haven interested me much. Am glad the precious boon of health is once more restored to you; hope you will not again be deprived of it.

Have turned over no new leaf in my life since I last wrote you. My school has increased in number and some what in interest. Am enjoying very little of the spice of life at present: indeed very little occurs to relieve the monotony of eating, teaching, and sleeping. And then I am surrounded with every thing uncongenial to my tastes and discordant to my feelings. I am *trying* to bear it with a very good grace however; for hope and expectation beckon me on to a more agreeable future. I think I told you in my last that I had applied for a situation in the college in Covington. Have received a *favorable* answer from the faculty, and now expect to commence my duties there as a teacher at the opening of the next term on the 16th of September. Am very much pleased with the idea. Hope to find a pleasant home there. I shall at least be favored with more refined and intelligent society than I now am; and that is *every thing* to me. Do you write to Anna Mr Lines? She does not speak of hearing from you in her frequent letters to me.

The weather is *oppressively* warm; and I am feeling very dul and uninteresting; which is my excuse for so poor a letter. Expect to remain here four or five weeks longer. Hoping to hear from you before I leave I am as ever

Your friend
Jennie A. A.

*   *   *

DIARY

Friday 23rd   There are services at Sardus Church to day and I had to dismiss my school for the week. Have been sewing very busily, and have at last finished my dress. Several ladies called on me this afternoon, but a *ceremonious* call is never much satisfaction to me. Had they been friends how much I should have enjoyed a talk with them. Have felt in a mood for chatting to day but have seen no one with whom it was any satisfaction to talk. This morning was reading in Psalms. I came to a passage that troubles me, which gave Satan an opportunity to put sinful thoughts and mischief into my heart.

His breath goeth forth, he returneth to his earth; *in that very day his thoughts perish.*[29]

What are thoughts but the *soul?* The soul surely can not *die.* What then does the Psalmist mean? Sometimes the thought of annihilation intrudes in my mind and almost forms itself into a belief. I have somewhere seen the idea advanced that the spirit is an emanation from God, and at death it returns to him from whence it came and forms a part of his being. That when the body dies the soul ceases to have a separate and *conscious* existence, but is absorbed into the great Author of its existence. At times this seems to me a reasonable and plausible theory. But O! how vain to form any theory; we are poor blind erring mortals. We can but trust all to our Heavenly Father. He will order all things *well.* I have to talk about these things to some one who is wiser than I am. To day I feel a strong desire for such converse; but am denied the privilege and can only *think*, and ask my God to help me to think aright, and to throw light upon a subject which is so dark to my feeble comprehension.

Saturday 24th   Have been alone nearly all day. Have been very busy and have not felt very lonely. Indeed I never feel so much alone or rather do not suffer from a loneliness in the retirement of my own room as when surrounded with congenial society. When boarding (as I always am) my *room* is my *home*, and in it I can *feel* at home, at least when I can feel that I am free from intrusion, Situated as I am this summer I can never feel sure of undisturbed quiet; but I hope it will not long be [?]; I must try and bear all things as patiently as possible. * * *

Sunday 25th   Well I have attended what they call a general meeting at Sardus Church to day. There were many people assembled together of all ages ranks and colors. The house would not have seated one fourth of them in anticipation of which an arbor had been constructed in a rude but very convenient and comfortable manner. It was not like sitting in a carpeted and cushioned church, but never the less it was a very suitable shelter for the occasion. This morning Mr Shaw an old school Baptist addressed the audience from these words "All things are of God." He seemed to be a very good man, but illiterate and unlearned. I was not much pleased with his discourse or his manner of delivery. His sermon was I should think nearly three hours long. The people were nearly all bountifully supplied with eatables, and those who were not, were invited to partake from the well filled baskets of others. After an intermission of an hour, the multitude again seated themselves in the arbor, or at least as many as could be accommodated with seats. A man from the state of Maine now rose to address them. Had I not been told that he was a northerner, should have guessed it. His language, the tone of his voice, his gestures and indeed his whole appearance appeared so familiar to me that I felt as if I was looking at and listening to an old acquaintance. He is an old school Baptist and reminded me so forcibly of Elder Hill, Utica, N.Y. that I might have closed my eyes and found myself there. His text was in the second chapter of Hosea 21, 22, & 23 verses. It was decidedly the best sermon in defense of the old school faith that I ever listened to. Should like to have formed the acquaintance of that gentleman and conversed with him much, but time and circumstances did not even favor me with an introduction. I did not remain until the services were over. I suffered nearly all the afternoon with a sever[e] headache which continued to increase until I felt obliged to return home and throw myself in the bed. And now the "big meeting" as they call it is over. It is only eight oclock, but the horse is shut up and the family has retired. I think in retiring so early one misses the most delightful hours either for meditation or social converse. It always gives me the "blues" to retire before dark or arise before light.

*   *   *

Friday evening [August] 6th * * * School would have passed of pleasantly to day; had not a snake paid us an afternoon visit, which attracted the attention of the children more than their books. * * *

*   *   *

Monday 9th   Something to make me feel very thankful and cheerful to night. A letter from my dear brother Ezra. One would not think from his letters that he was a patient in an insane asylum and he is not an *insane* patient, only when disease prostrates him in body, then his mind is prostrate too, and reason dethroned. How strange that Ezra should be thus afflicted. Not one member of our family bid fairer to enjoy life and do good in the world than did that dear brother. Truly the ways of God are mysterious and past finding out. * * *

Tuesday 10th   Very warm again to day. Usual number of pupils and they have made an unusual amount of noise and trouble. I fear I have been *rather* impatient with them, and *rather* cross too for I know I felt impresed with the idea that several of them needed a whipping; but could not nerve myself to administer it. My aversion to using the rod is decidedly against my own comfort and interest in the school-room for I have more to endure from troublesome children than I should if I were more severe in my discipline.

Wednesday 11th   O dear me! how many trials and perplexities the poor care worn teacher has to endure. It seems to me parents must think that *teachers* have an unusual amount of *iron* in their composition and are also void of *sensibility*, from the way they trample upon their feelings and *sympathize* with them in the annoyance to which they are subjected. I do believe teaching is the most thankless calling one can engage in. A little circumstance occured this morning which *un*nerved me for the day. I wish the parents in this neighborhood could feel it their duty to shoulder a little responsibility themselves and not put it all on poor me. A *hickory* was put in my school-room this morning. A *delicate* hint that some of my wild flock needed the benefit of it. I do not intend to give them reason to complain of my whipping their children as they did of my predecessor. I can man[a]ge them in a better way while in the school-room and in the play ground; and I do not consider it my duty to take charge of them else where. Really I can not help feeling impatient for my school to close.

*   *   *

Sabbath the 15th   Attended the Hard Shell Baptist church to day; and was interested and I hope benefitted, if not the fault was my own. The first sermon was not very interesting but the remarks which followed it by Rev. Mr. Walker were very good. I believe I am almost a hardshell in faith. I know I am [?] in some points of doctrine, and then in other things I can not see with them at all. I believe I ocupy a middle ground; am neither a Predestinarian nor an Armenian.[30] I witnessed to day what was to me a *novel* scene; but not void of *interest* or *solemnity*. The afternoon service included the administration of the Lords supper, and *foot-washing*, something I never heard of any denomination practicing. It seemed so strange to be amused; but such a humiliating scene soon made *me* feel humble too. I could then have gone forward and bathed their feet with my tears had it been a duty. They had two bathing pans, one for the brothers, the other for the sisters. The minister commenced the operation by laying off his coat, girding himself with a towel, and getting down upon his knees washed his brother ministers feet and then in turn his brother washed his. In this way all the members of the church washed each others feet thus showing publicly their humility and love for their brethren. The last hymn sung was very affecting and appropriate for the occasion. While the congregation were singing it Mr. Walker went round and shook hands with all the members of his church. There was a good deal of weeping and some shouting. Have enjoyed myself on this sabbath better than on any other spent in Monroe. It is now late and I must retire.

* * *

Saturday 21st   Am teaching to day; but have only 8 pupils. How little most of the people in this neighborhood care about educating their children! Really it is like "casting pearls before swine" to give them means and opportunities for improving their uncultivated minds and degraded condition. They are perfectly satisfied as they are, and take offence at any suggestions that tends to civilize or enlighten. * * *

Sunday 22nd * * * I have been reading in Pilgrims Progress nearly all day; and feel intensely interested in it. I can see many of my own trials and temptations in those which poor Christian had to encounter; but I do not bear trials with the meekness and fortitude which he displayed; nor do I resist temptation as he did. Have finished the description of his pilgrimage. He crossed the river of death, not without fear but safely at last, and was received at the portal of heaven. Am now reading the description of his wife and children's journey in the same narrow way. They too find trouble and difficulties.

* * *

Thursday 26th * * * Am going to send Mary a copy of my essay on the Voyage of Life. She says she is intending to have my Lifes Chances published in a Morrisville paper.[31] Surely it is not worthy to be put in print. It is dark and I must say good night.

* * *

Sabbath 29th   The eve of another holy day. Yes a calm sabbath night. Just the time when our thoughts should be raised from earth to heaven. From the creature, to the Creator. I am alone in my room, with nothing to disturb or prevent tranquil thought and peaceful communion with my Maker. But I find it almost impossible to fix my thoughts entirely upon divine things. And when I attempt to pray it seems as if God was so far off. I can not feel the sweet assurance that he is near and listening to my feeble unworthy words. Earth and it's vanities keep me at so great a distance from my holy Father. I desire to bow low at my Saviors feet to night and I know He will not spurn me if I go with meekness and penitence. I desire to concecrate myself anew to his service, to live continually at his feet. I feel that there is no other place of safety for sinful erring mortals. O that it were my privilege to bathe his feet with my tears and wipe them with the hairs of mine head, as did Mary of old.

1   Yes let me bow *low* at my Saviors feet,
    And bathe them with humble and penitent tears
    Perchance He'll grant me communion sweet,
    And a pardoning smile to dispel my fears.

2   Perchance His love for me He'll then reveal,
    And make me to know that my sins are forgiven,
    If low at his feet with *faith* I kneel,
    And *repentance* toward God my Father in Heaven.

3   O! Savior the *need* of thy pardoning blood *I feel*,
    To cleanse my heart from guilt, polution, and sin;
    To make me pure, holy and new within,
    The bruises and wounds of transgression to heal.

4   I'm pining in sadness, day after day,
    Hope sheds but a *feeble* and *flickering* light
    Oh! I know it is *sin*, that distresses and clouds my way
    And keeps my soul shrouded in the darkness of night.

5   From the bondage of *Satan* I long to be free;
    Too long at his shrine with homage I've knelt,
    With doubts, fears and terrors, he has wearied and distressed me
    A desire to be freed from his yoke how Oft I have felt.

6   And yet where e're I stay, where e're I go;
    What e're I think, what e're I do,
    I am still the slave of this deadly foe.
    Oh! tell me humble christian, is it thus with *you*.

7   Oh! my Savior am I *wholly* Thine?
    Hast thou *all* my sins forgiven?
    My heart renewed and filled with love divine?
    And can I *ever* hope to live with thee in heaven?

8   Oh! then *dear Jesus* hear me now:
    To this poor suppliant bow thine ear.
    While at thy feet I humbly bow
    Remove each doubt, dispel each fear.

9   Help me to know and love Thee more;
    Help me to walk in the narrow way;
    Until life's pilgrimage is o'er,
    Oh! help thou me to "*watch* and *pray*".

A *poor* attempt at writing poetry my journal. I can not express my thoughts in verse, this gift is denied me, although at times my soul is full of poetry; and I must be content to *feel* and not *write*.

* * *

Thursday [September] 2nd. Have just finished making out my report. Have earned $41,40 clear of all expenses since I left Oxford. Hope I shall be so fortunate as to receive it all. Shall to day close my labors as a teacher in Walton County. I think I can say with a *clear* conscience that I have done all I could for the children and youth who have been under my care. *Some* of them have made rapid progress in their studies; and I think they appear a little more civilized than when I first came among them; but perhaps I have become accustomed to their rude ways, and am not so much annoyed with it. Am not sorry to close school; on the contrary am very much rejoiced to bid Sardus adieu. Never have been pleased, and could not feel very happy here. Time has seemed long and passed wearily with me. I have been impatient for the weeks and months to pass away. I do not pretend to justify myself in not feeling happy in my place and under my circumstances where I could do any good; for I know I ought to adapt myself to my situation in which God saw fit to place me, and be contented therein; but I have not reached that state of perfection yet. This summer's campaign has taught me some things about myself that I did not know before. For instance I have often thought I would like to be a missionary and go among the heathen as a teacher. I will never flatter myself again that I am benevolent, self sacrificing and meek enough to take up that cross. I *know now* that I do not possess the spirit of a *missionary*. For if I could not content myself and find happiness for a few months in trying to do good to the children of ignorant unlearned people in this my own enlightened land; what could I do in a distant land, among savage nations. O no I now realize the painful truth that I am not good enough, am not enough like my Savior to teach his gospel to the dying heathen.

SYLVANUS TO JENNIE

New Haven, Sept 5, /58

Friend Jennie:—

Again I am seated—not to perform an unwelcome task, which were it finished and out of my sight would give me ease—far from it— although my procrastination would indicate as much, but rather do I consider it a source of pleasure to be permitted to commune in spirit with my distant friend, whom I hope soon to meet, and perhaps to converse with more agreably than it is possible through the seemingly cold formality of solitary musings.

I have delayed writing for some time in hopes that I should be able to answer your letter verbally, as I have been somewhat expecting to return to Georgia before this time. Mr. Mason wrote me some five or six weeks ago to know if I would come and take charge of an office in Fayetteville, Ga.,[32] to be started by a Mr. Looney, the Principal of an academy there. I accordingly wrote him that I would but have not heard from him since. If I should come, I shall be a near neighbor to you, as I think it is the town adjoining Covington.

Your reveries (which you was pleased to call *nonsense*,) interested me much. I have read and re-read them, for they called to mind the days that have passed, when, time after time, I have set in my room, while the evening shades closed around me, and my mind would wander back to what I would then look upon as a paradise, and ask myself why I had left the pleasures of a home and the society of friends to go among strangers, unknown and uncared for pleasures, it is true, that I had not fully appreciated until I was deprived of them; but the pleasures of *this* life are of short duration,—experienced, as it would seem, but for an hour and then passing, away, like the dew of the morning, but lest I should unthoughtedly call up sad reflections, I will forbear speaking of the *past* We are naturally and constantly looking to the *future*, with the hope that joy and happiness will be our destiny, but how many are disappointed, we set our mark in the dim future and strive to reach it, but alas! how few there are who finally attain that goal for which all are straining every nerve.

Nothing has pleased me more than to hear that you had been successful in obtaining a situation in the college at Covington; hope your anticipations will be more than realized in the change, for surely your associations for a year or two past have been anything but agreeable.

My health still remains excellent, for which I am truly thankful. I am at present employed on a morning paper which confines me very much, depriving me of my evenings' leisure, and compells me, if I write at all, to do it on Sunday. I am in hopes that business will improve in the South that I may return soon.

I visited New York last week to attend the great Atlantic Telegraph celebration in honor of the success of one of the greatest undertakings of the nineteenth century; it was a magnificent affair and was attended, as near as could be estimated, by over a half million of people.[33] While there I met several acquaintances from Atlanta, also a few from Columbia whose faces were familiar and made me almost think I was again in the South.

I received a letter from Cous. Anna some time ago, but have scarcely had time to answer it, but if you should write to her, tell her I have not forgotten her but will write soon.

I hope you will let me hear from you again soon, how you like your new situation, (as I suppose this will, barely reach you before you leave for Covington,) also your prospects for the winter

Resptly Yours   Sylvanus

DIARY

Monday 6th   At Oxford once more. Yes here I am where for many weeks been pining to find myself. The trials which I experienced in Walton are over. I have thrown off the burden and responsibility of a teacher for a few days; and am enjoying my freedom finely. Have not written in my journal since the day I closed my school at Sardus. The following day I went to Monroe accompanied by Miss Nancy Fretwell, Mr. Paxson and Frances. I presented my report to Mr. Michell the ordinary, and before him made oath as to the accuracy of my list. Went to Goodson & Raigan's store and made a few purchases. Just after our arrival in town a violent thunder storm came up, which [?] in the store until nearly night; it then abated in violence so much that Mr. Paxson thought it safe to start for home. We did not know what was before us or we should not have ventured to start. Mr. Paxson rode on horse-back as there was not room in the carriage, which threw the responsibility of driving upon us girls. Miss Nancy being the most accustomed to horses and having the most courage took the whip and lines. The horse seemed to know that one of the *"weaker vessels"* was guiding him, and he seemed quite disposed to frighten if nothing [else?] by continually threatening to kick. But this was not our only cause of anxiety; the rain began to fall harder than ever; the thunder roared and the lightning flashed *fearfully*. We found a stream which it was necessary to cross so high that it was hazardous and perhaps impossible to cross. We however were so anxious to get home that we concluded to run the risks, and drove into the water, Mr. Paxson going first and telling us to follow him, we reached the middle of the stream safely, then danger threatened us the water came rushing into the carriage and the horse began to throw up his heels, and for a few moments the fate of being thrown into the stream seemed inevitable. We were all mute with fright. Mr. Paxson had nearly reached the other side of the stream; but on seeing our danger and alarm came plunging through the water, and seizing the horse by the bridle urged him through the roaring waters. I think if I ever felt thankful it was when the wheels of the carriage were once more rolling on dry ground. The remainder of our ride was very wet and unpleasant, but we finely reached home with sound bodies and I *hope* thankful hearts, for surely we had great cause for gratitude after encountering so many dangers and being delivered from them all. Miss Nancy spent the night with me, and a wild one it was without. The morning however dawned bright and pleasant. I arose with a light heart for I had spent my last night in Walton. About eight o'clock I bid adieu to Mrs. Paxson's family and with bag & baggage started for Oxford. I did not manifest the joy I felt for fear of wounding the feelings of the Paxsons; for of course they could not feel so very well pleased to see me so much delighted to leave them. I shall remember the kindness I have received while an inmate of this family but shall never pine to be again a recipient of any pleasure or kindness received in Walton. * * *

Monday 7th   A few words upon thy pages before I retire my journal. Jennie and I have spent the day alone. This morning Mrs. Jennings left us to make some business calls in the country; we expected she would return before tea, but we had nearly finished when she came in, and then her appearance filled us all with alarm. She was dressed in the clothes of a stranger, the tears were rolling down her cheeks and her whole appearance bespoke grief and excitement. As soon as she could command her voice to speak she told us of the peril she had encountered during the day. In attempting to cross Big Gum creek in the carriage with Sam driving; they entered the water in the wrong place not knowing where the ford was. Before they could correct this dangerous mistake, the water nearly reached the top of the carriage and the horse seemed drowning for he could not swim being harnessed to the carriage. Mrs. Jennings and Sam both stood on their feet to keep their heads out of water, and for one hour called for help without being heard. Mrs. Jennings said she then gave up all hope of being rescued, and almost felt resigned to die then and there; but then came thoughts of the dear ones she had left a few hours before, and all the strong and tender feelings of a mother, well nigh mastered the submission of a christian. It was too rending to the maternal heart to die alone in the pitiles waters, without a farewell word and a parting kiss to her fatherless children. Ernest and fervent were the prayers she offered in that hour of peril; and just as the last ray of hope was fading, help appeared. Their cries had at length been heard by the nearest neighbors and a negro man sent to discover the cause. He instantly entered the water and reached the carriage side with only his head visible. He took Mrs. J. in his arms and bore her almost fainting to land; and then rescued Sam in the same way. By this time several persons had arrived to render assistance. A white man swam to the carriage and assisted the negro in leading the horse and draging the vehicle out of the deep water. It is useless to attempt a description of such a scene of danger. An eye witness alone could give one an adequate idea of so painful an occurrence. Mrs. Jennings stopped at Mr. Bakers where they showed kindness and sympathy by doing all in their power to relieve her suffering and soothe her agitated feelings. But she is still so much excited that we greatly fear the effect upon her nervous system. We hope however a night's rest will partially restore her.

*   *   *

Monday 13th * * * Last night our rest was somewhat disturbed by the illness of a little negro which Mrs. Jennings found it necessary to take into her room. Jennie and I indulged in sleeping until late this morning, and even then did not feel entirely refreshed on rising. This afternoon we have been to Covington, to choose a boarding place. I wish to get in a family of good standing, have a room to myself, or room with some of the teachers. I do not wish to be with the school girls; they will be no society for me, and I would rather be alone than in the company of very young, thoughtless and very likely rude school girls. But I doubt whether I can find a place where I can be thus retired. Shall go to Prof. Jones house on Wednesday, and if they take boarders shall probably remain, if not they will get me a boarding place. Jennie and I each received a letter to night. Mine was from my New Haven friend, and the most interesting letter I have yet received from that source. It was directed to Monroe, then forwarded to this place. * * *

Wednesday 15th   At Covington; but not yet settled, and do not know when I can be satisfactorily so. Came over this afternoon in the Hack. Called at Prof. Jones' and was directed to Pres. Fultons, went there and was introduced to Prof. Mosely who was to assist me in obtaining a boarding place. He spoke of one, to which I objected. He was very polite and mentioned several other places for me to choose from. We came to Mrs. Carrs where I am at present; but whether I shall remain or not is uncertain. I like the house and appearance of the people very well. The rooms are well finished and pleasant, but they are intending to take school girls to board, and I shall be obliged to room with several of them, which I know will be very unpleasant for me. I would not very much object to having one in my room, but I do not much like the idea of having more than one with me. * * * I am dreading to-morrow very much for I shall have to meet so many strangers, and of course be looked at and criticized by the pupils. How glad I shall be when I get settled in a boarding place, and accustomed to my school-room duties, and the rules and customs of the college. I am now rooming with a Miss Jackson a young girl of thirteen. She is very social and appears to make herself quite at home with every one. * * *

Thursday 16th   Rose early this morning, and was ready some time before breakfast. Miss J. and myself went to the college at eight o'clock. Spent nearly all the morning in the college office passing through the ordeal of an introduction to patrons, teachers and pupils. Went again this afternoon, but there was not teaching to be done, as the Prof.s were busy examining new scholars, and could not direct and assist in organizing and arranging classes. am still unsettled as to my boarding place. Called at Mr. George Carrs this afternoon and applied for board, but the same objection there as here; too many in a room. I do not know but I shall be obliged to room with ever so many romping girls after all. * * *

Friday 17th   Well my book what shall I say to night. Went to the college again this morning; all assembled in the chapel & had morning worship. I then went to my room and examined and classed my pupils in several of their studies; this afternoon finished that preparatory duty. Am now ready to commence teaching on Monday. * * *

Saturday 18th * * * There are two gentlemen boarding here. One is an *old* bachelor, the other a *young* bachelor. The former is the best looking, the latter the most social. Neither of them have any charms for my eye or mind. I dont know how I am ever to succeed in making a conquest, for I *can not* captivate, and *will not* be taken captive. Ah well it would be pleasant to have *one firm friend*; but I dont know that it will be my lot.

Monday 20th * * * This morning commenced my duties for the week. Went to the college at an early hour. At the ringing of the bell teachers and pupils assembled in the Chapel for morning worship. The teachers all take their seats on the stage. Each pupil has her seat assigned her. Prof. Erdman gave out a hymn, and played on the melodean; the young ladies accompanying it with their voices. Pres. Fulton then made some excellent remarks, after which all knelt while prayer was offered by the Pres. The rules were then laid down and commented upon; the young ladies were cautioned, advised, exhorted &c. We then separated each one going to their duty. I am well pleased with the behavior and diligence of my pupils for this the first day. I have got them classed, and the rules laid down. Now we are ready to proceed with our daily routine of duties.

JENNIE TO SYLVANUS

Covington, September 20th/58

To Mr. Lines

My Friend:—

For a few moments I am enjoying the quiet of my own room, and will sieze this opportunity to hold silent converse with a distant friend. Am boarding and rooming with school girls, which gives me very little quiet

˙ Your letter did not arrive until after I had left Monroe. It was forwarded to me however.

So many weeks had passed since I wrote to you that I began to feel anxious lest you were sick again or that I had wearied you with my uninteresting letters. Since the reception of your last favor however, I have the pleasant assurance that you are still my friend. After closing my school at Monroe I spent a week very pleasantly with my friends in Oxford. Came to Covington on the 15th. Am not yet thoroughly [settled?] in my duties and cares in college, therefore can not tell how tolerant and easy I shall find them. From a few days experience I imagine my task will not prove to be very light, as most of the girls committed to my care appear to be rude and ungovernable. But probably I shall enjoy as much peace and quiet as usually falls to the lot of *teacher*. Our path is a *thorny* one. During the summer I suffered a good deal from loneliness having no society whatever, that was congenial to my taste. I saw people enough, but they had no sympathies in common with me, and all their customs and manners were so different from what I had been accustomed to, that I shrank from intercourse with them, prefering solitude to *such* society. I hope it may never be my lot to live in *Crackerdom* again. Since I came to Covington I have seen so many new faces, and been introduced to so many strangers, who I felt were regarding me with an eye of *criticism*, that I have felt friendless and homesick. To be in a crowd and not see a face that is familiar, none that gives me a smile of recognition, always makes me feel thus: after becoming settled and acquainted I hope to feel more at home.

All summer I have been looking forward to coming here with considerable hope and expectation: but as "both pain and pleasure are blunted by long anticipation" I shall not perhaps realize all I have anticipated. I have learned by experience not to look for happiness on *earth*. *Earth-born* pleasures as you assert "are of *short duration*" and leave a greater or less degree of *pain*. Pain and pleasure roam hand in hand through this lower world. Happy are they who when this pilgrimage is over, can read their titles clear to *unalloyed* bliss in heaven. *There* the fondest hopes, and the most glorious anticipations are *more* than realized.

Some days have passed since I heard from Anna. Am now expecting a reply to my last. Every letter I receive from home bids me return without delay; but as yet I am not inclined to obey the summons, and do not know when I shall as anxious as I am to find myself once more surrounded with *friends*, and the associations of childhood and youth. I dare not trust myself to think of *home* and the *loved ones* that gather there; *such* reflections would unfit me for duty here. Mr. Lines your letters breathe such a spirit of kindness and friendship, that in replying I involuntarily express myself with the freedom I would in writing to a brother. Excuse me if I weary you with a catalogue of my interests. You are intending to return South it seems. I am glad to learn that. Shall hope to see you soon after your arrival. Hope you will obtain the situation at Fayettville if it is such a one as suits you.

Am glad your health remains good; if you wish to keep it so, you had better return to this warm clime before the chilling winds of winter. I shall hope to hear from or see you *soon*. Until then I bid you adieu.

Your Friend
Jennie

DIARY

Wednesday 22d * * * Thus far, I am well pleased with my new situation. Have at present no pupils under my care which are *un*manageable. A large class of Fresh[men] came into my room to recite; but I keep them busy while there so they have no time to take liberties if they were so disposed. The town is in great confusion this week as it is Court week. To night there is a show in town. An exhibition of animals, and circus performances. The former I would like to see, but the latter I should be disgusted to witness. Mr. D. invited Miss Jackson and myself to go, but neither of us could accept. College rules forbid her going and principle and tastes kept me away. * * *

Sabbath 26   Several days have passed since I wrote in my journal. I seem to have no good opportunity for writing. I am never alone in my room; and my room-mate is a young thoughtless frolicksome school girl. I can neither read, write, or think where she is. How I long to have a room to myself or a room-mate, more congenial, one with sympathies in common with me. I like my situation in College very much; but am not very pleasantly situated in regard to my temporary home. I do yearn daily for inteligent substantial society. I feel that I am constantly loosing ground in regard to *mental* culture. What little intellect I have is decreasing for the want of intellectual food. * * *

Monday 27th * * * The college has not adjourned but I have dismissed my classes, and am alone in my *dominion*. The dismissal bell is just striking; and what a rush! More than 100 girls all in haste to get home to their dinners. Many of them probably think more of feeding their *bodies* than minds.

Evening   Have just been gasping with wonder, admiration, and a *little* fear at the Comet which is visible. Its tail is longer and brighter to night than I have before seen it. There is also one to be seen at four o'clock in the morning. I do not rise early enough to see that.

* * *

Thursday 30th   Mrs. Carr has two new boarders. Miss Lamar & Miss Brooks. They are to ocupy the room with Miss Jackson and myself. It is not pleasant to room with so many. I hope soon to have a room with but one. * * *

* * *

Monday [October] 4th * * * The comet is very brilliant to night. Have just read a little of it in the paper. It was discovered last June is called D——.[34] At its nearest approach to the earth will be 52,000,000 miles from us, so there is little to fear from receiving a brush from it. It's tail is said to be 15,000,000 miles in length. When this Comet last made its appearance or when it will again visit us, can yet be calculated. Pres. Fulton took tea here; I saw him a few minutes in the parlor. Always feel more encouraged about my school after talking with him. * * *

Wednesday 6th   Dear journal, I cannot get one moment alone with you. Can not even be alone long enough to read my bible unmolested. I can not endure long to be thus obliged to be continually in the company of those with whom I have no congeniality. I do not think it is right to expect a teacher to room with school girls. We see and hear enough of their folly through the day; and at night we ought to be free from them.

I am so weary at night, and long so much for quiet; but not one moment of it do I have here. * * *

Thursday 7th   Joined the Clio society to night. Did not wish to join but the girls were *so urgent*. I see no great benefit in belonging to the society except that we have access to their library, which though not very extensive is well selected. Mrs. Carr expects two more boarders to morrow, if they come I shall move into another room where I shall have only one roommate; but that one is so rude I shall have but little peace. * * *

Saturday 9th * * * I am now in a very pleasant little room; if I only had it to myself, I might pass some hours very pleasantly. Miss Jackson is going to room with me, and I can not expect much peace or quiet. We have no sympathies in common, and she is so rude, and has such an ungovernable temper that I find it very unpleasant to be obliged to be continually with her. * * *

Sabbath 10th * * * Evening. Prof. Mosely called this afternoon to request me to attend the sabbath school at the college. I felt very little inclination to grant his request; but felt obliged to do so for to day at least. The pupils were not all there and but two of the teachers. I wonder if it is my duty to go there every sabbath. I do not feel inclined to do so. But inclination must not guide me for it would too often lead me astray.

*   *   *

Tuesday 12th   Has been a dark dreery day, although but little rain has fallen. I shall have to begin to lecture my pupils severely, they are trying me to see how far I will let them go; if I loosen the rein ½ an inch they will soon take a foot. I find it very unpleasant to be obliged to be so very strict with them but there seems to be no other way. I almost despair of gaining their love. * * *

Thursday 14th   We have all been very much frightened since school. Mrs. Carr came very near being burned to death. Her dress caught fire, and in pursuit of water she ran out doors; the wind increased the flames, which soon enveloped her. The boarders, the children and the servants were running in every direction, screaming and crying; but rendered incapable by fright of rendering any assistance. Miss Jackson jumped out of bed ran out at the front door, and frantic with fear she ran about the yard in her night dress and bare feet. A crowd of men soon gathered in the yard, and some of them soon succeeded in putting out the fire. Nearly all her clothes were burned off. She thought at first that she was not badly burned. but soon found her hands and limbs were considerably burned. She is now suffering the most excruciating pain, and is groaning most piteously. The house is crowded with people; the servants and children are in my room. There is too much confusion to write.

Friday 15th   My troublesome little flock have all gone, and I am enjoying the quiet of my school-room. The little immortals have worried me much this afternoon by their rudeness. What *shall* I do to tame them. Really I am quite at a loss. Some times I think the fault is in me. Then again I have the vanity to think I am doing as well as any teacher could with such ungovernable children.

   Mrs. Carr is suffering very much from her burn; the physician does not consider her dangerous however. * * *

Sabbath day 17th * * * Prof. Mosely called this afternoon to request me to go to sabbath school in the college chappel. I had just lain down as I was suffering from headache. I sent an excuse and did not see him, neither did I attend the sabbath school

SYLVANUS TO JENNIE

New Haven, Oct. 24

To Jennie

   There is no time in the ever-changing variety of the seasons more beautiful or more suggestive of emotions, painful and pleasant, than the twilight hour of a beautiful day so common in autumn. The mellow light fading away into the growing darkness seems to carry with it the fouler thoughts and worldly desires which have sprung into life during the struggle and tumult of the day, while the stillness and saint-like repose, in which all nature lies hushed, points the heart to the eternal peace and glory of that higher world to which in our serious states of mind the aspirations of our souls, as if drawn by some invisible attraction, are continually turning. It is the hour for those moments of self-examination which at times will come upon the most thoughtless.

From the very stillness of the quiet rise up and move before the spirit in airy procession the visions of long ago—phantom hopes and wishes of former years—ghosts of resolutions broken and higher purposes unaccomplished—sickening memories of what might have been—bitter memories of opportunities wasted of talents misused, of all the feelings which should not have passed away but passed away the soonest. Moments such as these are often turning points in our destiny when from the seasons of earnest heart communion or self-upbraiding we go forth to the conflict of life with nobler aims and renewed strength.

As I sat by my window this evening, feelings like these came upon me, but I was awaken[ed] from my revery by the thought that your letter was yet unanswered, and I at once concluded to write, for I shall want to hear from you when I again find myself among strangers. It is my intention to leave home on the 2d Monday in Nov. for Columbia, S.C. to remain there a short time, after which I shall go to Georgia and of course come and see you.

I suppose you have become more acquainted by this time in your new home and I hope find it more pleasant than it seemed at first, but we are too apt to raise our anticipations so high that in our failure to experience that degree of pleasure which we sought we become disheartened. Such seems to have been the result of your anticipations, but I am not much surprised that it should be so in a measure, for I have found it so myself and especially in the South.

Although I have found many friends among Southerners yet it was from a long acquaintance with them, for as far as my experience has been I have found them a peculiar race; they do not form an attachment for a person at first sight; when once their true friendship is gained none are more ready and willing to assist and sympathise than the Southerner, but on the contrary, when once their displeasure is aroused there is scarcely any bounds to the malignity of their disposition. They look with an eye of criticism upon strangers and for this reason no doubt you have found it very unpleasant.

Friend Jennie, in your last you paid me a high tribute when you spoke of my friendship to you as also in the manner of your replies to my uninteresting letters, and be assured your letters are received with a hearty welcome and always afford me much pleasure for the reason that they are so frank and openhearted. I like to hear from you, of your trials and prospects—would that they were more promising.

You write me that your friends are urging you to return home nor would I counsel you to the contrary—but should I again visit Geo. I shall feel much disappointed not to meet you there.

I received a letter from Cousin Anna last week from which I learn that she has about made up her mind to return North—I hope she will not attempt it before warm weather for she has become so acclimated there that I have no doubt she would share the same fate of myself. I shall endeavor to write to her before I leave home if my time should permit if not I shall remember her when I arrive in Columbia. I should think from her letter that she had really become homesick and tired of the South for her expressions in regard to the Southerns as also of the negroes were not of the most loving character. I use to think that she was *almost* a *native* of Geo. but if she talks in that way I shall be obliged to alter my opinion of her.

Jennie do you hear any thing from our friend Mrs. Cartnell, and Mrs. Welton, should like to hear of them but I seldom receive a letter from Atlanta and when I do nothing is said of them.

I fear that I am wearying your patience with my unintelligible scratches which have been written somewhat hurriedly, so I will stop for the present.

Truly Yours,
Sylvanus

DIARY

Thursday 28th   When I awoke this morning the rain was falling in torrents. I thought surely the college bell would not summon us to our posts on such a day. At ten o'clock however, the storm somewhat abated in violence, and the bell soon told teachers and pupils that we were expected to repair to the chapel through all the mud. * * *

Wednesday [October] 3d   I believe I am more timid and shrinking than any one else upon the face of the earth! This *extreme shame-facedness* keeps me down in my own estimation, and I am inclined to think in the estimation of others too. Were it not for this *blushing* I could hide my embarrassment, and I would patiently endure the uncomfortable feeling of *excessive* bashfulness if I could only hide it from others. A little incident of yesterday and another of to day have drawn these *timid* remarks from me my journal; but enough for the present on this subject, only I do wish I had a little more of a certain kind of metal in my face. * * *

Thursday 4th   Another letter to day, from *sister*. It has been a beautiful day. I enjoyed my walk to school this afternoon. What a strange thing is the *immortal* mind. What various moods and states it is capable of assuming. It is governed in some degree, but not entirely by external circumstances. Sometimes when all is bright and pleasant around us; when there hangs no *visible* cloud o'er our way; when we are surrounded by all that should tend to gladen the heart and enliven the spirit, there looms up before the minds eye, a dark forboding of coming evil. The mind, like an ocean-wave is tossed and troubled by the tempest of contending passions. At other times when troubles and perplexities *really do* assail us, the mind is strengthened and buoyed up by some unseen power; we think we can bravely meet our fate what e're it may be, for through the darkness a light gleams upon us from some unknown quarter. I know from experience the *quiet* and *disquiet* arising from these two frames of mind. I feel like writing more on this subject but time will not admit. "The day is past and gone" and several hours of the night. I must lay aside all daily occupation, and for awhile resting myself to the power of "Nature's sweet restorer"

*   *   *

Tuesday 9th   Cold very cold for this clime. Have not felt well to day, and in concequence the school-room has seemed a troublesome uninteresting place to me. Sometimes I feel that [any] occupation would be prefferable to teaching; but fortunately my feelings are not always in such a state. Have not sewed any this week; my bolt of cloth will not get made into garments very soon at this rate.

Wednesday 10th   A frost this morning the first I have seen this fall. The day has been cold but we have kept very comfortable at school; the furnace warms the room very well. Scholars have behaved unusually well to day. Prof. Mosely gave them all a lecture in the chappel. and I think it had a good effect upon *my* deportment at least. I like my school very well indeed, and like my boarding place as far as *physical* necessaries and comforts are concerned, but I would like a little society; so I might now and then have an agreeable chat with a pleasant acquaintance or sympathizing friend; but as yet I have found neither friend or acquaintance, to pass a leisure hour with.

*   *   *

Wednesday 17th   Sabbath and Monday found me in bed sick with roseolia. A new disease to me, one I never heard of before; but I know now by experience. Was not able to come to school yesterday but I was fearful my little flock would run wild without me, so I bundled up and nine o'clock found me at my post again. A letter from sister last night; she has left Col Harrise's and is at present at Cartersville where she intends to open a dressmaking shop. I hope she will succeed in business and find a happy home; but I wish she was nearer this place. * * *

Thursday 25th   Thanksgiving day; but I have been in school notwith-standing. I never taught before on that day. and did not like to do so to day; but as all the rest of the teachers were to be at their posts I knew it was best for me to be at mine. * * *

JENNIE TO SYLVANUS

Covington November [?] 1858

To Mr. Lines.

Your last truly interesting letter came to hand in due time. Your re-flections at the hour of eve, were perused with deep interest; for they gave utterance to thoughts which have often crowded my brain, to feel-ings that have often filled my soul, while enjoying that calm, yes *holy* hour when the last ray of sun-light fades away. It is indeed the hour for communion with our God, and with our own hearts. At this hour the angels seem to droop their pinions, and hover near the soul, whisper-ing *heaven*-born thoughts and desires. Then if ever our thoughts are lifted from earth to heaven, and borne on the wings of fancy, we almost forget we are yet sojourners in this lower world, and in imagination are mingling with the spirits of the just made perfect, and participating in their unalloyed bliss. Often at day's decline, when wrapt in pensive, tranqil meditation, has my spirit yearned to leave its clay tenement and wing its flight upward, and upward, until it reached the home of angels; there would it linger awhile holding sweet converse with the purified spirits of dear departed ones. Sometimes my listening ear has well nigh caught the sound of music, as with my mind's eye I saw the celestial choir gathered around the throne, casting their crowns at Jesus' feet and singing anthems in His praise.

But I am forgetting myself and perhaps wearying you with this long preamble to my letter. It is pleasant to know that others have thoughts and feelings in unison with mine; and I could not forbear mentioning that your last interested me much.

Writing is the only means of social converse which at present I am favored with, for I have not yet formed any acquaintances in Covington with whom I can feel much congeniality. But there are those who will in time I doubt not prove themselves warm friends. President Fulton's family especially, who have already kindly manifested an interest in my welfare. Were it not for the little sunbeams in the form of letters

which frequently cross my path, I should feel quite alone now that I am
so far from my sister. It seems rather hard that I can not be near her,
as I came South almost expressly for that purpose. But I am so well
pleased with my situation in college that I feel no disposition to complain although I am deprived of the society of my friends, which to me
is the goal of earthly enjoyment. When I first came here I was fearful
that the duties and cares imposed upon me in college would be greater
than I was [accustomed] to: but in that respect I am happily disappointed; never have I filled a pleasanter situation. 'Tis true I am very
busy from eight o'clock in the morning until dark; but so long as my
task is pleasant and interesting, as well as arduous I can perform it
cheerfully.

Young says "Life's cares are comforts". I agree with him. Without
care I should be wretched. I would not be a cipher in the world. To, I
would act my part in the great drama of life. I believe *all*, however in-
significant and obscure have a mission to perform. I often feel to re-
[gret?] that I have not greater talents; but this is wrong. I should be
grateful for what I have, and not as it were busy them in the dust, but
cultivate them, then at my Lord's coming, He can receive His own with
[?].

Mr. Lines I felt forcibly the truth of your remarks in regard to anticipation. I have always anticipated more than I have realized, and finally I have come to the conclusion that there is more happiness in
anticipation than in participation. Why is it that the past and future
always look brighter to us than the present? I know not unless it is that
in casting a retrospective glance over the past, we are prone to dwell
chiefly upon the brightest spots in our lives.

Hope is ever beckoning us on to the uncertain future, which touched
by the wand of fancy appears to our impatient and expectant gase to be
gilded with the richest lines of the rainbow. *Hope* would strew our
pathway with flowers; but the breath of *reality* too often without the
fairest of them, and in treading that path our feet are lacerated with
the thorn, where we expected the rose. But enough of this, I will cease
penning thought after thought which give rise to each other.

The idea of your being again in the South is an agreeable one; but I
can not feel sure of the fact until I see or hear from you. I hardly knew
what to do about writing to you, not feeling certain that you have yet
left your northern home. If you left on the end Monday, In Nov you
have of course reached your destination: if not this will not find you as I
shall direct it to Columbia; but it will be no loss, only you will not know
that I have written, and perhaps think me negligent. I received a letter
from my sister yesterday. She did not mention having heard from you.
She has had a great deal of trouble with the servants at Col. Harris,

and been very unhappy; but she is now going to give up the housekeeping, and devote her whole time to the children, which will be much pleasanter for her. I have no fears in regard to her returning North yet awhile. I do not believe she would leave me here; and I am not ready to go home yet, as much as I would like to find myself surrounded again with the friends and associations of childhood. I never hear from our friends in Atlanta. I wrote to Mrs. Welton last summer, but she did not reply. She promised to try and sell my [?] this fall; but I never expect to hear from it. I did intend to write to Mrs. Cartnell, but have neglected to do so. Mr. Daniel's children are in college. Two of them are my pupils. I wish Mr. Mason would send his children here. I loved that little [?] *so much*, I often think of her and wish she was again my pupil. She was so innocent and artless one could but love her.

Mr. Lines please reply to this as soon as convenient as I am anxious to know if you are again in the South.

With this accept kind regards
From Jennie

SYLVANUS TO JENNIE

Columbia, S.C. Nov 30

Friend Jennie:—

To day finds me in Columbia; I arrived safe on the Monday morning after I left Atlanta, nothing occurring to mar the pleasure of our trip. I found numerous friends and acquaintances whom I left here two years ago, and who *appeared* very glad to see me, especially my former landlady, with whom I am now boarding; she however has changed her name since I left here, but is nevertheless as courteous as ever, and I feel very much at home.

The "City of Flowers," for such it is called and I think rightly named, although somewhat seared by the autumn frosts, still looks beautiful, would that you could be here for you could but admire this beautiful city, with her magnificent gardens, her neat cottages, and her wide and capacious streets, lined with shade trees, not the least of which is her Palmetto tree, from which the State takes its name and for which she may well be proud.

I have been very busy since my stay here, scarcely having time for a moments' rest, and which is my excuse for not writing to you before. I anticipate remaining here until Christmas or New Years and then going to Washington for a short time.

Jennie (if you will allow me to be so familiar) I am anxious to hear from you,—of yourself personally, and also of your prospects of success, and pray do not think me inquisitive or formal as I consider myself identified, in a measure, with your present gloomy prospects. Have you succeeded in finding a good boarding place yet, and if so with whom.

Jennie, when I last saw you I requested the privilege of writing to you, can I now ask the liberty of extending that privilege, which if it were your will would afford me unbounded pleasure. Our acquaintance, it is true, has been but short; we are as it were almost strangers to each other, and it may be presumptious in me to make this request, and should you decline a correspondence with me I shall have no fault to find, but shall always cherish our acquaintance as one of relationship, for until now you have appeared to me as such.

I hope you will answer this request with frankness, that I may not trespass upon you unthoughtedly.

Until I hear from you again I remain

Very Resply Ys
S.D.F. Lines

DIARY

Wednesday December 1st   Autumn has passed and stern winter commences his reign to day. I have a ticket to a party at the hotel to morrow night. I feel some curiosity to attend as I have never attended a party in the South. It is cold and rainy to day. I think winter at the South although not so severe is more gloomy than at the North.

Thursday 2nd   I am think[ing] about going to the party but hardly know how to decide as Miss Atkisson can not tell whether she will go. Mrs Carr partly promised me she would go and Mr. Bowher has politely offered to escort me there, if I wish to attend. I am feeling nervous and excited as I always do when thinking about appearing in a large crowd.

Friday 3d   Well I went to the party last night, and through the polite attention of Mr. Bowher passed a pleasant evening. I was not very much pleased with the appearance of the company; they lacked sociability and I think politeness too. Miss Atkisson and myself were strangers, we were watched closely, and I presume criticised; but no one took pains to introduce or make us feel at home in their midst. Returned home at 1 o'clock with the same feelings that always oppresses after attending a gay assembly. I have another invitation for to night. A party at Dr. Hendrich's. I rather wish to go but shall not unless Mrs.

Carr or Miss Atkisson attend. Evening, I came home from school to night hesitating about attending the party. Mrs. Carr urged me so much that I finally consented and began to make preparations. Mr. Bowher had left an invitation for me at noon. I did not go out to tea. Miss Jackson came in to our room after tea and told me of a remark made at the table, which put a veto on my going. In a few moments Mr. B. sent for me and politely offered to escort me to the party. But my sensitive nature was wounded, and I could do no other than decline his offer. I thought from his remark at the table, that if he went with me it would be because he felt obliged to do so, as he had asserted that he had no inclination unless it be perfectly voluntary; therefore as politely as possible I positively refused to go; although Mr. & Mrs. Carr insisted upon my doing so. After Mr B. left I told Mrs. Carr, I could not under the circumstances go with Mr. B. but if she would go I would. While we were hesitating the Omnibus drove up and Mr. Jones a gentleman to whom I was introduced last evening came in to wait upon me to the party. I was not ready and of course had to be excused

Saturday 4th   Mr. B. has learned by some means that I desired to go to the party last night and thought of going after I had refused to go with him. Mrs Carr says he appears to be displeased; she thinks I ought to explain. I have written him a few lines of explanation which Queenie handed to him to night. Have done very little of any thing to day. This evening have been in Mrs. Carr's room.

* * *

Tuesday 7th   A visit from Mr. Lines to day. He came in the 12 o'clock train and has just left. Gave me a short call this noon, and has spent this evening with me. I enjoyed the visit much; but it was altogether *too short*; but I am so busy in school that I could not have had much time to spend with him had he remained longer. He appears like the same pleasant friend that he did when I knew him in Atlanta last year. Excitement has given me a head-ache   I must retire.

Wednesday 8th   Cold again. These sudden changes are very detrimental to health. I am not suffering from the effects of them. I have a very hard cold. Have been congratulating myself on escaping the influenza which has been so prevalent for a few weeks; but I have it now. I fear I shall not be able to endure walking through the wet and mud all kinds of weather I have not a large amount of *iron* in my physical composition. I believe Prof. Mosely thinks both teachers and pupils in this college have a good deal of that mettal, for he will not dismiss school for the worst weather imaginable. I can not write for sneezing and coughing, so good night my book.

* * *

SYLVANUS TO JENNIE

Atlanta, Dec 23

Friend Jennie:—

As I intend to leave this place the coming week and as it is impossible to visit you in the mean time, I shall be pleased to see you in Atlanta on Christmas day if it is convenient. Mrs. Welton says she should like to see you and will make arrangements for a Christmas dinner, as I told her that I thought you would come. As the time is too short for me to hear from you unless you should receive this in time for the mail tomorrow night, I shall be at the train on Saturday morning and shall be happy to meet you if it is your pleasure.

Very truly yours
S. De F. Lines

JENNIE TO SYLVANUS

Covington December 25th/58

Mr. Lines

Allow me to wish you a "merry Christmas" I should be most happy to spend it with you were it possible. Your note has just been handed to me; the train has gone two hours ago. Had I received it a few hours earlier I should have given myself the pleasure of accepting the kind invitation of Mrs. Welton and yourself: but I hope my not being able to do so will not interfere with your merriment at all. I am going to have a few days rest, and expect to spend them very quietly in my room. Last evening I attended a party at the Masonic Hall; and enjoyed myself just about as I always do in a gay crowd.

Received a letter from Anna last night; she is well, but not very happy.

Please give my love to Mrs. Welton, tell her I regret *exceedingly* that I can not dine with her to-day.

I shall be happy to hear from you when you are settled in your new home; I hope it may prove a pleasant one.

Yours in Haste
Jennie

PART THREE

TEACHING, COURTING, & MARRYING

1859-1860

DIARY

January 1st 1859   I can not realize that another year has passed away! that we are upon the threshold of 1859! The past year with it's record looms up before me; and almost involunterily my eye scans the list of blessings with which the past year has been fraught. How have I appreciated them? Some spirit of truth and purity seems to answer the question by whispering words of reproach in my ear: accusing me of misspent moments, foolish fancies, idle talk, vain amusements; of ingratitude, sinful repining, impatience. O! my sinful heart can it be that all these sins lurk within it? I must cry out with Paul. O! sinful man that I am! who shall deliver me from [?]? O! for wisdom grace, meekness, and patience to overcome these sins, and if my life is spared the coming year live so that at its close, when casting a retrospective glance over its serious incidents and changes, my good spirit may grant me an approving smile in place of upbraidings.

The past year has had its trials, it's vexations and it's discouragements for me; but my heart has not been crushed by my overwhelming affliction. The dear ones I left in my distant home are still spared, to love and bless me. Our dear Ezra still lives, and though disease still retains its hold upon his physical frame, his spirit is peaceful and happy. With christian resignation he kisses the hand that smites! But while my heart glows with gratitude for the life and health of the few dear ones that remain, and humbly submits to the loss of the many that are gone, it is also filled with keen anxiety and suspense for one of whose well-being we are ignorant   Not one word has reached our ears to tell us of the life or death, weal or woe of our Charley. O how my heart sinks with doubt and uncertainty in regard to him. Daily do I commit him to the care of One who is able to protect him amid danger, and shield him from every ill. O! that it may be His good will and pleasure to return him to us in safety 'ere long.

Have to day changed my boarding place. Am now at Mr. Hendersons.

a contrast in this and Mr. Carrs. There was noise and confusion. Here there are no boarders, no children, no family but old Mr. & Mrs. Henderson. Every thing is so quiet and still. No doubt I shall suffer somewhat from loneliness; but I mean to strive against the "blues" and try to feel cheerful and contented if not always happy. I have a very pleasant room and every thing in it to afford me physical comfort. I must make *books* my companions, and my journal must be my bosom friend. Upon thy pages I must pen the thoughts I would like to utter were dear and intimate friends at hand. I can not expect any one in Covington will take the trouble to visit me for no one here knows me, well enough to care for my company. I believe I must give up all social enjoyment until I return North, for indeed I have enjoyed very little of it since I came South. Mrs. Henderson seems like a motherly old lady. hope she will act like a mother to me, for I do indeed feel the need of a mother's sympathy and kindness. I have unpacked my trunks and now that I see my own things in various parts of the room I begin to feel a little at home. I must retire and try to [?] in the right frame of mind on the morrow which is a holy day.

Sabbath 2nd   How quietly this sabbath has passed; but I have enjoyed it more than any sabbath spent in Covington. [?] came down this morning and I presume would have spent the day had I not gone to church. Attended the baptist church, heard Mr. [?] preach. There is preaching to night, I would like to go if I had suitable company; but *company* is out of the question in Covington. It does not seem to be the fashion or custom to pay attention to *teachers* in this place. Not much of a compliment to their college I think. Any person who has a mind so [?], *since* views so *contracted* and *perverted* as to feel themselves superior to a teacher is in my humble opinion *vastly inferior* to any one who has the capacity and education to teach. But if I am treated with kindness and respect I will not complain. I did not come with the expectation of winning any thing more.

* * *

Tuesday 4th * * * Have been reading Bayard Taylor's travels in the Oriental world[1] since school; and in imagination have visited some romantic and interesting places in Germany   My desire to visit the old world is always renewed by reading the travels of others. From my earliest recollection this has been a day dream with me, and one which can never be realized I fear, certainly not unless fortune play some unexpected freak in my favor. If I was a man, I would start as Taylor did, with a cane in my hand, and knapsack on my shoulder.

O dear! it is impossible for *me* to keep the aspirations of my soul down to the common level of the every day life of a poor school teacher.

* * *

SYLVANUS TO JENNIE

Fayetteville, Jan. 9/59

Miss Jennie:—

Now that I am settled in my new home and have had a little opportunity to become acquainted with the people and also to satisfy myself as to the prospects for the future, I take the first favorable moment to address you.

I find this place all that I had anticipated, and I may say more, when I take into consideration the sociability and kindness of its inhabitants. My employer is one of the best men that it has ever been my fortune to deal with, and spares no pains to make my stay an agreable one. His school commences tomorrow under the most favorable auspices, and our little town has had, for a day or two past, the appearance of a city, by the constant arrival of students from all parts of this and adjoining States. Our village is pleasantly situated on rising ground with a park in the center, around which are numberous cottages, some five or six stores and one hotel at which I am at present boarding; it has much the appearance of a Northern country village, as much taste has been displayed in its laying out, planting shade trees, & contains some four or five hundred inhabitants. Should the business pay of which I have the charge I think I shall make this my permanent residence.

It was our intention to publish the paper the coming week, but on account of the non-arrival of a part of our material, it will be delayed for a short time,—when it is issued I will send you a copy.

I received the letter which you directed to Columbia while in Atlanta, it was long (not too long) and full of interest to *me*, and gave me unbounded pleasure in its perusal,—freighted as it was with the expressions of friendship for kindred and friends in a far distant land, together with a spirit of Christian resignation which alone can make me contented and happy, even in their most lonesome moments,—would that I had the same blessed assurance that, on the Lord's coming, *I* was prepared to meet him in his glory and majesty.

I was much disappointed in not seeing you on Christmas day as I had anticipated spending a "merry Christmas" with you, but your kind note in reply satisfactorily explained your absence,—however, I hope to have the pleasure of meeting you there before long.

My situation is such that it is impossible for me to leave but for a day or two at a time, or I should visit you at Covington, and shall endeavor to do so, with your permission, whenever an opportunity offers. It is my intention to visit Atlanta in the course of four or five weeks to stay a day or two, and as I have already written to cousin, I shall be happy to meet you both there; we might arrange it so that we could be there on Saturday & stay until Monday, what say you to it?

Hoping to hear from you soon   I remain as ever

Yours truly,
Sylvanus

DIARY

Wednesday 19th * * * Last Saturday Jennie Jennings came for me to go to Oxford. The invitation was extended to Miss Atkisson also, and she too accepted. We had a delightful visit, although the cold kept us in the house. Sabbath day we attended church; heard rather a dull, but good practical sermon. The congregation was rather smal; the cold weather kept many at home, and but few of the college students have returned. In the afternoon we rode through the college grounds, and paused before the monument of Col. Few one of the founders of Emory College. His remains lie in the grave yard; but his monument is erected near the college. His wife was unwilling to have his body rest beneath it, as she could not then be permitted to sleep beside him. * * *

JENNIE TO SYLVANUS

Covington Jan 22nd 1859

To Mr. Lines—:

Saturday finds me free from the confinement and duties of the school-room, and at liberty to spend the day as I please. I enjoy my freedom exceedingly, and try to make the hours as pleasantly as possible. To-day shall be devoted to the agreeable task of answering letters. Yours shall claim my first attention. It was received several days since, and came just in time to ward off [a] fit of the "blues" by throwing a ray of sun shine across my path. Accept my thanks for remembering me so soon after your arrival in Fayetteville. I was glad to learn that you were so well pleased. I hope your prospects will continue as flattering as they now are, and that you may realize all happiness and prosperity you anticipate. From your description I imagine Fayetteville to be a very quiet, home-like little town. I have no doubt you will find warm and *true* friends there, for there is generally less heartlessness and deception in a small place than in a large one. Having been accustomed to city life, you will undoubtedly miss its attractions and amusements, and perhaps feel at a loss how to while away your leisure hours; but should friends and fortune smile upon you! that will I doubt not reconcile you to quiet, unpretending village life. I am anxious to see your paper. We have one published here, edited by the young ladies in college. I will send you our next number. There may be a few lines in it from the pen of your humble friend. See if you can tell which piece it is.

Monday eve, 24th

Company prevented my finishing this letter on Saturday, and yesterday I was prostrated with the most severe head-ache that it has been my misfortune to suffer from since I came South. But through the kind attention of Mrs. Henderson I was so far restored this morning that nine o'clock found me at my post in college. This evening although somewhat wearied I will finish this sheet, feeling assured that you will pardon all its imperfections. I have changed my boarding place since Christmas; and have bettered myself decidedly. I can but congratulate myself in finding so pleasant a home. I am in the pleasantest part of the "city" and in one of "*the first families*" Every thing is done for my comfort and happiness, and as I am the only boarder, like an only child I shall probably be indulged a little and enjoy a good many privileges. I feel very much at home, and intend to make myself as happy and contented as possible. Miss [?] one of the teachers is my next door neighbors which makes it very pleasant as I can be favored with her society.

I hope it may be convenient for you to call upon me, for I should be most happy to see you at any time. I hardly realize that I have seen you at all, your call was so *very short*. In regard to taking a trip to Atlanta, I do not know what to say. If I should let my inclination decide it might say go; but my judgment says perhaps I had better not. I could not return until Monday noon unless I came Sabbath day and that I could not do; but I do not think they ought to complain at my being absent a day. "Duty before pleasure" is my motto, when teaching, but if you and Anna are in Atlanta at the same time I think very likely you will see me there too. We had one weeks vacation after Christmas, and now we shall have no more rest until next June. I will bring this scrawl to a close by subscribing myself

Your Sincere Friend
Jennie A.

DIARY

February
Wednesday 2nd Noon. At school. Did not write yesterday as I did not spend last night in my room. When I went home to dinner yesterday found Mr. Doolittle waiting to see me. He remained to dinner; there was also another gentleman there. A Mr. Heartsfield. After dinner I learned that he was a *widower* and one who had been recommended to me as being an intelligent well informed clever, and last if not least a wealthy gentleman: *decidedly* a "*good catch*" I am told. He has been a widower ten or twelve years, and has of course seen many fine ladies; but as none of them have been able to take his heart captive, I have not the vanity to think that such an *uninteresting, unattractive* little piece of humanity as myself could demand a look or a thought from him, or any one else. At night Mr. H. gave me a paper from the office. It was from Mr. L. It seems he occasionally thinks of me. After tea Mr. B. called   I went with him to call on Miss Atkisson. Spent the evening very pleasantly. Miss A. is so lively and interesting a gentleman can but feel interested in her company. I wish I could make myself more sprightly and attractive, I am too dull and prosy. I know it but can not *help* it. I think I expressed myself a little too freely on a certain subject last night. I will not commit myself again. * * *

Thursday 3d * * * Had quite a chat with Miss Fulton this afternoon. She is getting tired of teaching, and this is only her first year. She says she shall not teach after commencement, I do not blame her I would not if I was not obliged to. Am reading Madame Levert's travels,[2] do not like her style very well.

SYLVANUS TO JENNIE

Fayetteville, Ga.
Sunday Eve, Feb. 6th

Jennie:—

Once more I seat myself to perform a pleasurable task—if it is a task indeed, though I would rather call it by a softer name. If I can be the means of driving off even *one* "fit of the blues," how willingly will I devote my leisure moments in throwing a gleam of sunshine upon your (at present) desolate path; made so, perhaps by a long separation from the friends you hold most dear. Ah! how well can I sympathise with you in that particular. Although my situation is peculiarly a *pleasant* one, the people social; and the village quiet and delightful, yet there is something wanting to make life's rugged path a smooth one.

Were it not for the occasional letters which I receive from friends my life would be a disconsolate one,—but they come to me like a spring in the desert, and serve to cheer up my drooping spirits in moments of reflection.

In reading your letter I was pleased to learn that you have moved your boarding place for a better and, although I thought you was very very pleasantly situated where you was when I saw you. I shall be happy to call upon you, and only regret that I cannot see you oftener, as I have written before, my position is such that it is difficult for me to be absent scarcely for a day   I received a letter from Cousin Anna in the same mail with yours, and she writes that she will be in Atlanta on the 12th (next Saturday) if nothing happens, and expects to see you there, and I hope she will not be disappointed. It is uncertain whether I can leave here before Saturday morning, and as I shall probably drive there in a buggy you will arrive there before I do, if so please stop at the Atlanta Hotel and I will call there for you.

I anticipate much pleasure in seeing you and Cousin. I could not decipher the true meaning of your objections to going, but as you left it for me to conjecture, I have no doubt they were plausible ones. "Judgment," I admit, should always predominate over "inclination" as we are prone to do wrong and *conscience* is our instructor, but I hope you will not let trifles debar me the pleasure of seeing you there.

You may think strange of my requesting you to "meet me half-way," and well you might, but then I thought by such an arrangement we might all meet each other and renew old acquaintance and perhaps pass off a few hours agreeably.

I have sent you the two first issues of our paper which I think you will be pleased with. The story in the second number is well worth reading. I hope to receive your's when published. Hoping to see or hear from you again soon. I remain yours

Sylvanus

DIARY

Tuesday 8th   Had some trouble in school to-day, and to night I came home weary and discouraged; but the sight of a letter made me forget my fatigue and perplexities. It was from Mr. L.   he asks me to meet himself and my sister in Atlanta next Saturday. I should be most happy to do so but duty forbids. I have replied to his letter to night telling him my excuse which I hope he will accept. It is too late to write more.

JENNIE TO SYLVANUS

Covington Feb 8th 1859

Mr. Lines:—

To night I left the school room weary, and somewhat discouraged. My walk homeward through the rain, was cold and dreary. But on my arrival at my own pleasant room, the sight of a little messenger, revived my spirits, and made me forget the toil and perplexities of the day. Hastily I relieved the little traveller of its wrapper, and by the side of a cheerful fire, sat down to commune in spirit with its author. Very cheering to my heart were the expressions of kindness and friendship that greeted my eye, as with interest I perused line after line written by the hand of a friend.

A *friend!* how pleasantly that word falls upon the ear of a stranger in a strange land! for though it is two years to morrow since I left my Southern [sic] home, I still feel like a stranger; for I have not tarried long enough in one place to become very much attached, or to feel very much at home. It causes the heart many a desolate pang to mingle day after day with a busy crowd for whom one has no stronger, no warmer feeling that cool respect and *interested* kindness. I am trying to school my feelings into "passive fortitude", but it is a weary task. Sometimes I feel utterly lone and friendless, then a letter from you or Anna gives me the pleasant assurance that although so far from home, I have *friends* near me. Grateful indeed to my feelings is the sympathy you express for me. I know that you *can* sympathize, for you too are far from "those you hold most dear". But I must not write in this strain, lest my letter breathe a spirit of discontent and unhappiness, which I do *not* harbor.

You will think I am *too* punctual in answering your letter this time I fear, but I wish you to receive it before going to Atlanta, that you may not be disappointed and displeased at not meeting me there. For several days judgment and inclination have been at war, but the battle is over now, and *judgment* is the victor. Therefore instead of meeting my friends on Saturday I must remain at home, ready armed for duty on Monday morning. Mr. Lines *please* do not feel vexed with me, nor think I allow "trifles" to prevent me from going, for I assure you it requires no small amount of self denial to give up the pleasure. I have not asked "leave of absence," of course I could take leave if I chose, but none of the other teachers have ever been absent for an hour, and I want my reputation in regard to punctuality to be as good as theirs. I wrote to sister last week that I could not go. I have not heard from her since; probably she will meet you and I sincerely hope you will enjoy yourselves just as well, as if I was with you. I *will* be with you in spirit. Did I imagine you would not accept my excuse, I would go, whatever might be the result, rather than incur your displeasure, or detract from your happiness: but surely you will think my excuse not only "plausible" but reasonable. I suppose you will be in Atlanta frequently. We can meet there yet. We are going to have one more teacher soon, perhaps I can be spared better then, and the weather will be pleasanter too. I shall hope to see Anna in Covington before many weeks pass, for I can not survive much longer without seeing her. If I do not see you both here soon I shall fancy you are trying to punish me for not meeting you in Atlanta. I do *not* think "strange" of your requesting me "to meet" you "half way." It is perfectly proper under the circumstances, and gladly would I grant the request were it practicable. The papers have been received and read with interest. Please reply soon

> Friend
> Jennie A.A.

DIARY

Wednesday 9th   The weather has assumed a wild mood to night, and is shrieking and whistling in a most frantic manner. I am sitting close to the fire but can only keep one side warm at a time. So much for *fire-places*: give me a *stove* in cold weather either North or South. * * *

Feb Sabbath 13th   An unexpected pleasure to day in a visit from Mr. *Lines*. As sister and myself failed to meet him in Atlanta yesterday he thought he would not have his trip for nothing and not see either of us, so he concluded to give me a short call, for which I am grateful. He spent a part of the afternoon with me, and after tea he came again to remain until the nine o'clock train. We had just got nicely to talking when the omnibus came for him; and broke off our visit before it was hardly commenced. * * *

Monday [March] 14th * * * The teachers have complementary tickets to hear the Apollomans read to night; but I for one shall be obliged to remain at home, because I am minus a *beau*.

Monday 21st * * * Sunday received an unexpected visit from Mr.
Lines. He has been laid up with a felon on his finger nearly ever since
he was here before, which accounts for his not writing to either sister
or myself. He left on the train last evening; his visits are short but
agreeable. * * *

April 3d * * * Received a long pleasant letter from Ellen Dillow last
week. She expects to graduate the coming summer, then take upon herself the burden of a teacher. Ah she little knows what a burden it is; her
spirit is light and free now; then it will be bowed with care, crushed
with toil and trial. She seems to desire to come South, and I should be
delighted to have her near me; but I am almost afraid to encourage any
of my friends to come so far away from all their friends, and to endure
the hardships which a teacher must in teaching at the South   We are
better compensated here than at the North, but children and youth are
so hard to govern as well as teach that a teacher dearly earn their salary and a good deal more than they get. * * *

Monday 4th   The rain is over for the present. The day has been pleasant, but rather cool. School room duties have passed off as pleasantly
as I can expect in this school. One new pupil. Hope no more will come
for I have my hands full now. No letters yet. Am reading "John Halifax"[3] interesting and fascinating like all works of fiction. Have been
reading ever since school, and the time has slipped away, and here it is
bed time and I have done nothing but pour over a *novel*.

Tuesday 5th   Very very cold for April. We all received quite a fright at
college to day. We teachers were all up stairs in the college office at faculty meeting   One of the girls came up and said something was the
matter with the furnace. Pres. Fulton and all the Prof's ran in haste,
and soon discovered there was a *slight* cause for alarm since *little* danger of an explosion; the pupils all ran screaming out in the yard, The
gentlemen all set to work and cleared out the registers thus removing
the cause of danger. The pupils were so frightened that they could not
be quieted for the morning recitations to proceed and were dismissed.
This afternoon all has passed off as usual. Have been reading "John
Halifax" since school. No letter

Wednesday 6th   Warmer to day and very pleasant. Since school Miss
Atkisson have taken a long walk with our pupils: she took the fresh,

and I took the preps. The girls enjoyed the walk very much, and we enjoyed seeing them happy. We went about two miles out in the country returned home just at dark excessively fatigued. Mr. Bowker has been here since tea. I fear I was not very agreeable, I was so very weary.

Thursday 7th   Arose this morning not entirely recovered from my last nights tramp, felt therefore very little like encountering school-room trials and duties. On my arrival at college Miss Fulton informed me that our regular exercises would be suspended. and were to listen to lectures on Physiology by Dr. Lambert. Of course such an arrangement pleased both pupils and teachers, and we have been both interested and amused through the day. * * *

Wednesday 20th   Well my book a letter came to night and a great fright it caused me. It was from Sarah Harris, & was sealed with dark green. Mrs. Henderson thought it was black, and expected it was a messenger of sad tidings to me. She met me in the hall on my return from school, and handing me the letter begged me not to be excited. I ran hastily to my own room, and with trembling fingers broke the seal, and scanned its contents, expecting every line would pierce my heart with agony by revealing the dreadful fact that my only relative in Georgia was dead, but thanks to God the preserver of life and health no such news awaited me. Sister is alive and well. * * *

Monday morn, 25th   O! O! how I do dread to go to school and encounter the trials which I know are awaiting me. There goes the second bell. I have no more time to think of and shrink from duty.

SYLVANUS TO JENNIE

Fayetteville Ga.
April 30th, 1859

Dear Friend Jennie:—

Some time has elapsed since I have seen you, and I am almost ashamed to write after so long a silence but trusting to your forgiving spirit for my negligence, I will venture to trespass once more upon your patience.

I took a trip last week to Atlanta intending to visit you and Cousin, and as the trains suited my time best I started for Cartersville at noon of Saturday intending to return at night, but Anna would hear nothing to it, and as all my trips had been made in your direction she felt that she had a claim on me; so contrary to my *inclination* I was obliged to forego the pleasure of seeing you. I regretted it much as I am so situated that it will be very difficult for me to leave the office again for some time, though I am in hopes that we shall not be strangers to each other on that account.

I had much to say to you which I hardly know how to express in writing, and in fact I am almost certain of failing in what I would under ordinary circumstances say to you in person for to express myself in this way the language must necessarily partake *too* much of the cold formality which pervades the correspondence of merely a passing acquaintance or entire strangers, but if such be the case I hope you will attribute it to the fault of the *head* and not of the *heart*.

Jennie, we have met a great many times, apparently as one friend or acquaintance meets with another, but then you have ever appeared more like a sister or a cousin to me, and as such I have greeted you, I have never displayed a particular attachment in your presence beyond this, not knowing what your relations *might* be in another direction, nor do I know even now, but I cannot do less than to address you upon the subject. I have been strongly attached to you almost from our first acquaintance, and that attachment has grown upon me, until from the natural impulses of my heart I am prompted to lay it before you, hoping at no distant day to find a reciprocal feeling in you. I may be asking too much, from the casual acquaintance which you have had with me, to request the privilege of addressing you as an admirer, nay now, as one offering his hand in the consummation of those vows most sacred in human relationship, but I do so trusting that you will treat me confidentially and with candor in accordance to your own feelings.

There are many things that I should speak of were I conversing with you in person, and perhaps it is due that I should, but I will say no more at this time, hoping to have other and more favorable opportunities when I can express myself with that freedom which I should wish.

Hoping to hear from you again soon I remain as ever

Yours truly
Sylvanus De F. Lines

DIARY

Wednesday [May] 4th. Just a word to night my book   I am so in and out of school that I hardly have time to look at reading or writing. Two letters to night; one from sister, the other from another friend, the contents of which are of an important and serious import. and which require thoughtful heart probing, and earnest prayer. God grant me grace to answer it right.

* * *

JENNIE TO SYLVANUS

Covington May 10th 1859

To Mr. Lines,
    My Friend:—
    Yours of April 30 has reached its destination, and although but a few days have passed since its arrival, I find myself seated for the purpose of replying; thereby proving that your long silence is pardoned, although it *did* seem like neglect, and *did* wound my feelings, for I feared that through some inadvertency I had forfeited your good opinion.
    The import of your letter, Mr. Lines, was unexpected but not unpleasant. It is gratifying to know I hold a place in the regards of one whom I esteem so highly, and for whom I have ever cherished the most kindly feelings. I did not know that you felt any interest in me beyond that of friendship, for as you say, you have never manifested any stronger regard in my presence, concequently I have not allowed myself to become *too* much interested in you: but since by expressing your own sentiments, you give me a right to question my heart and know what feelings it entertains for you, I have done so; and now to be true to you, and true to myself, I must frankly acknowledge that I feel a deeper interest in you, and a stronger attachment for you, than I have ever admitted even to myself. Our acquaintance although of some length, has not been intimate; but I think I know your character and principles, and have found sympathy in the spirit which breathes through your letters.
    You wished me to reply with candor; I have done so. Indeed I would not do otherwise on this all important subject. I can not, and need not say more at present. Shall hope to see you as soon as your business will admit.
    I received a few lines from Anna soon after you visited her. She expressed her pleasure at seeing you. I am glad you remained with her, although it prevented me from seeing you. Gleams of sunshine rarely illuminate her path.
    I suppose your little town is smiling in the freshness and verdure of Spring. This delightful season has smiled on our "city" too. She comes with her flowers and birds, to cheer us with beauty and song. Nature in her beautiful robe looks glad and joyous. Involuntarily our hearts sympathize with the beauty and gladness of earth: bright hopes, and pleasant anticipations *will* flit through the mind notwithstanding the

crushing errors of other days. I do not have much time to enjoy this delightful weather, for my mind is so constantly occupied with my school. We are very busy preparing for examinations and commencement, which takes place in six weeks. I for one shall hail its arrival with delight and relief, for I was never more weary of confinement and toil. I went to Atlanta to trade a few weeks since; went up in the morning and came back at night. Enjoyed the trip finely. Called at Mrs. [?] to to see my little pet, Fannie Mason. She has the same sweet face and bird-like voice. The college bell summons me to duty, and I must hasten to close with kind regards,

From   Jennie

*   *   *

DIARY

Monday 23d. Well I have *worried* through one more day at school. My pupils *will not* behave quiet and orderly. I went to Academy Spring with them to night, intending to have them practice their pieces, but a crowd of boys and girls prevented. Have had a lovely day, just cool enough for comfort. Received a letter from sister at noon. Sad, sad was her heart when she wrote. Ah! she is passing through the furnace now, and will doubtless come out pure gold. Have just finished reading "The Last Days of Pompei"[4]   Am not *very* much pleased with it.

*   *   *

SYLVANUS TO JENNIE

Fayetteville, May 29 [1859?]

Dear Jennie:—

Tis Sunday night—the hour when humanity seeks repose, when all nature is silenced, when reflection holds in sway over the man and warns him that another day has passed and gone; 'tis the hour when last we parted and my mind wanders back to your quiet abode where the spirit is wont to linger,—and at this time I know of no one who should command my thoughts and reflections more than yourself— would that I were not compelled to communicate them through the medium of a pen, but so it is at present; shall it be always thus? In your last letter and then again upon our last meeting was I lead to hope that I had found *one* of all others upon whom my affections had centered, a sympathising and a congenial spirit,—one with whom I might ere long be happy—was I right? Nay more, Jennie, you already know my feelings,—you know, too, the *love* which I entertain for you, and I have only to ask, are your feelings reciprocal—can you love in return one so unworthy as myself? would you be willing to unite your destinies with mine in travelling through this voyage of life? if so then shall I again be happy.

To answer this may require time for reflection, for to choose a partner for life is no trivial affair—the destinies of the immortal soul oftimes depend upon the choise of a companion,—therefore weigh well the subject, and be true to yourself, to your friends, and to your God, and when you have done so, then may I hope to receive your answer. It is true you know nothing of my circumstances in life farther than observation would lead you to conjecture, and this is a matter of no small importance in the consideration of a question so momentous, for I am aware that many a one has been deceived in making their choice with the anticipation of bettering their condition of acquiring wealth, or at least a competency for a support,—and it is but right that you should know with whom you are connecting yourself, and in view of this I can only say that my circumstances are very limited—that I have nothing but what is acquired by industry—which is all I ask, and so long as my health is spared to me through God's blessing, I have no fears of the future. With this I leave it to you, hoping you will give the subject your earnest consideration and as I have endeavored to do, treat with that open-heartedness which is due to yourself.

Mr. Doolittle, of Oxford, passed through this place on Wednesday last and paid me rather an unexpected visit. I was very glad to see him, however, and made his stay as agreeable as possible.

Jennie, let me hear from you at your *earliest* leisure.—and believe me

> Ever Yours,
> Sylvanus.

* * *

Monday 30th   Have toiled all day at school again. A letter from home today. All as well as usual, and still treading the toilsome paths of life. Went to Oxford with Miss A. on Saturday. Had a pleasant visit at Mrs. Jennings; returned this morning.

Tuesday 31st. A letter from Mr. L. to day   He has confered a great honor upon me; one which I feel hardly worthy to accept. He offers me a stronger arm than my own to lean upon as I tread life's dark and tangled paths; a noble and faithful heart to give and receive the affections which is indispensible to *womans* happiness. For many years I have baffled with the storms of life single handed; My sensitive nature has often, O how often shrunk from the chilling [?] of this cold world. I feel the need of a stronger and better self. God grant me wisdom to decide in a manner which shall be *right* in the sight of Heaven, and which shall be for the good and happiness of him who awaits my answer.

DIARY

Friday [June] 3d   Had a long talk with President Fulton to night. It is doubtful about his remaining here next year. If he does he wishes me to retain my situation; but I am unwilling to if I can do as well or better else where. I do not wish to live over again the trials of the past year. I think Pres. Fulton appreciates my efforts and labors, that is some consolation.

JENNIE TO SYLVANUS

Covington June 3d 1859

Dear Friend:—

   The last two hours I have been enjoying the undisturbed quiet of my own room. After witnessing a glorious sunset, and watching the last golden line fade from the western sky, I sat by my window dreaming. Opening the storehouse of memory, I recalled and reviewed many reminisences of my life. The early days of childhood—Ah! how glad and joyous they were, until a cloud darkened my sky, and threw a shadow over my bright morning. My earliest and best friend, the charm of our home, my *mother* was laid in her narrow bed, and then I knew *how bitter* was the cup of sorrow. Ere I passed from childhood to maturity, another and another of the loved ones who were wont to fill a seat in the home-circle, passed away from earth; some in the bud of childhood, others in the bloom of youth. Thus were my earliest days clouded by sorrow and bereavement. I have not the light and bouyant heart which beats in the bosom of one who knows no suffering; but still I crave the boon of happiness, and ever do I find my self gaping wistfully upon the star of Hope, and ever does its cheering rays beckon me on to a future, which, touched by the wand of Fancy appears to be gilded with rainbow hues. My happiness does not consist in mingling with the gay world; I could not, and would not adorn the halls of gaiety and fashion. O! no, I would have a quiet and peaceful home, with a few to give and receive the hearts purest and warmest affection. I would not be surrounded with wealth, and all to attendant follies; but I would enjoy those comforts and pleasures which are bought with a competency acquired by industry and economy; then I should "*love to live*" Such is my idea of life Mr. Lines I have pondered *well*, the subject of your last letter. I feel myself highly honored by your offer, and unworthy as I may be to accept it, I should not be doing myself justice to refuse a noble and faithful heart; one which I believe capable of giving and receiving the affection which is indispensible to my happiness. From all I know I think I could be happy with you; but could I *impart*—as well as receive the precious boon? Are you willing to trust your happiness to one so imperfect as myself? My nature is extremely sensitive and sympathetic: I can not truly live only when surrounded by an atmosphere of love and kindred feeling: a harsh word or a cold look is like an "Alpine torrent" to my heart. I have sometimes thought I should never dare to unite myself with any one; fearing I should be too exacting, expect too much kindness and sympathy. But knowing my fault I should be doubly armed against it.

You tell me your feelings, and ask if mine are reciprocal: if I know myself they *are*. You tell me you love, and ask if I can love in return; why should I blush to own I *can*.

In deciding this important matter, I have questioned my heart, and sought council from my God. My friends are too far distant to seek their advice, but I shall ask their sanction, and that is all they require, for they can trust me to choose for myself.

That God may bless us, and grant that you may not have erred in choosing, nor I in accepting, is the earnest prayer of

Jennie

DIARY

Monday 6th   Nothing of note to day my book   Sent off a letter of *importance* this morning.

Monday 13th   My heart is lighter than when last I looked upon thy pages dear journal. My examination is *over*, and I am free from college duties once more. My pupils recited well and was highly commended by Pres. Fulton. I do not think there will be any concert, so I shall not have to drill my girls any more on their precis, as they will have no opportunity to speak them. Have commenced my silk dress this afternoon. Shall have time to sew this week.

SYLVANUS TO JENNIE

Fayetteville, June 13/59

Dear Jennie;—

It is with unbounded pleasure that I now sit down to address you; a pleasure that I have never felt before,—not that our correspondence has been unpleasant or unprofitable to *me*, but I now feel that our sympathies and affections are *one*; that in each other we can place our confidence, and that ere long we may walk in the same pathway the journey of life, cheering each other in the trials which we all have to contend with. But for the "Star of Hope" our lives would be a blank;— since the reception of your last letter how bright has it shone upon my heretofore desponding and lonesome spirit. I now feel that I may yet enjoy the happiness allotted to man, and I can but look forward to the time when I shall take upon myself, before God, the vows which shall unite us as one through life. Your picture of true happiness was but the echo of my own feelings, nor could I express them more beautifully. To be happy is the aim of us all—and it is for us to seek out the means whereby that object can be attained. I think I have done so. I pondered the subject well in my own mind before I ventured to propose to you— whether I did in truth *love?*—for without that there is no real happiness,—and I am frank to say that *I do*; and it shall always be my aim so to act that I may command your *love* and *affection*.

You tell me that you are "extremely sensitive and sympathetic," but with a loving companion this is a virtue almost indispenable. My feelings in times past have been similar and to some extent are now; but from mixing with the world, being thrown into all kinds of society, and often meeting with perplexities where I should look for enjoyments has served to blunt, in a measure, the finer feelings of my nature. To promise you that I will be everything that you would reasonably expect I cannot do, for we are all liable to err, but that your life may be a happy one rather than a burden to you will ever be my object and prayer. Should it be my privilege to stand by your side before the altar to unite with you in the holy bonds of matrimony, then the vows which I shall take upon myself will be to me the most sacred and with Gods blessing I shall endeavor to fulfil them.

I am anxious to see you, but I am so situated that it will be impossible for me to leave here till after our examination, which takes place the last of this month when I am in hopes to be more at leisure. I suppose you are fast approaching your commencement and will then be free for the present. Please write me of your movements and when you intend visiting Atlanta. I wish to see you before you make any arrangements for the future, and especially concerning your stay in Covington, provided you have not already engaged. I received a letter from cousin last week, and she seemed quite down-hearted, not knowing what she was going to do, and as they had already invited you to spend your vacation there, which arrangement might be frustrated by the absence of the family and perhaps her discharge. Now I hardly know myself what would be best for her, consequently could not advise. If matters were situated different with me I would not hesitate for a moment, provided I could get your consent,—I speak in reference to our early marriage and procuring a home of our own, where she too might make herself happy;—but in this place there is not a vacant house and boarding is the only alternative, and very scarce at that. For myself, I am engaged for the year, and how much longer I may stay is uncertain, wholly depending upon circumstances, therefore it would be useless for me to make any permanent arrangements, if in my power, whereby she might find a home with us, but let things turn as they may I shall do what I can for her should she need my assistance.

Jennie, I have not proposed a time for our marriage, and it may be premature for me to do so at this time;—much rather would I have *you* do so,—in fact, it is my wish that you should, not knowing your feelings upon the subject. As for myself, I am unhappy here, situated as I am alone, with but a lone star of hope to bring up my spirits, and is that star far in the distance? I leave it for you to answer; and at such a time as shall suit your pleasure and convenience shall I look for its approach with a pleasurable desire.

I would that I could converse with you upon this subject personally, but fate has willed it to the contrary.

But I will stop, for I fear that I have already wearried your patience, hoping to hear from you on the receipt of this, and do not think that I would let a letter from you remain in the office for a week before I' would receive it, for it will afford me much pleasure to hear from you often.

Good night.
Sylvanus.

DIARY

Wednesday 15th   A beautiful shower to day. The air is cool to night. Have sewed so steadily to day that I am very weary to night. Miss Atkisson has been with me this evening; she has just left.

A letter came to night from one who may perchance God willing one day be more to *me* than all the world beside; but I will not let Fancy gild the future with colors *too* bright, for well I know her [?] will not stand the breath of *reality*. I could write more on this subject dear book, but I do not feel like trusting my inmost thoughts and feelings, even to thy pages.

*   *   *

Sunday 19th   Attended commencement sermon at the college chapel this morning. Rev. Mr. Carter preached. His text was in Proverbs. Subject; what constitutes true woman? A very appropriate subject and it was well handled too. I think all were well pleased. * * *

JENNIE TO SYLVANUS

Covington June 20th 1859

Dear Friend:—

'Ere I take up the burden of the day, a little time shall be devoted to replying to your last. As I seat myself for this purpose, a feeling kindred to that which you express at your commencement of your last letter, renders my task easy and pleasant. Our correspondence has ever been a source of gratification to me, and from it I have derived both pleasure and benefit. But it has of course been characterized by a certain degree of restraint, which must of necessity pervade the communications of even near friends, so long as no bond of sympathy is felt or acknowledged. Each must feel conscious of a congeniality, and a spiritual affinity, or the heart must remain as a sealed book. I have an inate dread of intercourse with those whose natures are foreign to my own; concequently I have [?] a good deal within myself, not always from choice, for my heart knows no higher earthly bliss, than free interchange of thought and feeling with a kindred soul then as Tupper beautifully expresses it "As in double solitude ye *think in each others hearing*".

The assurance that there is *one* to whom I can open the door of my heart, and reveal its minor recesses has caused it to beat with new hope and new joy. I feel that I have a new aim in life; for should it be my lot to tread lifes tangled paths with you, next to serving God it shall be my object to render your life peaceful and happy. We need not look for perfect happiness, for *that* boon is denied to mortals; neither must we allow Fancy to gild the future too brightly, for the breath of reality tarnished the most gorgious as well as the less brilliant pictures in imaginations gal[lery?]. Mr. Lines am I doing wrong to express myself thus freely on this subject? My heart answers, no! your last letter authorizes me to write as I have done. I feel that expressing your own sentiments gives you a right to know mine, and I will not withhold them.

In yielding my heart and hand to you, Mr. Lines I yield *all*; yes poor as the offering be it is *all* I have to give. Neither beauty nor wealth do I possess. I do not speak of this thinking it would be an insurmountable barrier; no I deem you superior to such obstacles. I simply mention it as a fact, and that you may [?] for what you ask. You wish me to appoint a time for the consumation of our recent engagement. I can not do so without first knowing your will in regard to it, more definitely. I had rather you would decide, and whether it be sooner or later, your will shall be mine.

I have just received a letter from Anna, which is the first I have received from her in several weeks. She did not speak of having written to or heard from you. It seems I must [give] up my anticipated visit to her, which is quite a disappointment as I had laid all my plans in reference to it. I shall not now visit Atlanta in some time unless I hear something favorable in regard to a school. By the way sister says she has heard something indefinitely of a school there for one of us through Mrs. Candice.

Two days more our commencement will be over and the college doors closed for the next three months. I have not engaged to return. Pres. Fulton wishes me to do so if he remains, but I do not think he will. I think most of the teachers intend to resign; it is a hard, hard school to teach in.

I expect to remain here until the first of next month, shall then spend a few weeks in Oxford.

Write soon,
To Jennie

DIARY

Friday 21st   Well one commencement day is over; and this evening finished my part of its exercises; I can throw off responsibility now. My pupils acted their part in the concert this evening quite to my satisfaction. Prof. Walace says it was "the spice of the occasion."

Wednesday 22nd   The great day is over. The college walls are deserted for the present. The exercises were very interesting to day. After all was over there was many a tearful leave taking between pupils and teachers. Although I felt no particular interest in any of the girls, yet I could not restrain my tears at the hour of parting. This afternoon I went to the college and settled with Prof Mosely. he paid me $230,00 making in all $800,00 received for my years salary. Miss A. has just

been over to bid me good-bye   Our parting was sad and tearful. Shall
we ever meet again? I have learned to look upon her as a *warm* friend.
Many pleasant hours have we spent together. Throughout the year we
have had the same weary round of duties to perform   The trials we
have born together has served to knit our hearts more closely.

We are requested to remain another year but neither of us have decided to do so.

*   *   *

Monday 27th   Last Saturday I was very agreeably surprised by a visit
from Mr. Lines. We went to Oxford, and remained until last night. Mr.
L. was quite delighted with Oxford and the acquaintances he formed
there; and Mrs. Jennings and Virginia were very much pleased with
him; a favorable impression all round. I can not realize the engagement which exists between us; it seems as if it had been formed without any agreement on my part, but such is not the case. It all seems
like a dream now; but I shall doubtless awake to the reality in a few
weeks if not before. Mr. L. has just left in the train. I do not expect to
see him again until a new and important era in my life. Will it be the
commencement of a happy era? Time alone can answer. Fancy weaves a
rosy garland to adorn the brow of future; her flowers are a choice selection; all are fair and fragrant; but a stern sister by her side conceals
many a thorn beneath the green leaves. I do not expect to gather *thornless* flowers, such has not been my lot.

*   *   *

Thursday 30th   Have been sewing on a very important article to day.
When I wear it for the first time I shall probably take upon myself the
most sacred and solemn vows. I have felt sad and thoughtful to day.

Saturday 2nd.   Am about leaving Covington   Expect the carriage
every moment to take me to Oxford. Settled with Mrs. Henderson to
day for board. She made me a present of $5,00. She has been very kind
to me, and I shall ever remember her motherly kindness and care with
gratitude. I can not leave this quiet and pleasant home without pain,
and regret. I have become so much attached to my room; it has been my
home for six months. I shall visit for several weeks to come. I wonder
where my next home will be? and will it be a happy one? I will not
write more for a feeling of sadness is already stealing over me.

SYLVANUS TO JENNIE

Fayetteville, Ga., July 3/59

Dear Jennie:—

Slowly doth the hours pass away in this now more than lonesome place. Our commencement is over, and the bustle and confusion incident to such an occasion has subsided; the students have all dispersed to their respective homes and our little village has the *natural* appearance of a backwoods settlement. I once thought it a pleasant and pretty place, but since my recent visit to your, at present, temporary residence, I can see no beauty here, no attractions here; but one reason may be the object of my affections is not here, nor need I tell you where it is, for did you not command them I should not write thus freely.

Jennie, I have now only to look forward with contentment to the time when, if ever, our happiness should be complete, at least, so far as our earthly existence is concerned; and if I have not misjudged you I have no fears but that we may lead a peaceful and happy life here on earth, and I hope assist each other for a life in those blissful realms above, and thus make the words of the author whom you have quoted applicable, which read—

"O happy lot, and hallowed, even as the joy of angels,
Where the golden chain of godliness is entwined with the roses of love."

On my return home I found the letter which Anna had sent to me in which she says she has changed her mind about leaving her place, or rather, of their wishing her to, but she thinks she shall do so as soon as an opportunity offers itself, which may very probably be the case when she visits Atlanta, as Mrs. Welton thinks she may get the school she had in view now if she wants it; but then it wont do to place too much dependance upon what the people say there, if I can judge from your past experience.

I suppose you are intending to be in Atlanta in two weeks,—if so write me and if possible I will meet you there, also write me where I may be likely to find you. I shall be under the necessity of going up on Saturday and returning home on Sunday night.

Jennie, I would write more but I am unwell to-night and do not feel able to sit up. I hope to hear from you *soon*.

Please remember me to our friends in Oxford.

Yours affectionately,
Sylvanus.

DIARY

Tuesday 12th   In Covington again. Have spent a painful weary week in Oxford. At my urgent desire Mr. Doolittle brought me home yesterday. Have been very sick since I last looked upon thy pages my book. Was obliged to call in a physician while in Oxford, and am still taking medicine, which does not yet afford me permanent relief. Mrs. Jennings and Virginia were very much opposed to my leaving them, but I knew it was best. They were very busy preparing for a crowded house commencement, and the noise and confusion incident to such preparations worried me, besides I was fearful I should be a trouble to them, as I was sick and needed some care. Am glad to be in my own pleasant quiet room again. It is *home* to me, yes *all* the home I have in this strange land. I have felt very very sad to day; can not keep back the tears; they *will* flow. I am fearful from my present symptoms I shall not recover soon, perhaps not at all. O! why this anxiety? why can not I trust myself in my fathers hands?

Wednesday 13th   Am feeling very much better to day, almost well; hope soon to be enjoying my wonted degree of health. I feel that I shall prize the precious boon more highly, & feel more thankful in its possession than I have hitherto done. Mrs. H. has had a housefull of company to day; but I have not seen them for I have kept my room, only going down to my meals. The weather is excessively warm; some indications of a thunder storm, which would be very refreshing. Mailed two letters last night one to Mr. Lines, the other to Mrs. Candice.

Married—
August 17th. Have neglected my journal for more than a month: the occurrences of the last six weeks are only noted down upon memories page. There they are traced in indelible characters, *never* to be effaced. The most important event of my life has transpired since last I greeted you, my book. An event to which I have ever looked forward with mingled emotions; but it always seemed far away in the distance; something to be *anticipated*, not *realized*. It was a dream of the future; a future which *reason* told me had its sun-shine and clouds, its lights and shades, thorns and flowers. But *Fancy* would have me believe that it was the garden of Eden before the Tempter found his way there; that the sun always shone undimed by clouds, that light dispeled *all* shade, and *thornless* flowers decked the margin of its silver streams. Can it be that *far off* future which hope and fancy have so often gilded is present time to me now   Have I passed the gate? Am I entering upon that new

era in my life capable of so much weal or woe? Am I about to try the realities of another phase in my existence? Yes such is true and real, as much like a dream as it seems to me. What a change a few weeks have wrought! a change in my inner and outer life. I have a new hope, a new aim, a new object to live for; yes and new responsibilities, new duties, and new cares. Never since the glad days of childhood did life look so desirable to me as now; and why should it not? have I not found a kindreed sympathizing spirit, a noble and faithful heart with whom to halve the evils, and double the pleasures of life? I feel unworthy of the happiness which causes my heart to beat so lightly, but Ah! how well can I appreciate it. Life to me, almost from the dawn of my existence has had its shadows: but I will not dwell upon the past now, I will live in the present, while it is bright and cloudless   Experience has taught me it can not always remain so, clouds *will* rise. This new tie can not keep lifes clouds away, but will make them lighter pass, or gild them if they stay. Trials await, and ills betide mortals while on earth they stay. and to meet them with meekness and patience, how much christian fortitude and grace is needed! When I think of my own weakness and insufficiency, how helpless I feel; how entirely dependent upon Gods assisting grace; and in this new relation more deeply than ever do I feel that trusting in my own strength I can not and faithfully perform the vows taken upon myself at the altar. Not only would I be faithful and devoted to him whose life I would render cheerful and happy, but I would be a meek and humble follower of my Savior. O! that it may be our united object and prayer to live first for our God, to work faithfully in his vineyard; if this be our first great aim I know our Father will smile upon and bless us.

Tuesday 23d.   Dear journal I am neglecting you without a cause. In after years it maybe pleasant to look back upon the first weeks of my married life, and I should note down its incidents. Nothing yet has occured to mar our happiness, or ruffle the calm sea o'er which we are sailing. Very pleasantly do the hours pass in this new but peaceful happy home.. The village of Fayetteville which is our present home is all that one could desire in a quiet country retreat; the inhabitants social and friendly, kind and attentive to strangers. My room [neat?] and home like. All this is conducive to happiness, but it is not the great secret of mine. I have been as pleasantly situated before, but there was a void in my heart which *such things* could not fill. Now there is nothing wanting. I am *happy*. A few weeks since I did not know such bright days were in store for me. How thankful I should be to the Giver of all good.

Wednesday 24th.   Rained all day yesterday and until nearly noon to-day. This afternoon the sky has been cloudless again. Called on Mrs. Basworth and Mrs. Acton; found them social; enjoyed my calls well. Am alone this eve, Sylvanus has gone out on business, but he is coming now, I hear his foot on the stairs and must bid you good night my journal.

Thursday 25th   Nothing new to day. Our little [bark?] glides smoothly and peacefully on. O that it might ever be thus till we reach the haven of eternal rest.

Friday 26th   Have filled the pages of my journal and having no blank book at hand must make this sheet serve as a substitute. Have been writing letters to day. to Miss Van Deusen and Miss Beebe, warm friends of my girlhood, may they ever remain such. While writing to them it seems so much like other days that I forget I was [?]   Two ladies just called. Mrs Holiday and Mrs. Miss somebody else. They did not remain long enough for me to form any opinion of the [?].

Saturday 27th   Sylvanus has given me a new blank book to fill, but I believe I will fill this sheet before commence to sully its pure pages. How differently I am situated from that I was when I commenced this book; and how much happier I am; my [?] has found a *home* now; and is satisfied.

Mr. Mason called to day; he was full of humor and wit; says he is going to get married as soon as possible for he sees the ladies will *throw themselves away* and so he is going to take advantage of [?] folly. Emma and Fannie have been here [?]   Had a fine serenade last night. Are indebted to Mr. Loony for the compliment and treat.

Sunday 28th   The town is nearly deserted to-day. All have gone to the camp meeting ten miles from town. Sylvanus does not approve of camp meetings and had no desire to attend. In that case as almost every other our opinions are alike. It would have been a punishment for me to have gone to day. We have spent the time pleasantly and I hope prof-fitably in our own room. The Sabbath does not seem as long as it used to in Covington.

Monday 29th   Rather a cool dull day. Mrs. Tidwell returned to night from the camp meeting, very weary I suppose. Mr. Lines, I mean *Sylvanus* received a letter from his mother to-day   It contained a few lines to me expressing a cordial greeting and hearty welcome into her family. It made me feel that I had found more than *one* new friend. I wish I could see them.

Tuesday 20th   Have spent the day sewing and writing   This morning wrote a few lines to my husband's mother and *my* mother too but I can not rea—— it yet, but I did not feel that I was writing a stranger in addressing her. I already feel a [?] of interest in Sylvanus' friends because they are dear to him. I hope the time is not far distant when I shall meet them.

We are reading "The Prince of the House of David". one of my favorite works. Sylvanus has been reading aloud this evening while I ply my needle; thus employed the time has passed [?] away; and now it is time to kneel before the throne and our God for the blessings of the day that has passed and crave His protecting care during the unconscious hours of sleep. Good night dear journal.

Wednesday 31st. The last day of Summer. Have not time nor space to bid the Season adieu: Will write in my new book to-morrow. Have not felt well to-day

Since tea have taken a walk which has quickened my puls a little. Have spent this eve as we did last.

Tuesday [September] 6th   On Saturday last according to our expectations, we arose early and by six o'clock were wheeling toward Atlanta. The morning was cool and our ride delightful. Reach the city at eleven o'clock. Went to the Front House where we were furnished with a room. I threw off my riding habiliments and was soon resting myself upon a couch. Sylvanus had a good deal of business which kept him on the street hardly giving him time to dine. The dinner we found very palateable and refreshing after our long ride. In the afternoon went to Mr. Dill's for the purpose of having our pictures taken. Had two double pictures taken, and one of me alone. We wished to send a likeness of Sylvanus and myself taken together, to his home also one to my home; but they are so incorrect we shall defer doing so until we can have better ones to send. After leaving the Artists I done a little shopping, made a call on Mrs. Welton and attempted one on Mrs. [?] but did not find her

at home. Returned to the hotel and after partaking of refreshments prepared to turn our faces homeward. Sylvanus did not finish his business
so that we could start until six o'clock. Darkness soon overtook us; but
by the light of the moon and with a very gentle, careful horse, we proceeded on our way with little difficulty, until that luminary of the night
ceased to shed her light, then we found some trouble in keeping in the
right road. We reached home in safety however about two o'clock almost overcome with sleep and fatigue. I arose at the usual hour in the
morning and went down to breakfast. Sylvanus prefered a morning
which he extended until nearly noon. There were services at the Methodist church; and we regreted not being able to attend. Should have
done so in the evening had not rain prevented. * * *

*   *   *

Monday 26th   Just one week has passed since I have looked upon thy
pages my book. Nothing of note has occured. Yesterday I attended the
Baptist association at Flat Creek, some 7 miles distant, where a large
and promiscuous assembly were gathered; old and young, rich and
poor, high and low, white and black met together in a large arbor erected for the purpose. I enjoyed my ride, and on my arrival I was really
interested and amused, so vast and mixed was the multitude assembled. Had some difficulty in finding a seat, and when I succeeded in obtaining one it was very uncomfortable, and so far from the "preachers
stand" that I could not for the sea of heads intervening see the speaker
and a good part of the time the buzz of voices prevented me from hearing his voice. I can never appreciate a sermon unless I can *see* as well
as *hear* the preacher. After the morning service we were invited to dine
at Mr. Clements table, which was bountifully spread with substantials
and delicasies. We remained to hear another sermon after dinner, and
then returned home. In the evening there was preaching at the Baptist
church.

*   *   *

Wednesday 28th. Only 6½ o'clock, and supper is over and all the white
people in the house have gone to attend Prof. Ryan's lecture. A long
evening is before me, and I may spend it alone. Sylvanus has gone to
the Seminary & will perhaps remain to hear the lecture. I might have
gone but did not feel inclined to do so. I have been out calling this
afternoon

Thursday 29th   Did not spend last evening at home. While I was writing in my journal Sylvanus came in, and wished me to attend Prof

Ryan's lecture with him, I did so, and was highly entertained. His subject was *Beauty*. His ideas were *poetical* and *poetically* expressed. After his lecture, he interested us with reading poems from different authors, and personating different characters. As an elocutionist I should presume he rarely finds his superior. He is a perfect mimic, and kept his audience convulsed with laughter while personating "Job [?]" the hypocondriac and other characters. It was late when we returned home but we felt amply paid for the time and money spent; we expect to enjoy another treat to night

Friday [30th]   Heard Prof. Ryan lecture on the "Infinitude of Creation" last night   He went farther and deeper than any one I ever heard, on the subject. The citizens of this place are very much pleased with him; the seminary was crowded last night.

Saturday October 1st. Am alone this evening. Sylvanus has gone to a negro wedding, something he has never seen, and he felt some curiosity to witness their marriage ceremony, also to see how gaily the *fair* bride would be decked, so he has gone in spite of rain and wind.

* * *

Thursday 13th * * * There is a Hard shell Baptist preaching at the Court House. I fear I am becoming *heathenish*. I do not feel much inclination to attend preaching when there is any in town which is seldom. The preachers that I have heard so far are very *illiterate* and *noisy*; they certainly do not furnish food for the *intellect*, but doubtless do for the *soul* when the *heart* is *right*. Ah! me how cold and careless I am in regard to spiritual things. My heart sinks within me when I think what little progress I am making in the divine life.

* * *

January 2nd *1860*.   Once again after the lapse of two months, do I look upon thy pages my journal. I have neglected to note down daily occurrences for several weeks past; but with the new year I am going to resume the pleasant task. I do not intend to give up keeping a journal now that I am married. Perhaps my journal will not be all to me now that it has hitherto been. I need not now relieve my burdened spirit by penning it's grievances upon the unconcious pages; I have now a closer, dearer friend, into whose ever listening ear I can pour the trials and perplexities of every day life feeling sure of confidence and sympathy. Yesterday ushered in the year *1860*. I wanted to write, but I knew that

I could find no words to express the thoughts which crowded upon my brain, and the feelings which oppressed my heart. How differently am I situated from what I was one year ago! Well do I remember how sad and lonely I felt one year ago last night, as I sat alone in my room. Far from home, friends and all the associations of childhood and youth, with no one near, in whom I felt any particular interest, or to feel an interest in me; not one to whom I was bound by the tie of nature or the bond of affection. I was a stranger in a strange city. No wonder I was almost weary of life. I remember mentally saying, shall it be always thus? The past year has answered the question. I am neither lonely or unhappy now for while life lasts whatever ills betide I am sure of the love and protection of one who is more to me than all the world beside. *My Husband*

At the beginning of this new year we would unitedly crave a boon from the Great Giver of all good. That boon is *Grace*. Grace to enable us faithfully to perform our vows to each other; bearing with meekness and patience the infirmities and faults of each other. Grace to endure with *christian* patience the trials and perplexities which we must encounter in every day life. Grace to walk before the world in such a manner that they may *know* we are disciples of Jesus. Grace to *think*, *speak*, and *act* to the honor and glory of God.

Newnan Geo.[5] Monday January 9th 1860. Here I am in a strange place and among strangers again. We left Fayeteville on Friday afternoon the 6th inst., Rode in the hack to Fairburn,[6] where we took the cars for this place which we reached in safety at 3 o'clock. Met with Mr. Davis on board the cars; he conducted us through the rain and mud to the "Dougherty Hotel." The house was so full we could not get a comfortable room but feeling the need of rest and sleep we laid our weary frames upon a very hard bed, and soon forgot our unpleasant surroundings in "Tired natures sweet restorer" In the morning we were furnished with a comfortable room, where we or *I* rather remained until after dinner. Sylvanus then found a place which he thought would suit us for a *temporary* home; tea-time found us seated at the table of Mr. Brown.

Our room is not just such a one as we would like, but it is comfortable, and when cleaned and carpeted, I think it will be quite pleasant. We are much pleased with the family, and our *table fare*. I presume we shall find it a comfortable and pleasant home. I did hope we could have a home of our own when we came to this place, but circumstances are unfavorable, and we must content ourselves with boarding for the present. I hope the time is not *very* far distant when the goal of my earthly hopes shall be reached, and we shall know what home comforts, and home-privileges are.

There is a Presbyterian church in this place, am glad of that but regret to learn that there is preaching but twice a month. There is also a Baptist and Methodist church. We shall not lack for religious privileges, if we are only disposed to avail ourselves of them.

I received a letter from mother on Saturday, also a box sent by express, containing some articles I wished sent on to me from home. Sylvanus received a letter from Mr. Mason wishing him to take a situation in Atlanta which would pay him over $1,000, per year. I would like to live in Atlanta, but I do not want Sylvanus to take duties and responsibilities upon himself which will overtask his strength, and deprive him of health. He is far from being well now; last week's care & anxiety has almost prostrated him. For several days he has been so hoarse that he can hardly speak above a whisper; his cough is still very troublesome. I can but feel anxious about him.

* * *

Monday 23d. The weather continues delightful. Received a kind pleasant letter from President Fulton. He is now Pres. of "The Furlow Female College" in Americus. He tells me his family are still in Va. If they return to Ga, I hope they will find a pleasanter home in Americus than they had last year in C. Not one of that excellent family were appreciated there. Covington is not a pleasant abode for teachers. * * *

* * *

Tuesday 24th. * * * The first numbers of the "Southern Literary Companion" were issued to-day. Sylvanus brought me a copy For some reason my eyes are paining me badly to-night. I have been trying to sew, and trying to read, and am now trying to write, but I find I cannot use my eyes without pain so I will retire. I do not sit up for Sylvanus when he is detained late. Most *devoted* wives would, but I prefer to show my devotion some other way.

* * *

Saturday 28th * * * A little darkie has just burst into my room so unceremoniously that it has driven every thought from my brain, and I must lay aside writing. Servants in *"this country"* never think of knocking at ones door.

Tuesday 31st The last day of January. I arose a little earlier than usual this morning, and thereby made out to curl my hair before breakfast. I shall be glad when it is long enough to twist up, it is so much trouble as it is.

The rain is pouring down in torrents. How will Sylvanus get home?; as usual he is at the office. I have been reading the Companion this evening. There is a touching article in it by the Editor in regard to his blindness. None who read it can fail to feel deep sympathy for him, and an interest in his enterprise and success. I think that article alone can not fail to gain *some* subscribers. * * *

February Wednesday 1st   Last night a man by the name of Jones was found dead in the street; he was supposed to be intoxicated at the time of his death. Another victim of King alcahol! Another warning to all who tamper with the *fatal* cup. * * *

Thursday 2nd   Paid our washing woman $3, for one month's washing. * * *

Thursday 8th [March] * * * My afflicted brother has again been bereft of reason. After repeated visits mother was at last allowed to see and converse with him. She writes me that he is very happy and still clings to the hope that he will 'ere long be restored to health   It is a blessing that he does not realize his hopeless condition. Hopeless. how heavily the word falls upon my heart. The sad truth that he will never recover *will* force itself upon us. Years have passed since he became a patient of the Lunatic Asylum; he is no better now that when he left home. But through all his sufferings, never has a murmur escaped his lips: his mind though shattered, is tranquil and happy. Amid the ruins of his intellect, their remains one faculty undimed by the ravages of disease, and which shines brighter for the desolation which surrounds it. The faculty to love and worship God; to understand and *feel* the depth and riches of a Saviors love to fallen man, has survived the wreck. His only thought, aim and desire is to sit at the feet of Jesus. * * *

Thursday 22nd   Sylvanus and myself went to hear the Swiss bell ringers last night. I listened with delight to the music, and was pleased with the appearance of the musicians: they were dressed in [?] costume. The little girls sang very sweetly. Some very rude people were in the crowd, & made great disturbance. * * *

Monday 26th   Two days have passed since I have written. I must now note down the occurrences of Saturday. They are *indellibly* written on a page in "memory's book."

Although rather cold and windy on Saturday morning we decided to take our anticipated trip to Fayetteville. Started in a buggy about eleven o'clock. I did not feel anxious to go; on the contrary felt quite disinclined, and would willingly have returned to our room even after we started. A foreboding of ill oppressed my mind with vague and gloomy fears, which the bright sunshine, exhilerating air, and the thought of meeting friends, failed to dispel. Before we had proceeded five miles I had indulged in a hearty cry, because our horse proved to be rather fearful and freaky. But even tears could not clear my mental horizon; dark clouds still hovered over my spirit.

We proceeded ten miles which brought us to "Newell's mill," on "Shoal Creek" There was a bridge half across the creek, the remainder had to be forded. The bridge and ford were very near the dam, and owing to the recent rain the water was high and came rushing and roaring over the dam, with more than usual fury. It seemed dangerous to cross in the usual place with our freakish horse, and Sylvanus after permitting me to alight, and walk across on the foot-log-rode farther down the stream in search of a better place to ford. He entered the stream as he thought in a shallow place, but experiment proved it to be the *deepest*. At first the water reached to the hubs; when in the middle of the stream, it reached to the seat, and sent the cushons and Sylvanus' shawl floating. At one more plunge the buggy was out of sight and the horse with only his head and shoulders to be seen was resting his hind feet on the buggy, and his fore feet in the bank, which was perpendicular, and fifteen feet down, the water being on a level with it, made it appear shallow and like a usual fording place. The buggy was fast sinking to the bottom of this fearful depth. Sylvanus stood in it calling for help, with but little more than his head and shoulders above the water, and unless help had arrived within five minutes, swiming to shore would have been his only chance of safety. My feelings at that moment, words are too feeble to portray. Fortunately or *providentially* I should say, a negro man was within hearing and came to us with all possible speed. He immediately took off a line and threw one end to Sylvanus, which he tied around the handle of the valise, the negro drew it to shore, and again threw the line to Sylvanus telling him to "hold on tight" and he would "pull him out." It was not more than half a minute before he was safe on land. If ever a *thank God!* came from my heart it was at that moment. The negro man now left us and went to the house for more help; he returned with his master and several men servants. They all went to work to if possible to save the horse; after several attempts the horse made one desperate plunge and dislodged himself from his critical and painful, position and with one leap stood in a shallower part of the stream, and turning his head towards the other side of the creek he soon drew the buggy on shore. The gentleman then bade one of the servants take our valise & conduct us to the house. On our arrival a large fire was built and a lady we found there assisted me in taking our wet clothes; the valise was full of water, and every thing in it soaking wet. We had some valuable articles of dress which the water very much injured but did not quite ruin. After the gentleman had seen that the horse and buggy were put in a position to dry, he came to the house, and taking Sylvanus up stairs, he gave him a change of raiment and had his clothes hung out to dry. Despite the narrow escape he had just had, I could not suppress a smile, when he came down, clad in the habiliments of "mine host," almost hid in their *ample proportions*. We remained there until our clothing was dry and then after eating a nice piece of chicken pie we bade our host and hostess a kind adieu. Mr. Newell and his sister Mrs. Ward were the names of those to whom we were indebted for so much attention and kindness. Ever shall we remember them with gratitude. Mrs. Ward told me something of her history: it was a sad one. But doubtless trial and affliction had had a tendency to refine and elevate her character. She looked weary and downcast, but their was an air of humility and meekness about her. * * *

Thursday 29th　I am greatly disappointed about a very little thing to night. *Trifling* disappointments always annoy and disturb me more than weightier ones; and it sometimes calls for more self-control than my erring nature possesses to bear them with even a small share of meekness and patience. Such an acknowledgement is humilliating but true nevertheless. I know my fault but do not always guard against it. To night for instance I know I did not manifest a right spirit, and I fear lowered myself in the estimation of my *husband*; whose opinion is of more value to *me*, than, that of all other beings combined. No more my book for I am sad and discouraged on account of my *many* frailties & follies. Poor weak sinful erring human nature! How much grace we need to keep us in the right path!

Saturday 31st　March leaves us to day. He has sung in a wild strain through the leafless forrest, whistled a shrill tune through our key holes, and breathed forcibly against the windows, during his whole reign. *ladies* are certainly glad to have him resign his power, now they can venture in the street without having their skirts seized and whirled around in rather a ridiculous manner. Perhaps the gents, rather regret the departure of March, as he always favors them with a peep at *little feet* and *pretty* ankles. * * *

Wednesday [April] 11th   Have a new duty to perform; one which I fear is beyond my capabilities. I have consented with fear and trembling to take charge of the children's department, in the "Literary Companion." I [was] honored that Mr. Davis should select me, but I fear has too high an estimate of my intellectual powers. I have never written much for publication, and I fear my poor efforts will do but very little good, and reflect very little credit on their author. However I have given my word and will do my best; have my two first articles ready. It will be quite a tax on my time, as well as my brain   But as long as I have so little to occupy my time and attention I need not mind that. * * *

Atlanta. July 9th   Once again after the lapse of *three* months do I look upon thy neglected pages my journal. When I last wrote, I little thought so long a time would pass ere another line was written here. Many things of interest have occured, which I would were recorded here. My husband has been urging me to write from [day to?] day, but under the influence of procrastination I have thus far [avoided?] what I should deem a pleasure if not a duty.

We left Newnan rather abruptly. Our prospects in this city have not been and are not yet very flattering. I trust the clouds will soon clear away, and prosperity smile upon us again. How much faith is needed to look beyond the dark clouds of adversity. * * *

We have been boarding at Mrs. Gardener's[7] since we came to town. She is a widow lady from New York. She has several northern boarders, and we all feel very much at home. We now only take our meals there, and have rooms on the opposite side of the street at Dr. Youngs.[8] It is rather disagreeable crossing the street so many times a day this very warm dusty weather; but Mrs. G. had no comfortable room for us, and this is the best we can do. We have two rooms; our sitting & sleeping room is very nicely furnished.

Saturday 14th   Yesterday Sylvanus received a telegraphic dispatch from his mother, to return home, as there is plenty of business there. S. is quite undecided; we are both anxious to go, but feel that if business

was a little more lively here, it would be best for us to remain South
some time longer.

* * *

Monday 16th   This morning went with a crowd of ladies to a store
where goods damaged by the late fire were to be sold   Found a promiscuous pile of goods & a promiscuous crowd of people; Every lady
seemed to be doing all they could for *number one*. My purse being almost empty, I was more of a spectator than participator in the scene. I
remained until nearly noon, and came home thoroughly fatigued, and
very near sick. * * * Our circumstances now, are not at all favorable to
returning north; we should have to make considerable sacrifice to do
so, and then we have not accomplished what we intended to before returning, all things considered I had much rather remain here for the
present if this cloud which hangs so gloomily above us could only be
removed and the sun of prosperity shine once more upon us. * * *

Tuesday 17th   There is still no prospect of business here for S. at present; we do not know what is best to do; go to New Haven and take the
situation there, or remain here upon uncertainties. We are feeling very
much troubled. Sylvanus has just been home for a few minutes. A gentleman from Marietta has just called upon him, and offered him a fore-
manship; the gentleman who now has charge of his office does not give
satisfaction, and he wishes Sylvanus to take his place. S. has too much
principle to avail himself of this *timely* offer unless the situation can be
honorably and satisfactorily vacated   Thus our prospects are to-day,
whether thy will continue to brighten, a few days perhaps will tell.

* * *

Friday 20th   Forgot to write in my journal yesterday until after I had
retired. Nothing of note however occured so there was nothing of importance to record. Sylvanus does not hear from Cartersville or Maryetta, Our anxiety has been a good deal relieved for the last few days;
the star of Hope has been shining more brightly, but our sky is beginning to darken again: Ah! how uncertain, how delusive is every *earthly*
hope and prospect.

The weather remains the same, oppressively warm, and *very* dis-
agreeably dusty; vegetation is almost dead. The prevailing wish
throughout the city is for rain. I am trying to do some needle work, but
I do not progress very rapidly these melting days.

Evening—Since writing the above S. has seen Mr. Hunt from Mar-
etta and has engaged to take charge of his office in that place. He will

leave Atlanta Sabbath night; I shall not go with him, he will send for
me when he finds a place to put me. I fear he will find trouble again in
obtaining a comfortable boarding place. When I wrote this morning I
was in rather a disponding mood. I feel "*quite cheerful*" now, and I *hope*
thankful. Truly the sun is *ever* shining although it is *often* obscured by
threatening clouds.

Saturday 21st   Sylvanus wrote to his mother the first thing this morning; She will feel greatly disappointed, but I hope she will see that our
decision is a wise one at least to dim vision   We never know what is for
our good, we can only judge from knowing the present and imagining
the future. When we are led through dark paths, and not one ray of
light illumines our way, we do not trust the *unseen* hand which guides
us safely through all dangers. We tremble and shrink expecting every
moment to fall, and still our Father bears with our doubts and fears,
and leads us safely through to light again.

*   *   *

Tuesday 24th * * * I finished reading "Lena Rivers"[9] this morning;
like Lena's characters very well, but I think she was often too impru-
dent, it was however the kindness of her heart and her desire to do
good to others which prompted her to acts which were construed to her
injury. * * *

Wednesday 25th   Received a letter from my husband this afternoon,
and have just answered it. I do not know when I shall go to him; he
finds it almost impossible to find a suitable boarding place; the tone of
his letter is rather desponding, and I do not wonder that he feels thus.
    I was very much frightened last night about 1 o'clock, by some one
making an attempt to get into the room adjoining mine through a window opening on a low roof. I listened for a few moments until sure I was
not mistaken, then throwing something about me, ran down stairs as
fast as my trembling limbs would carry me. Dr. & Mrs Young had
heard the noise too. Dr. took his pistol went out in the rear of the
house where any thing on the roof would be discernible; he saw no one;
then we all went up stairs, but whoever had made the disturbance was
out of sight and hearing. I could not go to bed in my room again,
and begged the privilege of lying on the lounge in the sitting room;
but I was too nervous to lie there so I sat down on the carpet in Mrs
Young's door until day dawned, then I obtained a short nap before
breakfast. * * *

JENNIE TO SYLVANUS

Atlanta Wednesday July 25th 1860

Ever Dear Sylvanus:—

Your letter came to hand an hour since, and I hasten to reply, although I can not tell you what course it is best to pursue. It seems rather hard to have to lay out all your earnings for board. I should think it advisable to keep house, if we had the means to furnish *three* rooms comfortably, but as we have not, boarding seems the only alternative, unless they furnish for you, as they did for Mr. Williams. It seems to me if Mr. Hunt is so very anxious to obtain your services, he might help you in some way; surely he must know you are not able with your present income to pay $8, per week for food; then there is washing and lights *extra* I suppose. Surely there must be a few *private* families where we could get in. I think Mr. Hunt or Goodman ought to assist you. I would tell them I could not afford to stay at that price and pay so much for board; but then of course it is better to stay there at $50, per month, than here at nothing.

If we are *obliged* to go to the Fletcher House, I would make him give us as good accommodations as he has. Is there a closset in that room? if not he ought to put in a wardrobe.

A[t] lease see if the bed is *clean* and *sweet*. It is better to speak of such things before we go than after.

I am anxious to be with you, but if you think best I will remain here a few days longer, it is not costing as much as at that Hotel; unless you have engaged the room, if so I suppose he is charging you for it, and I may as well leave here as soon as you can send the money to settle, and still do not make any appearance to morrow night, you may know I am waiting a little longer, hoping to hear that you have found a cheaper home. I would like to be there by Saturday night however.

I do not like the idea of going to the Hotel, especially at that price, but if there is no other way, I will make a *great effort* to be contented & cheerful, for I know you have enough to trouble you without my tears and murmurs.

All are well—nothing uncommon has transpired except a delightful shower on Monday. No letters have arrived for us.

From Your ever loving w
Jennie.

DIARY

Saturday 28th   My trunks are packed, and in a few hours I expect to be on my way to Marietta. *How glad I shall* be to meet S.!!

Went up town this morning and made a few neccessary purchases.; viz. hoop, shoes, handkerchiefs, pocket book &c   We are having a very gentle shower.

Tuesday 31st. Left Atlanta on Saturday night at eight o'clock; reached Marietta about nine; found Sylvanus at the depot   He had been expecting [me] for the last two days, it is too bad I disappointed him, but I did not know that I was doing so. We are yet at the Marietta Hotel, and I fear we shall have to remain here, it seems impossible to find board in a private family. We are thinking of keeping house, whether we shall make arrangements to do, time will determine. * * *

JENNIE TO MARIA

Marietta August 1st 1860

My Dear Sister—:

You are doubtless wondering why I do not write, but I thought I would not do so until I was settled for the *Summer* at least. Sylvanus has charge of the "Advocate Office" in this place, and can probably retain the situation as long as he pleases; but he is not doing as well as he could in Atlanta with a permanent situation, and perhaps we may return in the fall.

We are boarding at the "Marietta Hotel" kept by Mr. Fletcher. It is the most extensive establish. of the kind I have seen in Georgia; it is also an *expensive* establishment, quite too much so for our limited means; but as yet we can-not find board in a private family! We are thinking of housekeeping; Mr. Hunt, the proprieter, is anxious we should do so; I suppose he thinks he should then be sure of Sylvanus.

We have a delightful room here, in the third story; we get plenty of good pure air, it seems very different from the heated, impure air in Atlanta.[10]

I am glad you are comfortably situated again; I hope it will prove a pleasant and permanent home.

We have not received that school money yet. I expect Sylvanus will have to take a trip to Cartersville for it. What a shame we can not have it when we are in so much need of money just now!

Marietta is the handsomest place I have seen in Georgia. I would like to live here as long as we remain South if we could do well, but we could not much more than live here. Sylvanus has received an offer of a permanent situation in New Haven at $10, per week which is good for the north. His mother was very anxious he should accept it and telegraphed for him to come at once, but we were too poor to give ourselve

that pleasure! I know they will all feel so much disappointed after waiting and watching, to learn that we are not coming at present.

Sylvanus saw Jessie Doolittle in Atlanta a few weeks since; he said
his father was very comfortable. Mrs. Jennings is going or has gone to
Atlanta to keep a boarding house for school girls.

I shall not write a long letter this time, for I have so many to write;
then I have no new[s]; I receive no letters, for I am in debt to all my
correspondents. Please write soon, tell me all about your new home,
cares trials and triumphs &c. direct care of Advocate office Marietta.

Accept kind regard from
Sylvanus & jennie.

DIARY

Sat. [August] 4th   Sylvanus received a letter from his mother this
morning. She is as we expected greatly grieved and disappointed that
we did not return north. Sylvanus feels troubled about it, but I do not
think he has reason to reproach himself for disappointing her; she is so
very anxious for his return, and not knowing our circumstances she
can not advise us for the best. I hope we may be prospered so that in a
year at longest we may be able to return. We shall never feel contented
and happy while we are roaming, and can not call any place home. I
want to settle some where and feel that I am to remain long enough to
identify myself with the place & people and form some attachment to
both. We are not satisfied in this place; boarding at the hotel does suit
our purse or meet our ideas of life. S. is very much dissatisfied in the
office, his patience is tried to the utmost, daily. I hope circumstances
will favor our returning to Atlanta in the fall.

A letter to sister to day   she is about as happy as ever.

*   *   *

Tuesday [August] 21st   We have a crowd here from Augusta. They
seem oblivious to every thing but their own comfort and amusement: I
think they are very disagreeable people. they sleep half the day and
then are prepared to sit up until midnight, singing opera music, dancing, talking and laughing in the highest key. We were very much annoyed by them last night. In such a promiscuous crowd as we find at a
Summer resort ones must needs meet all kinds of people; they must all
be well off for this worlds goods or they could not be here; but wealth
can-not and *does* not make them, either intelligent or agreeable, *some
few* of them at least. But I will not criticize too severely, I presume they
think me a very morose prosy little thing sitting up in my room all the

time; but it is too great a task to mingle with strangers, I prefer the solitude of my own apartment. Mrs. Manly & her sister Miss Willard have been in to see me to-day; they are northern ladies and very pleasant.

* * *

Tuesday 28   Have just finished a letter to sister. We have the prospect of returning to Atlanta. Sylvanus has just received the offer of a good situation, but he can not leave here until Mr. Hunt returns which will be in a few days. I shall go before he does in order to find a boarding place. Mrs. J.[11] is there and I wish to visit them and if they can accomodate us we shall make our home with them for the present. We had a delightful shower this morning, but it is still very warm. I must stop writing now and pack my trunks; they have been unpacked about four weeks; our stay here has been short, but long enough I am tired of hotel life and shall rejoice to leave

* * *

Thursday 30th   In Atlanta again, to remain I hope until we go north. * * *

Thursday [September] 19th. Have just returned from Dr. Youngs where I have spent the evening. Am alone in my room although it is near ten o'clock. Sylvanus has gone to the lodge, and if he does not return soon, I shall think it is a *lodge* in every sense of the word.

I am feeling quite well again, but not very ambitious and can not get up much interested in my sewing. I lay down this afternoon and slept a long time, but my sleep was disturbed by troublesome dreams. I dreamed my eye sight was nearly gone and I was groping my way through a strange house in search of water; but every room and article of furniture and even the two persons I met there, seemed familiar to me as if I had once been an inmate there. I thought I had faith in pre-existence of the soul, and remarked to the woman who gave me water that I had met her before in the same place and under similar circumstances in an earlier stage of our existence but that both her soul and mine were then inhabitants of other bodies that had long since mouldered back to dust. She seemed bewildered and unable to comprehend my meaning. In an adjoining room lay a gentleman on a sofa; he seemed interested in the subject of our conversation and began to converse freely with me but just as I was promising myself an agreeable and instructive tete a tete I woke with hard pain in my eyes and head, probably the cause of my dream of blindness. I had lain down with my face to the window and the light had been too strong for my eyes even through the lids.

*   *   *

Saturday 15th * * * This morning I went up town to do a little shopping, & after dinner went with Sylvanus to Mr. Young's furniture store to look at his beauroes. Sylvanus bought a handsome one for $22, he paid $17, and returned the dressing table which Mrs. Gardener bought   we shall pay her the price of that which was $5,00 then the beauro will be our own; so much towards keeping house. * * *

Nov 3d * * * There is now the greatest political excitement which has ever agitated our country since our brave forefathers achieved its independence.

Abolitionism is the *prime* cause; Why can not that set of fanatics mind their own affairs and let the South enjoy her rights in peace?

At the commencement of this political campaign the abolitionists set up a candidate which no honest & *honorable* southern man can vote for or hold an office under. If he is elected (and many think he will) the South will not submit to be ruled by the north, and a disolution of the union will be inevitable which must in all probability be brought about through suffering and death on the battle field and perhaps in our homes. I do not know how people can anticipate such an event. with so much calmness and unconcern. Surely christians should arouse themselves and besiege the mercy seat with the cry God save our country. Every thing moves on as if no such dreadful danger threatened us. Next Tuesday is election day. I for one will pray that Lincoln may be defeated. Of the other candidates I care not which succeeds I hope the wisest and best man will be placed in the presidential chair. * * *

Sunday 4th   We have been favored with delightful weather to-day. I attended church morning and evening. I did not enjoy the morning service very much; a little circumstance occurred just before I started that troubled my feelings. Caroline, Mrs. G's hired servant came to my room and asked me for a little camphor   I gave it to her without a word, also a piece of flannel. I do not know why I should have refused the negro surely it would have been very unkind had I done so. Mrs. G. came to me after she left and asked about it. I told her the simple fact which excited her very much. She said she should give Caroline a good scolding, she had no business to come to me instead of her. I begged her to say nothing to Caroline I did not wish her to, for she would think I had gone to her mistress with so trivial an affair, and as I told her, I do not want even a negro to loose confidence in me. I also told her if she reproved Caroline for it I should inform her that I had not told her mistress of so simple a thing.

On Saturday I saw that Caroline had a hard cold and I told her to bathe her feet and take some hot tea. Mrs. G. seemed displeased about that, and requested me to express no sympathy at all for the negro if she was sick. That would be acting against my nature and violating the most common law of humanity. I do not think it my duty to *outrage* my own feelings to please any one. When I have boarded with those who owned servants I could not please them better than to notice their servants kindly; but it is not so in this house. I have been very sorry that we ever came here to board and I certainly regret it now. We can not know people until we live with them   I am very much disappointed in Mrs B. She is not blessed with an amiable disposition and even temper, but she is a professed follower of Jesus and I must think that the principle of religion is in her heart and is continually striving with the carnal nature. But enough of this, perhaps I have done wrong to write about it.

Monday 5th * * * I hope politicians are doing all they can to defeat Lincoln and thus save our union from blood and strife. This is the last day they have to work in the cause. To morrow they must cast in their votes. I can not have much ambition for work or peace of mind until after the decision, then perhaps I shall feel worse than I do now.

Tuesday 6th   Election day has passed, and all say very quietly. All places where "a drink" could be obtained have been closed by order of the mayor of the city. If they are open to night, I fear there may yet be trouble.

*   *   *

Thursday 8th   The report is that Lincoln is elected. Wo to the union if he is! It does not seem possible that there are abolitionists enough in the United States to elect a president   I hope the report is *false*, but fear it is too true! Times are getting very hard. Sylvanus can-not get monney to pay board. What are we going to do? "Put your trust in the Lord," says a monitor within. Would that I could! I know it is my privilege and a *precious* privilege too. if I would avail myself of it; but alas poor earth worm that I am I can not trust confidingly in the unseen hand that can [guide?] me safely through all dangers & trials. I know that I need all the trouble and anxiety that is perhaps awaiting me. I have wandered from the straight and narrow way, and need something to bring me back. O! that my heavenly Father will enable me to bear meekly any and every trial that He is preparing for me!

Friday 9th   We hear nothing talked of but "hard times" and disunion. This state and several others are taking steps to withdraw from the union, whether they can do so peaceably, a few weeks will decide. The "Wide awakes" at the north and the Minute-men here are preparing to meet on the battle field if war is declared.

Saturday 10th   Well I have been so busy to-day I have had not time to think of Lincoln's election or the prospect of perilous times in concequence thereof. I have been washing starching & ironing. My collars undersleeves & handkerchiefs are all clean now. * * *

Sabbath day 11th   Attended church this morning and heard an excellent sermon from Mr. Rojers. He alluded to the National trouble in a very appropriate and feeling manner. * * *

Tuesday 13th   This afternoon went to the printing office with Mrs. Lyon, Miss Usher & Mr. Noles. *Mr. Lines* showed a good deal of politeness and gallantry in waiting upon us from room to room, and explaining the wonderful art of printing. I felt quite proud of his gentlemanly and dignified bearing. Since tea I have been over to Mrs. Wing's. I left Sylvanus in our room writing, but I find he has finished and gone out some-where. I do not think he likes to stay in here when I am absent, and I am glad of it. I like to feel that *I* am the greatest attraction for him at home.

*   *   *

Thursday 15th   Attended the concert last night and was very much pleased. The singers were 4 children from six to fourteen years old. The youngest is the sweetest little thing I ever saw; she sings so sweetly too. We are going again to night. Sylvanus does their printing and they favor him with complimentary tickets. When we can enjoy such a treat *gratis*, I think best to avail ourselves of it.

*   *   *

Tuesday 20th   Last evening went to hear the Holmans again. The Atheneum was crowded, probably there were 600 people there. Soon after the performance began we were startled by the cry of fire! Every one were on their feet instantly and many crowding to the door supposing or fearing at best that the fire originated in the Atheneum. The greatest excitement prevailed for a few minutes, but order was finally restored and the mayor [12] of the city informed the excited audience that they were perfectly safe as the fire was on White Hall in the Calhoun House. There were some pale faces among the ladies and I am sorry to say, harsh words among the gentlemen. If anything *unmans* a gentleman in *my* estimation, it is to hear him speak in an *authoritative unkind* manner to a woman under his protection because her nerves are not *iron* and she shrinks and trembles and perhaps *cries* when danger threatens. I heard one man in the crowd say to his wife in no *mild* tones either, "*Behave yourself cant you*" Shame on any man to speak thus, when if ever soothing arm is needed! I am *grateful*, and *proud* to say, that though I grew pale and trembled with fear, my heart was not made to bleed! No! *my* husband spoke gently, and threw his arm protectingly about me. That is one of the moments of my life which will *never* be forgotten and it left an impression on my heart which *can never* be effaced. Little acts of tenderness; little words of love, how dear they are to womans heart. The day is very pleasant. Nothing of importance is transpiring to interrupt the even tenor of my way. The political world is in great commotion. The dreaded crisis has arrived. The Union will probably be *disolved*. Whether it can be done peaceably or not, time will determine. Lincoln's election has already caused a great amount of trouble and anxiety. Business of nearly all kinds is nearly defunct. Hundreds are thrown out of employment in the South and many *many* more at the North. Probably this winter will be a time that has no paralel in the history of our nation since the revolution. Crime famine and pestilence will steal abroad in our once happy land. All this trouble had been brought upon us by *rabbid abolitionists*. Would that they alone could bear the penalty of their evil doing.

Wednesday 21st * * * We must prize our comforts while we enjoy them, the cry of "hard times" is continually ringing in our ears, I almost tremble for the future. The prospect for peace, plenty and happiness is *very dubious*.

Thursday 22nd   A dark rainy day. After dinner I went with Sylvanus to Cutting & Stone's and bought $10, worth of dry goods. We were obliged to get it on Mr. Seals act', he is owing Sylvanus and we could get no money. This evening I have been very much interested in listening to a speech of Mr. Cobb of Athens.[13] in favor of *immediate* secession. He talks like a true *man* and *christian*. His speech was delivered before the legislature of this state; it is published in pamphlet form. S. read it to me.

* * *

Tuesday 27th * * * Mrs. G. has been in my room this morning recounting her trials with Caroline. Negroes seem to be a *necessary* evil. If abolitionists *knew them* surely they would not wish to abolish slavery, & give them liberty to roam at large through the country.

Wednesday 28th To-day was appointed by the Gov.[14] as a day of fasting and prayer. There is preaching in all the churches; but mud and rain will prevent many ladies from attending. * * *

Thursday 29th * * * Mr. Peck came to see me to-day. He is principal of the Masonic Institute in Greenville Ga.[15] I have engaged to teach for him if Sylvanus decides to go into business with him. I like Atlanta and would prefer to remain here if we could do well, but if we can-not, we must go where we can. Mr. Peck does not object to giving me $400, a year, consisting of 40 weeks, I should feel almost rich to be earning $10, per week; but I wont count my money yet.

Friday 30th *Lost!* Some where in my room, about noon to day, my patience and *temper*. The missing articles are *very much needed*, and the finder will be *liberally* rewarded. Well my book this advertisment shows you that I have lost something *very valuable*, and somethings which I had *sometimes* flattered myself were in my *own* keeping. Mrs. G. takes the liberty to dictate to me, and reprove me in a way I do not like. There are but four persons in the world from whom I will accept a dictation or reproof. My husband, father, mother and sister-in-law. The first is too indulgent to do either, the second & third, do not take it upon themselves, but the fourth does *both gratis* whenever she finds occasion. * * * I have written a note to Mr. Conyers to-day inviting him to call on me, I wish to see him for old acquaintance sake and also to make inquiries in regard to the "Atlanta Female Institute" If we do not go to Greenville I am anxious to get situation to teach in this place. * * *

Saturday December 1st * * * Sylvanus has gone to the Union meeting to night.[16] I have just finished my evenings work, and I wish he would come home so that we might retire early and feel bright & fresh for the sabbath. Sylvanus gave Mrs. Gardener a $20, order on McNaught & Ormand [sic] which she traded out for butter and groceries.[17] Last night she bought two pairs of shoes at Dimicks[18] at $0,90 amounting to $1,80. on order. The eighth of this month we shall owe her $0,20 for board. I am glad to be so near even. I do not like to feel indebted to any one much less *such people*.

Sabbath day 2nd   I hesitated this morning about attending church on account of my old bonnet. Pride said it looked so shabby. Conscience said "it does not look bad enough to justify you in remaining home from church." I listened to the voice of the ever faithful monitor and went to the house of God morning and evening; heard two excellent sermons from Mr. Rojers. The day has been very pleasant.

Monday 3d * * * Sylvanus has been reading a speech of Mr. Stephens.[19] He is a union man. He *reasons* well, and talks more dispassionately than Cobb. but I do not think him quite so eloquent.

*   *   *

Thursday 6th   I have trimed over my travelling bonnet with plumes and ribbon for a winter bonnet; the times are so hard I can not afford a new one. Mr. Rojers came after tea and the evening has passed in a pleasant & proffitable manner. Sylvanus and myself expect to join the church next Sabbath.

*   *   *

Tuesday 25th   Christmas day has rolled round again. "Christmas gift," "Christmas gift," is continually ringing in our ears: but the times are too hard to answer to the cry of every one. Mrs. G. has received some valuable presents from several of her boarders. I do not think she ought to feel as she does about keeping boarders, looking upon them almost as intruders upon domestic peace and happiness; surely she must feel reproved now that they have remembered her so kindly. Miss Corbit[20] was here to dinner. Sylvanus and myself are feeling lonely to-day. We have few sympathies in common with those around us, and do not feel like associating with them more than politeness requires   The holidays make us homesick. We know there *are* those in the world who would gladly have us in their midst when friends gather around the

festal board. It costs a good deal of self denial, and a good many heart-
aches to live so far away from all we love, and all who love us. How
pleasant and heart cheering to meet old, tried friends and exchange
greetings and good wishes when these rejoicings come round! * * *

                              *   *   *

Thursday 27th   Another lovely morning. I have nothing special to
write now. I may have before night: we never know what the events of a
day may be. There are some fears of an insurrection among the negroes
during the holidays but we have seen no manifestation of it as yet, and
I trust we shall not.

Friday 28th * * * I do not write any thing about the state of our country lately. I hear a great deal but do not investigate matters so that I
have no decided views of my own on the subject. South Carolina has
withdrawn from the Union and Georgia will doubtless follow her soon.
A good many are trying to destroy the Union and a good many to save
it. I hope our national trouble will soon be settled amicably in some
way. * * *

Saturday 29th   A letter from Mr. Peck to day; the contents were satisfactory to Sylvanus, and he has decided to go into business with him in
Greenville I did hope to stay in Atlanta, but, the prospects for business
here are dull and in Greenville quite flattering. In a pecuniary point of
view we may do well, and we ought to for we sacrifice for everything
else in leaving this city. Atlanta is the only place I want to live in in
Ga. A country town has no attraction whatever for me. * * *

PART FOUR

WARTIME

1861-1865

DIARY

Greenville[1] January 18th 1861   Many days have elapsed since my husband presented this book to me, but we have been so unsettled that I have had neither opportunity or inclination to note down passing events upon its' pages. We left Atlanta on Wednesday the 9th of the present month. Arrived in Grantville[2] about one oclock P.M.; remained until eight oclock the next morning, then started in a hack for this place; arrived about noon; dined at Mr. Pecks', and being informed by Mrs. Peck that it was impossible to find board in town, we decided to remain with them, without making any attempt to find board elsewhere. They have rented a hotel which is very much out of repair, concequently they could not give us a desirable room, and having very little furniture could not make it comfortable for us: we have to go to the trouble and expense of painting papering and whitewashing our room, besides buying new furniture and carpet. On Friday morning the 19th Sylvanus went to the store and bought paper for our walls and after dinner commenced putting it on; and by nine oclock Sat. night three sides of the room were covered; and after bringing up our bureau, the room presented a more cheerful aspect. Sunday was rather a dull lonely day to us; we did not attend church. Monday Sylvanus went to work arranging the office; he has two rooms joining this building. I commenced my duties in the school-room; had but few pupils Monday morning, and in the afternoon it rained so hard I remained at home; unpacked our trunks and bureau and regulated our things. Tuesday had a few more pupils, but not enough to busy me, and the seven school hours seemed long and hung heavily on my hands. Wednesday and Thursday no accessions, and nothing of note transpired. I finished a long *blue* letter to Anna and S. commenced a letter to his mother which I finished this morning, and he has just mailed it, also one to Dr. Young in Atlanta, ordering furniture for our room. It rained so hard this morning I did not go to school, but it has cleared off now, and I must go this afternoon. I do not know how I shall like Greenville yet, but our surroundings in this dreary dilapidated old building are any thing but neat, cheering and pleasant. Thus far I am completely disheartened and dissatisfied with our change. I can not see that our prospects are any brighter in a pecuniary point of view, than they were in Atlanta, and certainly the facilities for enjoying ourselves are less here than there. I doubt very much if we have bettered ourselves; board is as high here as in Atlanta, and we expected it would not be more than half. We're paying $30, per month just for our room and what we eat. But I will close my book before I enter more bitter complaints. O that I could adapt myself to all kinds of circumstances!!

* * *

January 21st   A very cold day! Three accessions to our school. My duties are not numerous or wearisome at present, neither are they very interesting as my pupils are quite young, and can only read.

Georgia has seceded! We no longer live in the United States. There is great rejoicings to night; firing of guns illumination of houses and stores, speaking &c. I think their jubilee will be of short duration they will soon feel the need of uncle Sam's and aunt Columbia's care and miss the roof that has sheltered them so long.

Children are not justifiable in leaving the paternal roof in anger, because brothers and sisters have trampled another's rights. There is so much noise in the street that I can not write connectedly and legibly so will lay aside my pen for to night.

* * *

Friday 25th   A long letter from sister to-day. She lectures me a little for giving way to discouragement and low spirits. Have spent the evening down stairs. The weather is still cold and gloomy it rains almost constantly.

Sabbath 26th   The sun is shining once more! It is very cold but the sky is cloudless. I hope we may have a few days of fine weather   Sylvanus has gone to Atlanta. I wish I could have gone with him, and to *remain* there too. Never should I sigh for a sight of Greenville again! O! dear I wish I could feel more contented and satisfied here. I know Sylvanus must blame me mentally, for murmuring, but I can not help giving vent to my feelings some times when I am so unhappy. I do want to enjoy life, I believe that is a desire natural to all, but *staying* as we are at present is to me bare existence, it is not living. It seems to me I do not crave a great deal of earth's goods and pleasures to make me happy, and at times it seems almost hard that I can not be situated a little while as I would like. My husband, the privileges of religion, the society of friends, and a little home where my surroundings bespeak comfort and refinement, is all I ask on earth. I do not want wealth that would give me a passport into the society of the gay and fashionable. But I am forgetting myself and writing in my journal when I should be writing to Anna.

*   *   *

Wed. 29   Our furniture came last night. A bedstead, mattress, six chairs, a large rocking chair and towel rack. Our room much better but it can not look well until we get a carpet. The weather is very fine. One accession to our school this week. All passes off pleasantly. my heart is lighter this week than it has been since we came to Greenville.

*   *   *

Tuesday [February] 5   Poor Sylvanus sat up all night, also Mr. Peck and Mr. Wells. They all looked weary and sleepy this morning. They accomplished their task; The Georgia Weekly[3] is issued at last. Success to it and it's faithful, energetic enterprising and able Editor and publisher. Two new pupils to-day. No letters from friends. S. is down stairs directing papers with Mr. Peck. he wanted me to go down but I excused myself having letters to write.

Wed 6th   The weather is charming rather cold but clear and bright. School-room duties have passed off pleasantly; nothing of note has occured. I am alone this evening. Sylvanus' duties keep him confined in the office. I rarely get a glimpse of him except at meal time.

*   *   *

February Sat 9th   Have had a pleasant day. This morning washed my morning dress; am going to make it over, and as it has faded very little it will look almost like new. After dinner went out shopping; Sylvanus went with me. Bought some bed-ticking, ten yards for a straw mattress,—a remnant of delaine to trim my morning dress,—a calico dress and a bottle of cologne. It is the first new dress I have had since my marriage. I had all the articles, except the bed ticking, charged to me; am going to keep our accounts separate, I want to see which is the most economical S. or myself. * * *

Wednesday 13th * * * S. is hard at work in the office. Poor man he is having a hard time to get the Georgia Weekly started. Charley is better to-day, but not able to work.

Thurs. 21st   No school to day; on account of the funeral of old Mrs. Harris; she was buried this morning. Mr. Peck did not think it advisable, to open school this afternoon. * * *

Friday 22nd   Mr. Peck went to LaGrange this afternoon, and left me in full charge at college; had no trouble; pupils behaved well. * * *

Mon. 25   No accessions to our school to-day. Our number is rather small to busy two teachers and to pay them too. I should think Mr. Peck would feel discouraged. If I was a man I should rather do any thing than teach. Little Mertis Peck is very sick to-night. Mrs. P. thinks her nurse has given her something indigestible to eat. What a vexation negro servants are; and yet it seems impossible to live without them in this part of the country. Mr. P. gave Hannah a severe whipping to night; perhaps she will do a little better now.

Tues 26   Has been rather a hard day in school; scholars have been troublesome. Weather warmer, prospect of rain. Mertis is some better, but still very sick. Mr. & Mrs. P. sat up all night with her: he could not have felt much like going to college this morning; but teachers must always be at their post; there are always those in every community who seem to be watching for some short coming on the teachers part; and are ever ready to criticize and find fault at the least delinquency. * * *

Sat. [March] 2   Went out shopping with Mrs. Peck this morning. Have already spent about $10. since we came to Greenville. I do not like this *credit* system; one never knows how large their bill will be until *pay day* and then one is sure to have the "blues." Am going to keep an account of every thing and add it up occasionally.

Mon. 4   Much colder. Am feeling "blue" to day. Two new pupils in my department. Mrs. Rice the ornamental teacher came to-day; she is to board here. Lincoln takes his seat in the president[i]al chair to-day; I wonder what will be the result, peace or war?

* * *

Fri. 8   Friday again, how soon it has come round. Am tired of school-room duties. To morrow's rest will be acceptable. Wind from the South which always causes me to feel depressed in body and mind. The prospect is we shall have *war*; the thought fills my mind with gloom and horror.

* * *

Thurs. 14th * * * The wind is high and the air cold to night but not withstanding the inclemency, Mr. & Mrs. Peck, Mr. Wells, Sylvanus and myself, have taken quite a walk since tea; went down to Mr. Simontons where we spent an hour or two very pleasantly. Mr. Simonton appears like not only a gentleman, but a *good man*. Mrs. Simonton is very lady like, and interesting in conversation and personal appearance. Greenville can certainly boast of good society.

Sat 16   Our carpet was brought from LaGrange by the mail carrier to-day. It is not as fine as we expected to get for $0,75 per yard, and the figure is not just what I would have chosen; but Dr. Young was kind to get it for us, and I am satisfied. Have sent it to Mrs. Floyd to be made. I am impatient to see it down. Mrs. Peck made some of the best egg nog to night that I ever tasted

Sat. 23   A busy day in my room. Have had one negro man white-washing, and another painting. The carpet is down now and our room is a little paradise to what it has been. There is nothing in it now to remind us of the dismal dirty looking room we came into. How can people live in such uncomfortable, unpleasant rooms and houses as some of them do, when a little trouble and expense would improve them so much! We have been having quite a merry time down stairs to night. Mrs. Peck made some delicious egg-nog, and we all manifested our appreciation of its merits by making it disappear rapidly. It is very late, and I am very weary so good night my journal.

* * *

Mon 25   Quite an excitement prevailed here this morning. Mrs. Peck found all the clothing her children wore yesterday had been taken out of the house during the night. Mr. Pecks boots, and the childrens shoes were also gone. Some negro was, undoubtedly, the thief. I hope whoever it was will be found, and made to suffer as the crime deserves. This will be a lesson to all of us to keep every thing under lock & key. It is hard to live among negroes, and hard to live without them in this part of the country. * * *

Sun 31 Attended church to-day and heard the poorest apology for a sermon that it was my misfortune to listen to. I think such preachers desecrate the holy office of priesthood. Perhaps I am wrong, but I do not feel that it is one's duty to go to church unless we can be edefied; for the *example* however it may be duty to assemble with the people of God in His sanctuary even if we are neither instructed or interested.

* * *

April Sun. 7th Something of note *has* occurred to-day. Mrs. Peck has *another* daughter. She slept with me last night; got up about day light and went into her own room; the child was born about ten o'clock. Her nurse said she suffered as little as possible under the circumstances.

* * *

Greenville, Ga., Aug. 11th, 1861.
Dear and loving Jennie,—

Another year has rolled around, and a second anniversary of our marriage is upon us. When I look back upon the past how varied are the reflections which crowd upon my mind:—of the pleasures and sorrows which in their turn would meet us in our pathway. Though we have had many difficulties to encounter,—many crosses to bear; yet I feel that they have served but the more closely to cement our affections to each other, and taught us to look above, to Him who alone is able to bear our burdens, and through whose grace our hearts may rise above the vain and transitory things of earth to a home in Heaven.

Our lives have been marked by many pleasures, for the past two years, and it is with gratification that I look upon them, and say with truthfulness that they have been the happiest years of my life and you, Dear Jennie, have made them so. When the world seemed to frown upon me, then it was that you stood ready, with words of encouragement and sympathy, to cheer me; when worn down by fatigue, how often have you bathed my fevered brow, and by many acts of kindness revived my drooping spirits.

I have spoken of the *past*; of the *future* I have only to say—May Love and Affection govern our actions to each other, and Love and Obedience to *God* our faith and practice.

Your Husband

August Monday 12th   I prevailed upon Sylvanus to celebrate the anniversary of our marriage as he did lastyear, by writing a page in my journal. He was loth to grant my request, because I had so long neglected writing myself, but yielded when I promised to be more faithful in future. Indulgence *ever* characterizes his conduct toward me. This book is now more valuable to me than ever. It contains two pages that breathe that constancy and affection of a devoted husband.

We have had one month's vacation. I enjoyed my freedom and rest very much. I was very busy with my needle all the time, but the change was pleasant. We have taught one week on the present term. The weather is cool, and I feel more like teaching than I did before vacation. * * *

*   *   *

Tuesday 20   S. and myself are feeling very unhappy & discouraged. Indeed we have reason, situated as we are. Never did we strive more earnestly to avoid every thing in word or action that might cause hard feelings & disturbance, and yet we fail; we can not do right; we are not appreciated or understood. The One who seeth and knoweth the hearts of all, is our judge and not sinful mortals. How thankful I am there is a God in heaven who judgeth righteously.

Thurs. 22   It rained very hard last night, pleasant to-day however. Am still feeling very sad, and expect to while I remain here. God help me to bear every wrong with christian forbearance. Never did I have such trials as those to contend with before. I have always said and thought that one might live peaceably any where by doing *right* but I find I am mistaken. If I have given cause for the censure and insult I have received from Mrs. P. I am unconscious of it; it has been an error of the head and not the heart.

Tues. 27   A cloudy day, no rain until sundown. Am very much troubled with dyspepsia, and as usual it affects my mind as well as body; feel gloomy and discouraged. How much I want a sincere female friend to whom I can go for advice and sympathy. Never before have I been without one. I presume there are those in this place whom I could trust if I was better acquainted, but situated as I am I have but little opportunity to form more than formal acquaintances. Bugs of almost every variety are flying and buzzing about the lamp; I can not write with the troublesome things in such close proximity to my face.

*   *   *

Wed 4 * * * Sylvanus took a ride to-day with Dr. Floyd.—, went to a picnic about seven miles from town where the Anthony Grays are camping. He returned just at dark pleased with his ride, and all he saw and heard. * * *

*   *   *

September Frid. 13. *Very* warm. Am feeling weary in body and depressed in spirits. Was up until a late hour last night. We all attended a concert given by the young ladies of Greenville for the benefit of the "Confederate Invincibles." I was very well pleased with the musical part of the entertainment, and thought the ladies done themselves credit.

Rev. Mr. Leek delivered an address which was altogether too long and to me was very dry and uninteresting for I was too weary to follow him closely enough for my mind to become interested in or appreciate such a sound and classical speech.

I am so glad it is Friday. School room duties drag heavily; I feel very little like performing them. I think of resigning my place in College on account of my health & for some other reasons. I think Mr. P. will be willing to accept my resignation, for there are so few pupils he can easily teach them all himself, and it will decrease his expenses too. * * *

Monday 16   Have resigned my place in college. I think Mr. Peck was quite willing to release me, for the school is too small for two teachers, either to employ all their time or pay them for it. I feel quite relieved now that I can throw off the burden of a teacher once more; my situation here however has been a pleasant one; but I have taught so many years I am quite willing to give [up] my profession, unless necessity compels me to resume it. I was quite sick again last night. S. called in Dr. Donnelly. He gave me medicine which relieved me for the present, whether the cure will be permanent or not I can not say. Am feeling pretty well to-day. S. is worn down with work and almost sick.

*   *   *

Sat. Sept. 21   The "Anthony Grays" came to town this morning. The ladies prepared dinner for them in the grove near the Baptist church. A shower came up about the time the people assembled and drove them into the church where several speeches were made. The table was then prepared and the soldiers arranged on one side, and ladies on the other. All satisfied their appetites and the servants then feasted on the fragments. * * *

* * *

Wed. 25   Prof. Tucker lectured at the Methodist church this morning on the wants of the soldiers. I did not feel able to attend. I understand he had a large and attentive audience. * * *

* * *

Frid. [November] 8   Truly we know not what a day or a night will bring forth. Last night we all sought our pillows thinking only of quiet and refreshing repose; but ere our eyes were closed in sleep, the alarming cry of "*fire*" caused us to spring from our beds, and the bright red glare of flame and the suffocating smoke told us we were very near the fearful element, and it was already making dreadful ravages upon property. We expected every moment that the roof which sheltered us would take fire and we should have to fly for our lives. We lost no time in packing our trunks and having them and our furniture removed. Providentially the wind changed its course and before the morning dawned the fire was stayed in its course of destruction, and we could with safety have our things brought back to our room. About dawn Sylvanus and myself lay down completely exhausted by fatigue and excitement. S. worked very hard taking goods out of the burning buildings. I fear he will yet be sick from over exertion. Mr. Boswell worked until he was prostrated and had to be brought home; for some time we thought he would die. We are all feeling "the worse for wear" to-day. One block of buildings, containing three dry goods stores and two groceries was burned to the ground. Have not yet learned what the loss is estimated at. Every thing in our room and our trunks was thrown into such confusion last night that it has taken me all day to regulate. No one knows how the fire originated but it is supposed to be the work of an incendiary.

Sat. 9   We have all felt somewhat refreshed from last night's rest. I have felt very gloomy all day, and feel still more so to night. The mail came this afternoon and brought alarming news. Several thousand Federalists are about to land on the coast of Georgia. Citizens are fly-

ing from their homes in Savannah. O that God would stay the sword in
our land and let peace once more reign.

*   *   *

January 13th 1862   The dates in my journal are few and far between
for the last few months. Indeed I have written very little for the last
year. This book which my husband presented to me one year ago ought
to be filled, but most of its pages are yet unsullied. I have been plying
the needle so industriously for many weeks past that I have not given
myself time to write to friends or note down incidents in my journal.
We are still in Greenville and shall remain here until we have a prospect of doing better some where else, which may not be soon in these
war times. Since I last wrote have received letters from Mrs. Gardner,
Miss Atkisson and the *bride* Mrs. Fitz. I ought to answer them all before I am *down* but my sewing is not all done yet and when I feel able
my fingers must ply the needle instead of wield the pen. Have just
finished a letter to Sister. Probably the last I shall be able to write to
her for the present. I feel that my hour of trial and anguish is drawing
near. God grant me strength of body to bear me safely through agony
which I have never yet experienced, and fortitude to bear it all with
meekness and patience, and may I feel resigned to His will whatever it
may be concerning me.

January Tuesday 14th   Had a severe attack of cholera morbus last
night. S. called in Dr. Terrell about one o'clock. Have been in bed all
day; feel better this evening and am sitting up. Mrs. Peck has been
with me all day. Mrs. Winslow spent this afternoon with us. Weather
cold and rainy.

Wed 15   Am feeling quite well again; have been busy all day: cleaned
my room this morning and made a little garment this afternoon. Feel a
good deal wearied to night. Am alone in my room and expect to be until
bed time. S. is down stairs playing whist. I wished he did not like to
play cards so well. I can not feel that it is right for church members
to identify themselves with the world by joining with them in such
amusements. Have had several annoyances to-day and am feeling discouraged and discontented. I do not like to write on thy pages dear jour-
nel when I feel thus, so good night.

Thurs. 16   Poor women what sufferers they are! I did not know until
now what our sex had to endure. Last night I did not have one hours

undisturbed repose; this morning just as I was about to loose myself in
sleep I was much alarmed by the cry of fire! The tannery was burned to
the ground. I was relieved to find it was not a dwelling house. Have
hardly recovered from the fright to day; been sick all day. Sylvanus has
just been out to consult a phys[i]cian but did not find the one he
sought. * * *

* * *

Sabbath morning January 19th   All but the children, servants and
myself have gone to church. It will be many weeks ere I can enjoy that
privilege, if *ever*. *That* thought *will* come into my mind. But God has
brought so many, many through the same trial that I may trust *hope-*
fully that He will bring me safely through the hour of suffering and
danger. I feel that life and health is dearer to me now that I have the
prospect of having more to live for than ever, and I pray that God will
graciously spare my life and grant the priceless boon of health. Yet still
I would say, "not *my* will O God, but *Thine* be done"

Mon 20   This morning while dressing I learned that Mr. Cone was
dead! I was greatly shocked for I had not heard of his being ill. He fell
like many others, a victim to *intemperance*. A sad warning to many in
this town who are rapidly approaching the same dreadful end unless
they heed the warning & dash *forever* the poisonous cup from their
lips. Mr. Cone leaves a wife, five children and brothers and sisters
to mourn his premature and untimely end. I have felt gloomy all
day. * * *

* * *

Feb. Thursday 27th   Five weeks have passed since I looked upon thy
pages my journal. It is with feeling of deepest gratitude that I once
more take my pen to write. God has been so kind and merciful to me.
He spared my life through hours of agony & danger; and I am once
again enjoying perfect health. He has entrusted to our care a little immortal being. O that we may feel deeply the responsibility that rests
upon us and seek daily at the throne of grace for wisdom to guide and
train our little one aright. May God spare our little daughter to be a
comfort and pleasure to our hearts, a blessing to her race and an honor
to His cause. Our darling is five weeks old to day. Never was a brighter
or more precious jewel sent to gladden parent's hearts. Truly "A babe in
the house is a well spring of pleasure." Her birth has unsealed a foun-
tain of love and tenderness, hitherto unknown to us. We have not yet

decided on a name for our little pet but think of calling her *Forrest Lillie*. Received a letter from Anna this week and have just finished the eighth page to her. The weather is delightful. Spring will soon be here.

Tuesday Feb. 28th * * * To day was set apart by the President of the Confederate States for fasting and prayer.

JENNIE TO MARIA[4]

Greenville Feb. 20th 1862

My Dear Sister,

* * * Well dear sister I have filled one sheet writing about my baby: now I will try to think about something else. Sylvanus went to Atlanta three weeks ago. No prospects of business for him there at present. We do not know what to do. S. will get no money if he remains here; but we are getting our board and washing, and S. is going to get a set of teeth on Mr. Pecks account; that is his only chance of getting paid. Now this is certainly an accomodation to Mr. Peck for by S.'s remaining and taking his pay in teeth it insured him the tuition of Dr. Floyds two daughters which he would otherwise loose. Mr. P. considers it so. His wife wants him to give up the office; he told her he would keep it up this year at any cost; she replied if he did, she would make it pretty hot for him: but she seems to be venting her spite on us. Before I was sick she treated me kindly, Since my baby was two weeks old she has treated us both with the utmost indifference and coolness; acting as if everything she had done for us was a hardship and almost as if every mouthful we eat is a loss to her. She says Mr. P. will not pay her our board but still she admits that she has received about $70, on our board for this year, but because most of it was in produce she counts it nothing; she wants every dime in her hand. We are the only boarders for which she will receive one cent until the end of the year and yet we are treated worse than objects of charity. A lady told me that Mrs. P. said she was satisfied to have us remain until I got over my trouble and now she thought it would be better for Mr. P. to have Mr. Lines leave: then he could get some one cheaper. Now how could it be better, when he pays S. no cash and would have to pay a cheaper hand *all* cash, unless like S. he was unfortunate enough to need a new set of teeth. Perhaps *she* would *make* him advertise for a young man who had decayed teeth. Anna if I could tell you how she has served me about tea, that one act would make you despise her character. She appears to object to my having *two* cups of *wheat* coffee even. Last week she made herself so disagreeable that we concluded we had reached that point where for-

bearance ceased to be a virtue, and I decided to tell Mr. P. on Monday to fill his place; but she suddenly changed from December to May, and we shall try it awhile longer. She charges us $5, per month for our washing; since Christmas we have furnished our own wood, so you see our expenses are about $40 per month, how can we ever lay up any thing at this rate? We are anxious to keep house; then we can economize and live according to the times. Now a word about visiting you. I should be *delighted* to do so, but dare not go to the expense, unless we should think best to leave here and run a risk in Atlanta; then it would be best for Sylvanus to go a few days, or two weeks in advance of me so to engage a house, that we need not have a hotel bill to pay. In that case I should be paying board here and might as well use the same money to defray my expenses to Columbus provided I should not be on expense while there. I fear the managers would think me an *intruder* and *sponging* would they not? I heard the other day that the citizens in Columbus were preparing to leave, thinking the city would be taken by the federals. Is it so? I am afraid to go to Atlanta even. I had rather stay in this little country town until the war is over, if we could live here independent of this establishment. I want you to think over all I have written on this sheet, and tell us what *you* think our best course would be. We *cannot* stay after S. gets his teeth paid for, and that will only be about four months. Do reply to this soon,

Excuse all imperfections and believe me

Your loving Sister
Jennie.

JENNIE TO MARIA

Atlanta, April 30th 1862

My Dear Sister—:

I am so distressed because we do not hear from you! What can this long silence mean! I dreamed a few nights since that you was *dead*; the gloomy thought has haunted me ever since. I wrote to you soon after our arrival in this city; I think you cannot have received it, or surely you would have replied. Sylvanus has not received a Georgia Weekly since we left Greenville and yet they have been sent regularly. There is no certainty about the mails or any thing else in these war times. Perhaps you have written and it has failed to reach us. I presume you were disappointed because I did not visit you after we decided to come to Atlanta. *I* certainly was, but I thought it too much of an undertaking to travel alone with a young babe and the care of my baggage: and then too I could not make the trip with out extra expense and I assure you we had not a dime to spare for pleasure. It costs *enormously* to go to keeping house these times. We have not got a cook stove yet. Our new kitchen is finished and our little stove is in it. We have got to pay $25 for a stove which one year ago we could have bought for $16. We were very glad we had a little furniture to begin with; we have been and are still buying what other things we need by degrees as we have the means. I wish you could see what a comfortable pleasant little home we have. Our carpet nearly covers two rooms. Our sitting or *parlor* is very pleasant, and with our carpet, chairs center table books &c looks neatly. There are two large windows in it. We put up our paper curtains and white ones over them. Sylvanus has made some cornices of board and papered them with bordering, and loops for the curtains to match, so our windows look really *genteel*. We have a nice large bed room and pretty furniture to put in it you remember. Our dining room is just large enough for a small family. I have nothing in that but a safe and dining table. The safe is the prettiest I ever saw; it is like a side board on the top. The floor is painted so that looks very well without carpet or oil cloth. Our kitchen is new and concequently clean, but I am not sure it will remain so as I have a servant in it. I got along alone for a month; work and the baby kept me trotting all the time so I had no time to sew. S. had to bring every thing from town and makes fires in the morning, and we both got tired of doing drudgery.

We have a negro girl sixteen years old. She is large enough and strong enough to do everything, and I mean she shall if I keep her. We pay $4 a month for her besides clothes; that you know is cheap for a grown woman. I get her at the price in consideration of teaching her to do *every thing*. Thursday May 1st   Little Lillie is taking her morning nap and I will improve my time writing a few more lines to you. When she is awake I do not have much time to write or any thing else. She is very good however, especially at night. She goes to bed about eight o'clock, and we hear no more from her until five or six in the morning; then the little dove wakes us with her gentle cooing, and always greets us with a smile. She grows pretty every day, *we* think; her blue eyes are *bewitching*. We weighed her the day she was three months old 14 lbs.! Is she not a fine baby? I tell you we have astonished every one. I wonder when you will see her. I am impatient to have you.

We have planted our big garden: it cost about $5, I hope it will yield at least that sum. If you know any *cheap* nice dishes I want you to send recipies. How do you make bag pudding? Butter is $0[?] per pound and every thing else accordingly. I intended to write another sheet, but I believe I will send this off hoping you will reply *immediately*. S. and baby joins me in sending love to sister, cousin and auntie.

Ever yours,
Jennie.

JENNIE TO MARIA

Atlanta July 15th 1862

I cannot forbear writing to-day, dear sister, although I shall not mail it until I have a long letter finished. The increased postage will prevent my writing to other correspondents, but not to *you*.

I hope this letter may end with better news than it commences. We have lost our cow and calf! Sylvanus bought one last Wed. for $60, Saturday some bad boys let the calf out and we have seen neither since. The cow has not yet given but one gallon of milk a day, the man we bought her of said she would give two gallons. It is the richest milk I have tasted in Georgia almost equal to thin cream. I milked her: S was trying to learn so that he could milk in wet weather. He had a cow pen made which cost nearly four dollars. Yesterday S. was on foot nearly all day looking for her, and this morning he left home about six o'clock that he might go and see the man he bought her from. He went there yesterday, but did not find out the name of the man Mr. King bought her of. Yesterday was a day of anxiety and suspense. I know you will feel sorry for us. At present prices we can but just live, and to lose $60., how can we feel reconciled to it? It is hard to drink rye without milk and we can not afford to buy it. People have raised on that too. Our cow was very gentle, and I think we should have been pleased with her in every respect. I churned Saturday; only got two table spoons full of butter from 1 gallon of milk, but I do not think it was churned long enough. I have got a nice little stone churn. I was intending to churn the milk, for I do not think I could get pans to set it, if I could they would cost so much that it would not pay to get them. But I fear my churning is all over now. The disappointment is bad enough, but the loss is still worse.

I have not felt so hopeful and so ambitious since we commenced housekeeping as the few days we had that cow; but S. and my self are "out of heart" now I assure you. When Matilda told me the calf had gone, my first thought was, well that loss and trial is nothing compared with what it would be if our dear little daughter was taken from us. I felt for the moment that I dare not murmur lest a greater trouble come upon us. I have not shed a tear yet, but I tell you my heart aches. Poor Sylvanus! I dont believe he feels very ambitious to day. We had talked so much about the cow, and laid all our plans. He was going to give me $5. every week and all I got for milk to pay you. It is no use to lay any plans for the future is it?

Dear little Lillie was threatened with croup last week. Our hearts trembled then. The little darling was highly amused at her own coughing and sneezing. She is such a merry good natured little thing. I wish I could place her dimpled arms around my neck; she would press her little face to yours and coo so sweetly. her kisses would be wet however. When I am caressing her I forget our troubles. Enough for to-day.

Wednesday 14th   Has been a worrying day. We have been ironing. Matilda knows very little about it. I have ironed a fine shirt for the first time in my life. I tried last week but had to put it with the dirty clothes before I finished it. Have had to iron over a good many pieces after M. She is so lazy she will not put out her strength.

Have had a hard thunder shower this afternoon. It will do our garden good. Our onions have not come up. Shall we keep sowing seed until they do? S. came home to night weary and almost sick. The walk is too long for him. I had a very nice pork stew for supper.

Thursday 15th   Spent the afternoon at Mrs. Gardeners. Took nurse and baby. We have got a cook stove at last. It is nearly new and a pretty looking stove if it was not for the greese and filth which covers it. S. had to take an old knife and *dig* for a while before he could make out what year it was made in. The stove cost $18. It will cost about $10. to furnish it. S. paid $3. for a small tin bailer: that is cheap the way tin is selling. Took supper at nine o'clock. Had boiled potatoes fried pork, milk gravy, bread & tea.

Sat. 17th   I wish you could see how clean my house is: I washed the windows; Matilda do all the rest. Her kitchen floor is white enough to eat on. My oven bakes well to day: Made some fried cakes, but had no lard to fry them in, so I baked them. Strange to say, they did not taste much like *fried cakes*; but they go well with our corn beer. That constituted our dinner. S. took his with him. Came home very hungry to night. Had boiled pork and peas rice, warm biscuit swat cakes, & a good cup of tea for supper.

Sunday 18th   A delightful day. S. has gone to church. I did not feel able. Fear I am going to have an attack of dysentery. How I wish you could dine with us. We are going to have some nice soup, beef, potatoes, biscuit, rice pie & corn beer. *Dear* little Lillie is taking her morning nap. Am in too much pain to write more now.

Monday 19th   Washing day again. Have been trotting to and from the kitchen all day. Am weary to night. Took a dose of oil yesterday; feel but little better   S. heard of a cow to day that he may get. She is said to give three gal, a day. Price $50. We have nearly that amount in gold and silver, but do not like to use it because we can not replace it in coin and it is not very safe to lay by bills. Now if you have it to spare, and feel disposed you might loan us that amount, and hold a mortgage on our *bank* in case anything happened so that we could not pay you in the course of two or three months. It is so hard to live with[out] butter or milk. Buttermilk is five cents a quart, and it costs considerable to

get enough to cook with. Please write immediately and tell us what you
think about it

Have I told you our city is under marshal law?

JENNIE TO MARIA

[fragment, written during the summer of 1862]

Tuesday 16th   Do bring your work and sit with me a while dear Anna.
I am alone and we could have a quiet, confidential, sisterly chat   Have
sent Matilda to search for the cow again. No news from her yet. S.
walked several miles yesterday. besides doing his days work. He is very
much cast down. He remarked last night however, that "with all our
troubles we have much to be thankful for while God spares us to each
other and grants us health and the means of obtaining a comfortable
living". We sat chatting in the dark last night until bed time. We were
talking of days that are past when S. used to visit me in Covington. In
speaking of the past and present he paid me so many compliments that
I almost imagined he was a lover again.

Dear little Forrest she's asleep in her crib   She looks so entirely different from what I thought *my* baby would. I expected it would have
very light skin, light hair, perhaps red, and quite light eyes. Her complexion is between that of a blond and brunette; her eyes dark blue
with a sharp bewitching expression. I never saw a baby have such intelligent expressive eyes. Her hair is dark and very abundant. You
know most babies loose all form when they become very fat   Not so
with her; her little leg is as trim and tapering as any you ever saw on a
doll. By the way baby sends a kiss and her thanks for the doll you have
for her. I wonder when she will see it. Well I must sew a little while she
sleeps. Wednesday. Made a mistake in the date yesterday. To-day is the
16th   We are rejoicing in the return of our cow. Advertising was the
means of our finding her. She had been taken up about three miles in
the country, fed and milked. S. went immediately for her on hearing
where she was; brought her home about ten o'clock. Now I want you to
answer a few questions. How often ought I to churn the milk instead of
setting it? Must I stir it up well every time I strain the new milk in?
How much meal must I give the cow at a mess? Is it best to scald it or
mix it with cold water? How many boiled peas shall I give her at a
time? Do you think it the best way to give her her mess while I am
milking? We think the calf is a perfect nuisance; if S. can find a pasture
inclosed he is going to sell the calf, or would you advise us to keep it to
corn for us winter beef? You see we want to manage just right with

your cow, & I want you to answer all these questions. I do not like the
plan of milking a little then stopping to let the calf take a little but that
is the way she has been managed.

Have just received a letter from Virginia Fitz. She is spending the
Summer in Oxford with her ma. Erly is taken *prisoner*, Did you know
uncle Doolittle had lost his youngest son? S. has gone to Union, I mean
Typographical union meeting to night. The printers are going to strike
for higher wages. We can not get along comfortably on $15. per week.
Thursday 17th   The Union have raised S's wages to $18. but whether
Mr. Seals will be willing to give it is uncertain. He may discharge him
at once. Then what *shall* we do? Shall not mail this until we know the
result of the rise. It is perfectly just, but still it may be the means of
men loosing their situations. The proprieters are getting three and four
times as much as did in good times, and yet they expect their hands to
work for just the same.

Anna the cow wont give down her milk. How can I manage to make
her give down, so I can milk all at once?

Our garden is a *failure*. We have had one good mess of potatoes, two
small messes of peas. and cucumbers several times. Fear we shall have
very little if any thing more.
Friday 18th   Churned befour breakfast. The butter was very sweet
and nice, but their was a precious little of it. The milk is *very* rich how
is it I dont get more butter? Dear little Forrest sits on the carpet playing with her toes. She has but recently discovered that she has them.
Virginia says she wants to see "that little monkey." I dont thank any
body for calling *my beautiful baby a monkey*, even in jest. Auntie how
old ought she to be when I put short dresses on her? My neighbors
think it ridiculous to let her wear long clothes any longer, but I have
her summer clothes made, and think it best to let her wear them until I
put on winter dress in the fall. Mrs. Richards baby is over one year old
and *he* cant walk, although he has had short clothes on ever since he
was *four months* old. I dont want my little daughter to be too smart. I
sometimes fear she is *too good* & *too smart*. Now *laugh*; I know you
want to. I expect S. thinks I write very foolish letters to you, but I want
to write as I would talk. Enough for to-day.
Saturday 19th. Seven oclock A. M. Rose a little before five. Gave my
baby "maternal nourishment," milked, made a fire & got breakfast. I
suppose you will wonder where Matilda is. She is here, but such a mope
I never saw. She pretends to make a fire but it often goes out as it did
this morning. As too cooking I do not let her poke over my victuals. We
have eaten our share of negro filth. Anna I do *despise* the race. I wish
the abolitionists had to eat sleep and live with them. until they had
enough of their "colored brothers and sisters." "*Poor oppressed, down*

troden colored individuals" Dont you pity them? I think it is a pity, they cant be made to feel a little of the care which oppress white people these hard times. I should not wonder if monday morning finds every printer in the city out of employment. The proprieters hold a meeting this morning. I must save this space to tell you the result.

Monday 21st. Sylvanus retains his situation at $18. a week. An increase of three dollars will help us. Anna in your next please answer all the questions I have asked and tell me how to make short cake. also cheap tea cakes. I wish to write much more but it is time I mailed this scrawl. Love from all, to Sister, Cousin, Auntie.

Jennie.

JENNIE TO MARIA

Atlanta December 2nd 1862

You requested us to write by "return mail" dear Maria, but it was impossible to do so, as yours came to hand Saturday night, and Sylvanus was sick all day Sunday; yesterday I was obliged to go to shoe making as Lillie was almost bare foot. She wears out a pair every two weeks. Have just made two pair. You ask me what I should do with all your cares. I answer I could not and should not. do at all. Nothing but stern necessity or absolute want would make me take such a situation. I could teach and control one hundred children in the school-room but I should not want to cook, wash, iron and sew for them. Strange as it may seem to you I have all that I can do now, and sometimes it seems to me a good deal more. I am not and fear I can never be a thrifty "house wife". But Sylvanus, poor deluded fellow, thinks I am the best of wives mothers and housekeepers. Well whenever I fail in coming up to my duties in either of these positions it is an error of the head not the heart, for I love my husband, my baby and my home to well to neglect either of them. I presume you think I ought not to keep help. If I did not I should have to pay out the same amount for washing. True we should save the food and clothing but I do not believe we should save one dime more. Besides I could never look nice myself, keep my baby or my house clean. Sylvanus dont want me to do kitchen drudgery in this country—says he will break up house keeping if I insist on doing without help. If we ever get *home* I expect to do as others do. I do not want your Lula. I would not take her from you dear sister and then she is not what I want. One ten years old would do. But I have concluded it is best for me to have a negro. It would cost something to fix up a bed for a white girl. To dress one fourteen years old is out of the question. I want a *little* negro, but fear it will be as it was last year impossible to find one. We are trying to find a house nearer town, but there are so many refugees in the city that houses are in great demand at exorbitant rents. Our only neighbor, Mr. Grubb's family, are now in town,—moved last week. Close to them is a house at twenty dollars per month which we have engaged in case the present occupants leave. It is larger than we want so if we get it Mr. Grubb's family will change with us. The one they have is a neat little white house with green blinds, has a hall three rooms, kitchen and smoke house. I am very anxious to get it, and Mrs. G seems equally anxious to have us for neighbors again, says if we get the large house she will change with us any day and pay the difference in the rent which is four-dollars a month.

Sylvanus has bought nearly fifty dollars worth of wood. We hope it will last the winter. S. bought a sack of flour a few days since for $22.50!! His sallery is going to be raised this week probably to $25. per week. Our miserable cow is still on our hands. It costs from thirty to forty cts a day to keep her; she gives about one teacup full a day. I am writing on these pieces of paper to save them. They have been folded so it is difficult to write. * * *

I took what little soap greese I had saved, the other day and made about ten pounds of excellent soap. I sent to the slaughter pen yesterday and bought ten pounds of greese at five cents a pound. It smells so badly I can not make it in the house in my dinner pot. Shall have to borrow a kettle and make it out doors. Have got my cook stove in the dining room; it saves fuel. By making our own candles we have saved sixty cts on a pound. Lillie can pull herself up by things. Well I must bring this to a close. Write soon to those who are ever interested in your welfare.

Jennie.

DIARY

Atlanta January 23d 1863. Since I first began to keep a journal I have never neglected it so long. Almost a year has elapsed since the last date. My dear little daughter is one year old to-day. I will celebrate her birth-day by looking once more upon thy pages my book. One year has passed since God commited to our care an immortal being. How we love and prize his precious gift   I often fear that in loving the gift we shall forget the Giver. We have every reason to thank God for the little one He has given us. She is perfect in form and feature, and *beautiful* in our eyes. O that God will graciously spare our darling to us, and spare us to her. May she live to enjoy many happy birth-days, and may her parents be spared to see the promising bud unfold its beauties, is my earnest prayer this day.

I ought to have kept a journal the past year, for it has been fraught with strange, sad and frightful incidents in the history of our country. This dreadful war which is scourging our land affords a sorrowful theme to write and think upon. I often try to put the subject far from my mind, but there is too much to remind one of the terrible state of our country to forget it for an hour. How thankful I am that my husband has business which exempt him from the duties of a soldier. We have every thing to be thankful for. A pleasant home, all the comforts of life, and good health. O! if our Father will continue these blessings until this war ends, and then permit us to return *home* and look once more upon the faces of our aged parents, our brothers and sisters, and our early friends! How often are our hearts sad when we think and talk of the dear ones from whom all intercourse is at present cut off. We will daily pray for a speedy termination of the troubles which have brought untold misery upon our once happy and prosperous country.

Have taken upon me the cares of housekeeping since I last wrote in my journal. We were then residing in Greenville. Have now been keeping house in Atlanta ten months. We find it pleasant to have a *home* after boarding so long. My little Lillie stands at my side begging me to take her,—must lay aside my book.

Saturday 24th   Nearly bed time. This is the first opportunity I have had to write to-day. Now I am alone and all is quiet. Sylvanus has gone up town on business. My little pet has just fallen asleep, and Beckie is taking a nap too. I have a younger servant than I did last year, concequently I have more to do myself, and am obliged to watch her all the time; like all negro help she is a perfect eye servant. So long as I stand looking at her she can do very well but if I leave her she has her own way of doing things. I think if the abolitionist were obliged to live with their "colored bretheren an[d] sisters" a little while they would feel less sympathy for them. Saturday is my baking day. To day I baked three loaves of bread, four mince pies, one potatoe pie, a soft cake and some ginger cookies. We live well considering the times; have to pay fabulous prices for every thing we eat and wear. High prices is not our greatest trouble. If the sword could be stayed, and disease checked, then could our hearts beat with the calmness and hope of other days. We know not when we are safe. Destruction wasteth at noon-day, and pestilence waketh in darkness. I am almost constantly depressed in spirit, and my heart often trembles with fear. O! for an affectionate confidence in God—christian resignation to his will. Why can I not feel safe in his hands? Am I a christian? How often the question arises in my mind. If I am why am I not willing God should do any thing He pleases with me and mine?

Sabbath 25th   A lovely day. Wanted to attend church with my husband, but felt unwilling to leave my baby alone with Beckie. Our pastor offered his resignation after the services were over; it was accepted, and now we have no settled minister. The flock is without a shepherd. The pulpit will probably be supplied from sabbath to sabbath, until the presbytery meets in April, when we shall probably have some one sent to take charge of this branch of God's Zion.

I am sorry to loose Mr. Rogers. I like him both as a preacher and as a gentleman. While S. was gone to church Dr. Thurmond, a phys[i]cian appointed to vaccinate in this ward, called here to see if any members of our family wished to be vaccinated. I had my baby, my servant and myself vaccinated, I was almost afraid to do so fearing the matter was not pure. Small pox is spreading in our city, and the citizens are now not only requested to be vaccinated but compelled. Sylvanus was vaccinated last Summer and had a very sore arm but I doubt if it was any thing more than a common sore. I do not feel that he is safe. I hope it will take well in dear little Lillie's arm. This evening Sylvanus has been reading over some of my old journals. He is anxious for me to continue to keep a journal but I have so much to engross my time and attention I fear I shall not write often now that I have commenced again.

*   *   *

Wed 28   Still very cold and blustering. Can not have my baby's washing done. Have just finished her a pair of morocco shoes. Thus far I have made all her shoes and stockings. Every thing is so high we have to be very economical and save a dime in every way we can. Each member of our little household is quite well to day. How thankful we should feel! There are so many sick people in Atlanta.

*   *   *

Sat 31 * * * Have heard of two deaths from small pox in town this week. Can not help feeling troubled.

The weather is much warmer; looks like rain again. Sylvanus bought me a pair of shoes to night for which he paid $14. Dont think I ever wore a pair before that cost over $2. Never expected to see the day they would cost what they do now. For 25 cts wort[h] of straw we have just paid $1.50. Just so it is with every thing. Can not lay up a dollar although S. is doing so well. Once we should have considered four dollars a day a large income.

Sab Feb 1st. Rained all day. Mr. McCann called in the afternoon to vaccinate himself from our baby's arm; but could not do so as it was not far enough advanced.

Mon 2   Washing day. Gave up my washing woman last week on account of small pox prevailing in that part of town—was afraid to send Beckie with the clothes. Have had it all done at home to-day, had to do a good deal of it myself. The clothes are all dry and look very white.

* * *

Sat. 7   Beckie has sorely tried my patience to-day. She is so slow I do not know what to do to make her move more briskly. She has been all day doing what ought to have been done in two hours. Negroes are a great trial and nuisance, yet it seems impossible to get along without them in this country. We expected to pay $5. a month for Beckie. To-day her master told S. he must have $8. I had been so tried with her all day, that my first thought when S. told me was that I would give her up before I would pay such an exorbitant price for a girl twelve years old. We have been talking it over however, and have concluded it is best to keep her as we do not know where to get another. I want to go *home* where people can live independent of negro help.

Sab 8   Weather very pleasant again. Did not rise until very late this morning. Neither S. nor myself have attended church. Mr. McCan came this afternoon to vaccinate himself from the scab on our little daughter's arm. Sylvanus has vaccinated himself and me—hope it will take well on both this time. Beckie tried to run away this afternoon. Sylvanus overtook her before she got to town; all she gained by the undertaking was a severe whipping. I fear she is a bad negro. S. and I have been talking about going home tonight. I pray God we may live to see the happy day when our faces shall be turned *homeward*!

Tues 10   Sometimes I get almost tired of housekeeping; Things can not always move along just right; I ought not to expect it, but I get discouraged when they do not. Have been trying out tallow, am now making candles. Have to watch Beckie and the baby too while I write—can not write one line uninterrupted—think I had better lay you aside my journal for the present.

* * *

Thurs. 12   Very windy. A hard shower this afternoon. Finished making candles to-day. Made 88. Commenced burning them to night. Paid 75 cts a pound for the tallow in the leaf; an enormous price. Candles, common tallow candles, are $1.50 per pound. Have done no sewing this week. I think I must be very slow for I get but little time to sew; takes nearly all my time to attend to my little daughter and household affairs.

Sat. 14   Baked bread and cake to-day. Have nothing to make pies of. I made mince pies until we became tired of them, but should still make them occasionally if I could get apples, either dried or green. Beckie has got along very well with her cleaning to-day. She improves. Perhaps she will in a few months be just the help I need. I can make her do my work just as I want it done, which I can not do with an older one. My cozy little dining room is very clean to-night. I have undressed my pet and had a frolic with her. Beckie is now getting her to sleep. Papa has gone to typographical union meeting. It is more than a week since I received a letter from sister; have not yet commenced an answer— must do so to-night if Lillie will let me.

Mon 16   Rained all night and has continued all day. Could have no washing done but have caught plenty of rain water to wash with when the storm is over. Our well diger came this afternoon and worked a little while—hope he will keep at it now, if the weather permits, until we have a well of our own. It is not very pleasant to depend on neighbors and often be denied a pail of water. Have been knitting all day—not for the soldiers, but for my husband. God grant he may never become a soldier. When I read and hear of their hardships and sufferings my heart aches for them all whoever they are. It seems to me Abraham Lincoln will have more to answer for than the vilest catholic priest. He has been the cause of nearly half a million of deaths. How many hearts he has caused to bleed! how many homes he has desolated!

*   *   *

Thurs. 19 * * * Last night Sylvanus had a large sum of money in his possession belonging to Mr. Seals. I felt so much afraid of *burglars* that my rest was very much broken. There seems to be a good many of this profession about our city just now. Whether guests or residents we know not. S. says I need not feel at all uneasy, as no robber would think of entering our little unpretending abode. *I* think there *is* danger, for we both carry good gold watches, and many a house has been entered for a less booty   The well digers are here to day.

*   *   *

Mon. 23 * * * Sylvanus came home earlier than usual to-night—was quite unwell—hope he is not coming down with any of the diseases that are prevailing in our city. Can not help feeling alarmed if any of us are indisposed. Small Pox is said to be abating. Mr. G. told me scarlet fever was raging quite extensively.

*   *   *

Thurs. [March] 5   Sylvanus bought three coats for himself yesterday. A green merseiles, a brown checked linen and a brown checked alpacca. All cost $24. Very reasonable for these times. He bought a pair of shoes the price of which was not so reasonable. $15. Boots have got beyond his means. $40. Prices are constantly rising. Sugar is 75 cts per pound. Molasses $5. a gal. Pork from 75 cts to $1. Flour $45. a barrel. Milk $1. a gallon. Verily these are times to be remembered. The present generation will have many strange tales to repeat to their grand children.

Sat 7   As usual alone with my little pet all day. Sylvanus came home very weary to-night. It is hard for him to be shut up in a printing office day after day, secluded from the sun shine and the fresh air. I wish he had capital to go into business. Perhaps it is wicked pride in me, but I do not like the idea of his being an employee. We enjoy all the comforts and many of the luxuries of life that can be bought by strict economy and close industry, but not quite satisfied I sometimes sigh for riches— enough at least to make us independent of a cold selfish world. * * *

*   *   *

Sat 14   Have been busy baking bread pies and cake. Did not have very good success with any thing. Every thing is so high that I am obliged to economize in cooking—can not make things as palateable as I would like. Prices continue to rise. Flour is now $75. per barrel. Irish potatoes $20. per bushel. Rice flour $20. per hundred.—Corn meal $3. per bushel. Bacon $1. per pound. Beef 50 cts per pound. Tea $12. per pound. Coffee $3.50 per pound. The last two articles are beyond our reach. We use rye as a substitute for coffee. Sylvanus bought ¼ lb of tea and occasionally we treat ourselves to a cup of the refreshing beverage. * * *

Mon. 16   Three oclock A.M. finds me watching by the cradle of our dear baby. The dreaded hour has come! The hour I have feared must come, when we should see our little one prostrated by disease—when our hearts should tremble lest the treasure be torn from our arms. Do we love her too well? Have we made her our household idol? Have we given her that place on our hearts which should be dedicated to our

God? If we have committed the sin of idolatry O Father forgive us, and not rebuke us in Thy hot displeasure. Spare O spare our darling! But if it is Thy good pleasure to bereave us give us christian resignation. Teach us to say and *feel Thy* will not *ours* be done. *Sweet little Lillie* seemed quite well on Saturday until about three oclock, when she had a high fever and seemed very dull and sleepy which is unusual with the bright playful little darling. She did not rest well on Saturday night—Sunday morning found her no better. About ten oclock while Sylvanus was holding she became convulsed and had a hard spasm. Sent for Mrs. Middleton—she was not at home—then sent for Mrs. Hall—she was at church—thus we were alone with our darling. She was better in a few moments, and S. went up town hired a horse and buggy and brought Mr. Gardner out then went for a physcian. Brought Dr. Alexander. He said teething was the cause of her sickness, and assured us that after the medicine he left had taken effect she would have no more spasms. She had a very hard one about two oclock. O what agony to see our little pet insensible—the sweet face so purple and distorted. The medicine operated freely about four oclock; then the little one seemed much better, and remained so until midnight. Since then she has been very restless—the little hand[s] are constantly moving. O I am so fearful she will have more of those dreadful spasms. The Lord prepare us for whatever He is preparing for us! Mrs. Gardner remained with us all day. Sylvanus took her home just at dark. He paid $6. for a horse and buggy   It was a satisfaction to have her here. O how hard it is to be away from all our kindred in the hour of sickness. Mrs. Middleton was very kind—she came in very often, and sent in a lunch for Mrs. Gardner thinking I was in too much trouble to have cooking done at home. Mr. & Mrs. Hall called in too. They are strangers to us. I slept until twelve oclock. Sylvanus is now taking a nap. Little Lillie is resting better now.

Tues. 17   Our darling is much better. She is dressed and trying to toddle about, but she is too weak to walk much. I am suffering from tooth ache. They commenced troubling me last night at the supper table and have not been easy since. Sylvanus had two patients last night. He watched Lillie and waited upon me until two oclock. He must feel very little like business to-day—but as he remained at home yesterday he felt obliged to go to the office this morning. Hope we may all have a good nights rest to-night.

Wed. 18   We all arose this morning a good deal refreshed. Little pet seems almost well, except that she is very fretful which is so unusual with her. My teeth are troubling me badly. If a dentist was near I should certainly have several extracted. Our washing and ironing is done for this week. Made Beckie do nearly all the ironing to-day. She has done it very well too.

Thurs. 19   O! dear me how I do suffer with my teeth. I feel almost tempted to do as I heard Mr. McCan. Take hammer and nail and knock out the painful offender. * * *

Mon. Apr. 6   Have not written in nearly two weeks. Have been suffering so much with my teeth face and throat that I have felt unfit for any things. And now that I am feeling much better and suffering but little pain I lack ambition and energy. Every thing seems like a burden— every duty weighs heavily upon me. Am trying to get ready to go to Columbus to visit Sister, but can not even nerve myself to feel much ambition for the pleasant task of preparing my sweet little daughters wardrobe. I think this state of feeling must arise from prostration of my nervous system caused by suffering so much pain, and loss of sleep. Have just finished a letter to Anna. Must stop writing now and see to getting out the clothes—hope to get them all dry to day.

* * *

Columbus May 8th   Here I am in Columbus at the Female Orphan asylum visiting Sister Maria   Left home the first day of May—have been absent just one week. Sylvanus accompanied us but returned the next day. I expect he finds it rather lonely home alone. * * * I am enjoying the visit with sister very much when I can have her to myself a little while. As Matron of this institution she has so many cares and duties devolving upon her that she has but little quiet leisure. This is a delightful place. The building is handsome, large and commodious, situated in the suburbs of the city and surrounded with a hedge of the cherokee rose. There is a great deal of shrubery and a great many flowers in the garden and yard. It is a pleasant refuge for the poor orphans who find a home within its walls. * * *

Saturday 9th   Sister and I went out shopping this morning. I spent $18.50 and brought home my purchases in my hands. One has to spend a great deal of money for a very few articles these times. I think the merchants here are more polite and obliging than in Atlanta. Some articles are cheaper. I bought a very good hoop for $12.50 which would be at least $20. in Atlanta.

Columbus is a very pretty place—think I should like to live here.

* * *

Tues 12   Suffered greatly with my teeth last night. Resolved to have them out early this morning. Anna started with me immediately after an early breakfast. I felt quite courageous, but after walking in the sun two hours to find a dentist my strength and courage failed. Dr. Fagle was neither polite nor kind. After sitting down and having the tooth examined I could not feel brave enough to have it extracted and came home with the troublesome things still in my mouth. Bought a bottle of toothache drops which relieves me for the present. * * *

Sat. 16   Felt quite unwell all day. Received a letter from dear S. in the afternoon which cheered my somewhat drooping spirits. About five o'clock went to Dr. Cushman's office and had two teeth extracted—hope I shall have no more teeth ache for the present. Anna says I bore the operation like a brave soldier—did not make the slightest noise through it all. * * *

Tues. 19   Have been very much alarmed to-day. My gum commenced bleeding very suddenly, and bled almost constantly and quite profusely for several hours. Anna went with me to Dr. Cushmans—he crowded in some cotton saturated with something that stoped the bleeding. Hope and pray it may not commence again to-night. * * *

Sat. 23 * * * Am still suffering with my face. Dr. Cushman told me the plug of cotton would come out in a few days. There is no appearance of it's loosening at all yet. Can not help feeling uneasy. * * *

Mon 25   Intended to go to the dentists to-day to have the plug of cotton taken out of my gum, but I succeeded in loosning it myself and I now hope it will work out without further trouble or pain. * * *

June 16   At home again—yes and have been for the last two weeks but have neglected my journal. Left Columbus the first of June. Spent one month with sister. Enjoyed my visit as well as I could away from home and husband—was glad to get home again however. * * *

Thurs [June 20]   A negro man came to white wash this morning but rain began to fall and prevented my having it done. Have had the carpets taken up in readiness. Sylvanus engaged a cow when he was in Greenville and has been looking for her to arrive every day for the last week—fear she will be nearly dry when we get her from being so long without care.

Friday [June 21]   Has been a pleasant day. Have had Beckie washing windows. Our cow has come at last—like her looks very well—hope she will prove to be a good one. S. paid [$125.00] cost him $25. to get her here.

*   *   *

Sat 27 * * * Our cow was nearly dry when we got her—she is improving but is not yet what we expected. She gives nearly one gallon a day of very rich milk. Have just churned—shall have mush and buttermilk for supper. I wonder what our Northern friends would say to our eating buttermilk something they consider only fit for the pigs. It is delicious to our taste notwithstanding.

Mon 29   Do not feel like writing in my journal. It was once a relief to unbosome my feelings on its pages—a pleasure to note down passing events and comment upon them, whether fraught with joy or sorrow. But then I felt alone and my journal was my hearts companion—now I do not as then feel a comfort in committing to its pages the "ups and downs" of my inner as well as outer life. I have one now to whom I can "think aloud." * * *

July 1st 1863   Oppressively warm to-day. Have been ironing Not *very* cool work. Beckie makes me a great of trouble ironing days. She is so careless and stupid. What absurdity for any one to talk about the negro possessing mental faculties equal to the white race. I consider them but little above the brute in many respects. * * *

*   *   *

Sat 11 * * * Sylvanus wants me to put up some preserves even if sugar is $1.25 per pound. It will undoubtedly rise much higher now that Vicksburg has fallen. The fall of that city is not very encouraging to the Confederacy. It seems to me the prospects for peace grow darker every day. * * *

Wed. 22 Very *very* warm. Have not ambition and energy enough to nerve me to write. Hope to get a letter from sister to night. Am going to make apple dumplings for supper and I expect it is time to have Beckie make a fire. Have done nothing but mend to-day. The hard times give me plenty of that kind of amusement. Shirting is three dollars a yard, but S. will soon have to buy some for shirts. Patching and darning will not avail much longer to keep a shirt on his back. I am knitting me a pair of confederate hose. I never wore coarse unbleached stockings before but am thankful to get them now. The cotton to knit them was a present from sister when I was in Columbus. She is always giving me something useful. Ladies white cotton hose are only $3. a pair; just such ones as I have bought at the North for 15 cts.

Shall use the last flour I have in the house for supper. It is still $40. per barrel, but we must have it   S. can not eat corn meal.

Friday 24   Beckie has not yet returned from her blackberry excursion. Where she spent last night, I can not imagine. How troublesome and annoying to have a servant one can not trust out of sight. Beckie is probably giving herself the pleasure of visiting her friends. Possibly she may have lost her way in the woods, but I hardly think it probable. I have all the work to do to-day and as I have not much taste for certain kinds of house work my task is rather irksome as well as wearisome. Sylvanus left home this morning with the intention of hunting up our faithful (?) domestic, but as she has not yet *darkened* my door, I expect his search was fruitless. * * *

Sun 26 * * * Sylvanus heard a good deal about Bec yesterday but did not succeed in capturing her although he was on her track. He authorized the people at whose houses she had stopped if she visited them again to lock her up until he came to-day. He has been and just returned without the negro. She was probably skulking around in the woods yesterday and saw Sylvanus and concluded to make her escape from that neighborhood.

We shall now give her up to her master. He must find her. If he gets her in a few days I shall be willing to take her back bad as she is. She understands how to do my work as I want it done. I have had a great deal of trouble in teaching her and do not feel like going through the same trouble with a new servant. I find it very hard to be alone and do all the drudgery myself. * * *

Tues 28 * * * Just as I got my kettle of preserve ready to put on the fire
S. came home and brought the unpleasant tidings that we could no
longer have the services of Beckie as her master had decided to sell her
on account of her running away. That news did not tend to restore me to
an amiable and pleasant state of mind. I have had a hard siege teaching Beckie to do my work and it is certainly very trying to loose her
just as she becomes servicable to me, and have the same trouble with a
green hand. * * * Perhaps we shall find a better servant than Beckie
was—one I can trust out of sight.

Wed 29   No servant yet. Both S. and myself find it hard to get along
without one. S. says he will break up housekeeping if he dont find one
soon. We have boarded so long that we appreciate the comfort of a home
and should be loth to relinquish them for the "cold charrities" of a
boarding house, but still there are many troubles and perplexities in
housekeeping which we should escape in boarding. Sylvanus was intending to look for servant to-day—hope he may be successful. Wish I
knew how sisters poor hand is to-day.

Death of Lillie,—
    Never did I take up my journal to write with so sad a heart. I have
been defering communication with my book for weeks hoping to be able
to write calmly. But when I think of the great bereavement that has
filled our heart with life long sorrow how can I be calm! I wonder that I
am sane. When I last wrote in my journal I was a happy mother. A
sweet prattler was ever at my side, or nestling in my bosom. Little pat-
tering feet, a soft infant voice was ever making music for our hearts.
Now the stillness that reigns in my room almost maddens me. Here is
the precious little crib, the dear little high chair, in that drawer is all
the little clothes, yes and here is the little hat she looked so sweetly in.
But where O! where is my baby? My precious, my only, my idolized
child is dead! O what a wild cry of anguish those words wring from my
heart—my poor, broken, bleeding heart that yearns for its lost treasure. Nearly six weeks have passed since I heard the bird like voice of
my sweet little darling or looked upon her beautiful expressive face.
How lonely, how desolate is our once happy home. Time and duties
drag heavily with us. Life has well nigh lost its charms for our poor
bereaved hearts. Our earthly hope, joy, comfort and idol is hid beneath
that little coffin lid. We often feared our little Lillie was too bright and
pure for earth and shudered lest the lovely bud should be broken from
the parent stem and transplanted in a clime where we could not watch

it unfold. We fondly hoped mid all our fears that the blessed little treasure was given us but alas she was only loaned for a few short months. We saw our darling laid away in her little narrow bed one day before she had completed her twentieth month. *Dear little prattler*! how sweetly she used to say "nineteen month old" when we asked her how old she was. She talked as plain and as fluently as a child four years old; she had such a sweet winning way of saying every thing; she called herself papa's busybody and mama's chatterbox. I taught her the child's catechism. If I omitted a question she would instantly remind me of it. She loved to sit in papa's or mama's lap and listen to pretty little verses and nursery rhymes. She was so bright and beautiful, our fond hearts were filled with pride, hope, and joy. We had great anticipations of future as well as present happiness with our interesting child. O how anxiously, how impatiently we looked forward to the time when we could visit our friends at home and show them our dear little one. I wanted to place my darling in my dear fathers arms that he might love and bless my treasure. Our hopes are blighted—the light of our eyes and our home is quenched—the joy and pride of our hearts departed. So suddenly, so unexpectedly came the messenger. On Thursday night the 17th I laid my gem in her crib apparently in usual health, before morning she had a violent spasm, in a few hours it was followed by dysentery. We called in one of the most skillful physicians in the city but nothing he gave her checked the disease; she continued to grow worse until monday afternoon a few minutes after six an angel came and bore away the pure spirit of our loved one: the jeweled gates of heaven were thrown open; our darling entered and commenced her song of triumph. I wonder if my sainted mother knew my little one and folded her to her bosom. O how I sometimes long for one glimpse of heaven and its inhabitants, but that longing can not be satisfied until this mortal toil is laid aside. Sing on my sweet, sweet, blessed little one in harmony with those I loved and lost before I knew the happiness I experienced when you nestled close to my heart, and before I knew the overwhelming, desolating sorrow that sweeps over my soul now that you my only little darling have left me. When my mother sisters and brothers were taken from earth my young heart was almost broken—I thought the cup of sorrow was indeed a bitter bitter one; but now I have drained it to the dregs and find it tenfold more bitter than then. Sweet, gentle, loving little daughter papa and mama are so sad and lonely without thee—we miss the patter of thy little feet—the sweet prattle of thy innocent tongue—the sweet kisses of thy soft lips—the loving caresses of thy dear little arms—we miss thy merry laugh, thy infant glee, that once made our home so bright and happy. *We miss thee* O! my baby when and where do we not miss thee? Life is not now what it was when we had our little Lillie to live for. But this life will have an end; the weary months and years will soon pass away and then if we have "fought the good fight of faith" we shall be admitted into the world of light and immortality where our sweet one now dwells. The thought of being reunited with our darling is indeed a blessed, comforting one: it weakens the pang of present separation. My little angel was so patient through all her suffering. Not a murmur escaped the sweet lips. When we asked her to take medicine she would say "no maam thank you" and when we told her it would make sweet Lillie well we hoped she would turn to us in such a coaxing winning way and say "papa eat it mama eat it." but when we told her to take it for papa and mama she would open the dear little mouth and drink the last bitter drop and say with an air of triumph "meddy all done now." The affectionate little lamb would do any thing for papa and mama.

Only a few hours before she died she saw me weeping over her and put up her sweet lips to kiss away my tears saying "Ninnie so sick make poo mama ky." I never knew what great agony the soul can endure until I saw my idol fading away from earth. O how I longed for the power to snatch my darling from the cold arms of death. I could not then and can not yet say "The Lord gave and the Lord has taken away blessed be the name of the Lord"

O! I could write pages about my little one. Thinking, writing, and talking about her is all the comfort left me now. O how I *loved* my baby, how I did want to keep her here, how I prayed every day that she might be spared to me hoping God would grant my petition when He knew how much my child was to me. She was so beautiful too in form, feature, and complexion. Her beautiful blue eyes spoke more of heaven than earth in their expression. How I loved to curl her silken hair, how beautifully the fair curls clustered around the finely moulded head, just reaching the little white neck. O what happiness was mine when I had my little daughter here to love and care for. And now that happiness all gone yes all gone. O! how can I be calm and resigned. The grace and love of God alone can make me submissive.

Dec 17 I can not write in my journal now. I often take it up with the intention of doing so, but when I look over the pages and read what I wrote in happier days when sweet little pet was with me, and remember how full of love and joy my heart then was and contrast it with the sad bleeding one that now beats in my bosom I lay my book aside with sighs and tears, and thus day after day has passed and not a word written.

Three months ago to-day I bathed and dressed my little Lillie and curled her hair for the last time. That day was the last that the dear little feet pattered over the floor—the last day of her childish frolic and glee. That night after being unusually merry at the supper table, she came and laid the little fair head in my lap and said "put Ninnie in tib." She seemed drooping—did not even want to rock in papa's lap as usual. I felt uneasy but she soon fell into a sweet sleep, and I comforted myself with the thought that my darling was only weary. Would that it had been so! O! I can not be reconciled to the death of my lovely little one.

Mon 21   Three months ago to-day our sweet little one left us. O the terrible anguish that pierced my heart and for a time dethroned my reason when the pure spirit left my darlings precious clay and I looked upon the sweet face so cold and white and the motionless lips that but a few hours before had tried to kiss away my grief. They dressed my precious one in her little white dress that she always looked so sweetly in. Incased the dear little feet in the tiny black slippers—put on the little white merino sacque, curled her soft fair hair and laid her in her crib in the parlor. O! how lovely she looked. Even death could not mar the angelic beauty of the little sleeper. How I listened for the patter of her little feet and the music of her sweet voice all that time that she lay so still in her crib. How often I imagined I saw the little white hand move and involuntarily I would hasten to her side to see if my baby had awoke. Perhaps it is wrong but how earnestly I wished a mirracle could be performed and my treasure restored to my yearning heart.

Tues. 22   Three months to-day since I looked upon the sweet face of my darling. Three long, weary, sad months since we followed our only child to her lonely little grave. I see her now as I saw her when I took the last fond, earnest, yearning look. The fair curls clustering around her intellectual forehead—the little white hands folded on her bosom, holding a bouquet of white rose buds: delicate white buds and blossoms were strewn over the white dress and around the inside of the tiny coffin forming a wreath around the dear little form. Surely the little angels in heaven can not look more beautiful than did the precious remains of my darling. With our human vision we can form no conception of the beauty and appearance of spirits in heaven. In imagination I often try to look through the portals of heaven and among the happy group of little ones recognize my Lillie; but I always see her as she looked when she was with me, with her sunny curls, blue eyes and fair complexion—her sweet expressive face lit up with a happy, innocent smile. Then again my minds eye looks down deep in the grave and looks upon the dear little face and form lying so quietly, sleeping so calmly there. Then this comforting thought soothes my anguish, *she will rise again.* That same little mortal body will put on *immortality* that same little corruptible body will put in *incorruption.* Such are the precious promised in the bible.

Thurs. 24   Have been doing just what I done one year ago to-day. Baking for Christmas. My hands have been employed the same but my thoughts are in sad contrast. Then my little Lillie was with me and I was constantly talking to her, telling her what mama was making for sweet pet. I filled her little stocking that night, although she was only eleven months old and could not understand and enjoy Santa Claus presents. If she was with us now I think to-morrow would be the happiest Christmas of my life. I have been thinking all day what I would make and buy for my darling if she was here, and with how much eagerness and delight she would examine the contents of her little stocking—how sweetly she would prattle and how she would love and caress papa and mama for the toys and candies. O I can imagine it all, and as I think of the happiness I feel the sad weary look pass away from my face and a happy mothers smile lights it up for a moment, but then comes back the crushing reality and again my face is sad and my spirit bowed.

Frid. 25   Christmas day. Sylvanus and I remembered each other last night and slipped a small token of our great love in each others stocking. But O! how inexpressibly sad have been our bereaved hearts to-day. Our thoughts have been with our sweet child. Sylvanus intended to take help and go to the grave yard to-day and have our lot improved. We want to set out choice flowers and make the ground where our sweet one sleeps look as cheerful as possible. The day was very cold and Sylvanus could get no one to go with him, so was obliged to give it up. Hope it need not be neglected much longer. We received a letter from sister this morning. Have not heard from her in nearly two months. She is well, but her husband is in very poor health. We had a very nice dinner. Sylvanus invited a wounded soldier to dine with us. Hope he enjoyed it.

JENNIE TO MARIA

Atlanta February 11th 1864

My Dear Sister:—

I will now commence a reply to your last which came by Mr. Mason. I can not write much to-day however, as I am suffering from head ache and depression of spirits. Tears blinded my eyes so that I could not sew, and I laid aside my work (which is a quilt for *sweet Lillie's crib*) to take up the pen, but the tears will continue to flow. I spent yesterday at Mrs. Gardners. When I see her alone and can unburden my sad heart I find sympathy and comfort, for she has drank deeply from the *bitter* cup, but she has sought and found grace and strength to bear her burden at the throne of mercy, where never yet a sin and sorrow laden soul applies in vain. Her heart is deeply scarred, but the wounds are healed with the Great Physician's balm. Yesterday the girls were at home and their hilarity was painful to my bowed spirit. so today finds me sadder than ever. I believe I have never told you how kind Mrs. Gardner was in the first hours of our great anguish. She tried to soothe and comfort me with all a mothers or sisters tenderness. For several hours after my darling left me I was only conscious at short intervals, and then it seemed as if my mind comprehended the sad calamity but my heart could not and would not receive the dreadful truth. I plead with them to bring my baby and lay her on my arm, but the fair head could nestle there no more.!

Kind hands dressed my little one in her prettiest clothes—her beautiful little white dress, the little white merino sacque and the tiny black slippers—curled the fair hair and laid her in the parlor in her crib. I did not see her that night but early the next morning papa and mama bent over the little crib and kissed the unconscious brow, cheek and lips of the lovely little sleeper. How often that day I imagined the little hands moved, and involuntarily I hastened to the crib to see if my sweet one was waking. How still the house was that day! No sweet infants prattle, no little feet making music all day! O auntie I wish you could have looked upon the dear little one before she was laid away. Sylvanus telegraphed for you; it would have comforted our sad hearts if you could have mingled your tears with ours over the precious remains of our little Lillie. * * * We have got about settled in our new home, or as much as we can until I move the stove in the kitchen. Our house is a very pretty one, nearly new, and nicely finished. It contains but two rooms and a wide hall. There is a good double kitchen in the yard. One of the rooms I shall use for a dining room in the Summer. The other room which will be my kitchen has a closet in it which will be handy. We have a good smoke house and cellar, a barn, barnyard hog-pen and horse lot, and last but not least an excellent garden spot. Not so large as to discourage one, and plenty large enough to promise a good supply of vegetables.

It is just such a spot as you would delight in. for you could supretend it without much fatigue or labor on your part. Sylvanus is anticipating much pleasure, proffit and good eating from his garden, but he will have no sweet Lillie to run after him and prattle while he works. Our calf died last fall and then the cow ran away, but we subsequently received $200. for her by the man who drove her out of the county with his own cattle. Since then we have had no cow; it is not very comfortable getting along without one, for we can not by milk. Buttermilk is seventy five cents per quart—butter from four to five dollars per lb. S. bought a nice little pig in the fall but it froze to death about Christmas. We have a good place for hog cow and hens here but it costs so much to buy them I expect we shall have to do without them. I wish the house was larger and you was here keeping house and we were boarding with you, or that we were keeping house together. You know I have not much taste for household duties, especially when I am so troubled with a bad negro. It may be a fault in me, but it is nevertheless true. I think if I had some female friend to talk with about my household arrangements and take an interest with me, and for me I should like it better. I do not often see a lady to speak with from one weeks end to another. * * *

I grieve to say I do not dress in *black*. I shall never cease to regret it. While under the stunning effects of the dreadful blow I was advised not to attempt to get black as it was impossible to buy any thing but calico. I remember feeling a desire to put on mourning, and intending to do so, but like a child I yielded passively to whatever they said; but when mind and reason were fully restored the very sight of my collered clothing made my grief still more poignant. I could have procured mourning for I had some things, and dresses that could have been dyed, and then I could have sold some of my collered dresses. I can not bear to wear my clothes now, and do not wear in the street any thing but my black silk and my traveling dress. Am going to sell my blue challie, I can never wear it. O my only sister you ought to have been with me in that trying hour to have told me what to do.

Monday 22 * * * Last night we sent Cris to bed early, and then S. and I went to church. This morning she did not rise at the usual hour and S. went to the kitchen to see what the trouble was. He found the door locked as usual, but entered with his private key; Cris had made her escape through the dining room window some time in the night. This is the third time she has run away. I do not want her back. I do not know what we shall do. I wish we were boarding in a good family, where we could get something palateable to eat. * * *

Sylvanus has changed his situation. He is now foreman of a newspaper and exempt from military service. He gets [?] per week with the promise of more as prices go up. We are much obliged for the seed—we have now a good supply. * * *

Jennie.

Dear Cousin

As Jennie has written you such a long letter I will not weary you with anything but a short Postscript. Atlanta was panic stricken this morning—the effects of the new currency Bill. If you have any money on hand, I would spend it if it did not buy much. Everything has gone up here from 23 to 33 per cent. since Saturday & it is impossible to get a $10 bill changed in the city   Direct your letters to me care of "Atlanta Register"

Sylvanus.

A terse entry from Maria's journal[5] recorded the circumstances of the effects of Sherman's invasion on the Lines family:

Mrs and Mr Lines were driven from there pleasant home in Atlanta by the canon and shells, They found a home with us [in Columbus] and she has given birth to a fine little girl[6] yet she feels the loss of little Lillie.

PART FIVE

READJUSTMENT

1865-1871

JENNIE TO MARIA

New Haven Sept 1865

Dear Sister,

Do you begin to think we have lost ourselves in making our escape from Dixie? We had a long and tedious trip but met with no accident arrived safely "bag and baggage" after eight days of almost constant travel. We took the western route by the way of Nashville which although tiresome we found very pleasant. The scenery as we traveled through Tennessee, Kentucky and Indianna was wild and romantic— charming to the eye of one who has a taste for beauty and grandeur fresh from the hand of Dame Nature before Art and Civilization have introduced fashion and refinement. When we reached the Eastern and Middle states the green hills, the meadows, fine apple orchards and the neat dwellings were objects of interest to those who had been exiles for years. The cars were constantly croweded with passengers bound for the North, There was one large party from Columbus another from Athens, and indeed it seemed as if there were parties from every portion of the South, so much for their determination *never* to patronize the North again. Let me ask right here. Do you know Mrs. Michell of Athens, member of Dr. Hayts church? We were in company with her all the way. Her sympathies were all with the North. She only came on for a visit but said she wished it was to remain.

October 8th   I commenced this letter several weeks since but have had a very sore finger which disabled me for some time; but it has been well long enough for me to have written to you several times. I never had as much to say to you as I have now and it was never such a task to put my thoughts on paper. I feel so broken up and unsettled, so *homeless* and *homesick* that I can not collect my thoughts to write a respectable letter to any one. I intended to write you a lengthy description of our travels and visits, but if I wait to write a legible and interesting letter you will not hear from me at all so I will say just what I think

215

will interest you most and in as few words as possible so that I can finish it to night while the house is still and I am alone which is not often the case. We came directly to New Haven, spent a day or two with sister Jane Lane, then went to Prospect to visit mother Beecher—found her very comfortably situated—a nice house and nicely furnished, and a nice old gentleman to support, comfort and protect her. While there I attended church and passed the place where you was born. At church mother introduced me to the lady who lived in the house with your mother at the time of your birth. I felt curious to know if she dressed you the first time and while mother was getting into the buggy I ran back and asked her, she said she *did* so of course I felt quite well acquainted then and wanted to stand and have a long chat. I saw your uncle Jessie Doolittles wife and several persons who are distantly related to you. We spent a week with mother, returned to New Haven spent a little more time with Jane then went to Newark and made Mrs. Gardner a visit and from there to Utica.

I had written to father and mother but they did not receive the letter so we took them by surprise. I met father first. He did not know and it took some time to convince him that it was really his long absent daughter returned. Mother was so bewildered and surprised that she could neither open her mouth nor close her eyes. I stood there crying and trying to convince them I was no imposter. Sylvanus stood in the background with very moist eyes. Little Daisy was in his arms looking on, at first with wonder and then alarm—finally she screamed so loud that she brought us all to our senses. She did not seem disposed to claim kindred at first; grand pa's long white beard and gran ma's black cap frightened the little lady. In a few moments Eddie came home—not the little Eddie that you and I used to love and pet so much but a tall lad of sixteen. He knew me at a glance and expressed a great deal of pleasure in his merry laugh and sparkling eyes, but he did not climb in my lap and ask me to tell him about old time as he did the last time I saw him. What a change a few years make! While at home I involuntarily called Eddie, Charley and my own little baby I called Eddie; It seemed as if by gone days had returned and I forgot I was a wife and mother. And now dear sister I have *sad* news to tell. sad to us but not to our dear brother Ezra. His spirit is released from its suffering clay— the vail of darkness which shrouded his life here is removed. He has gone *home*. He died at the Asylum in one of those dreadful fits which had wrecked his body and mind. It would be sinful and selfish to wish him back, for we know that he is now with the redeemed in heaven. Brother Charley has not been heard from for several years and we fear that he too has passed away from earth. Uncle is living just where he did, and just as he did. He inquired very particularly about you. Father

& mother took a great fancy to Sylvanus; father could not bear to have him out of his sight, and could not go anywhere without S. accompanied him. He is very feeble and very childish. Mother has had the misfortune to loose the fore finger on her right hand; she had a fellon and was obliged to have the finger cut off. They keep a fancy store— have quite a good stack of fancy articles and dry goods on hand, and are very comfortably situated. Eddie is clerking and boards at home. He seems to have his own way in every thing, but I was glad to see he seemed disposed to do right. They all sent a great deal of love to you and want you to write. Mother says she loves you just as well as ever and is anxious to see you once more. Sylvanus went to New Hartford with father and visited the graves of our relatives. The myrtle you set out on Josephs grave has spread so that it covers not only that mound but several others near it. I fully intended to go to New Hartford for the purpose of visiting the old burying ground, but we only staid a week and the days flew so fast I did not get there and feel quite dissatisfied about it. Gran pa, gran ma and uncle E. seem to love little Daisy dearly. Gran pa's eyes would fill with tears and his voice tremble almost every time he took her in his arms. He said he never expected to see such a sweet baby come from the south. They had given up ever seeing us, and our arrival was such a happy surprise to them. I wish we could live in Utica, I know it be would such a comfort to father and mother. Mrs. Gardner is very pleasantly situated in Newark. We have not met with a more cordial welcome any where that we did at her house. They were all so glad to see any one from the South especially those who had lived in Atlanta. They are all very homesick. I think it is generally the case with those who have returned North. It certainly is with us. Most earnestly do I wish we were going to return this fall. We should be satisfied to settle down for life there now. Do you know that I almost envy you in that old Asylum just because you are in the South. O how I long to visit you in that *same old place*. I want to see all those little girls too. Why I verily believe I could enjoy a chat with a "Georgia cracker," or an old corn field negro. How keenly we should enjoy it if we could spend a sabbath with you and your good husband as we spent many a one last year. How much we should have to talk about. *We* should not be laying plans to get out of "Dixie." People from the South meet with very little sympathy here. They seem to think we have had little to eat and wear during the war and ought to be very humble in our aspirations and desires when we come to reside in the land of our *conquerors*. Really Anna I do not like these Yankee people. They appear so cold hearted and distant. When in the South I refuted the assertion that they were less hospittable and warm hearted than the Southerners but I must own it is so now. The women are great

workers I believe they think the greatest virture in a womans character is to be able to do a great amount of hard drudgery. I do not think it
is any disgrace to work, neither do I think it shows much cultivation
and refinement when one does kitchen drudgery for the pleasure of it
as many seem to here but enough of this. I am willing every one should
follow their own inclination and I should like the same privilege. We
are boarding with Sylvanus sister Jane; she has twenty five in family—keeps one Irish woman. She is doing well—dresses herself and
Kathe; her only child, in good style and has her house handsomely furnished. She is better off than when her husband was living. She is like
you in many respects but a greater talker. I have not seen sister Mary
yet. Mother Beecher[1] is the youngest old person I ever saw; she is
younger in many respects than I am. I have seen uncle Johnson Payne;
he inquired very particularly about you as do all the rest. We wanted to
go to keeping house this fall but can get no house. O I am so anxious to
have a home again. I presume we shall feel more contented when we
get a home to ourselves, but I do not feel now as if I should ever feel as
well contented here as I should in the South. When I think of dear little
Lillie's lonely grave my heart yearns to be near it. You would not know
our sweet little Daisy. She looks very much as little Lillie did. She
walks and begins to try to talk. Sylvanus brother in law, Mary's husband, is thinking of going South this fall and will probably pay you a
visit. I want you to reply to this immediately and tell us every thing
you think we want to know. Give our love to all the children and keep a
good share yourself.

Yours as Ever
Jennie A. Lines.

DIARY

December 21st 1865   It is possible that I have once more opened my
neglected journal? I hardly know what to write we have passed through
so many changes since my last date. We were then in our Southern
home suffering the privations and hardships of civil war. Peace is restored and we are now with our relatives in the North. We have seen
the faces of our aged parents again in the flesh. My afflicted Brother
Ezra has passed away. I bid him adieu when I left home nine years ago
but he was not here to welcome me on my return. I believe that his robe
were washed white in the blood of the Lamb and that he is now with
the redeemed. Sylvanus too mourns the loss of an *only* brother. My
brother Charley & Eddie are still living. Charley is a wanderer—it is
many years since any of our family have seen him. We are now residing

in the beautiful city of New Haven, Sylvanus early home. We are boarding with his widowed sister Mrs. Jane Lane.

When I last wrote in my book I was a bereaved mother mourning the loss of an only and idolized child. I still mourn the loss of that precious one, but I am not still childless. No *thank God* the sweet music of infant glee and the patter of childish feet is again heard in our room. Our Father in heaven heard our prayer and sent another infant daughter to bless our hearts & home. Our little Forrest Daisy is a little more than 16 months old. It occurred to me a few days since that if this little one should live she might some day look over her mothers journals, and I have not yet even recorded her birth on its pages I resolved to begin now and try to atone for past negligence.

Our second little daughter is in form and feature a counterpart of the first. Some times as I sit at my sewing and recall the happy days when little Lillie played at my side, I almost feel that I have but to look up and I shall find my little angel is still with me; but no the sweet little face that always meets my gaze with a smile is not just like the one we saw hid beneath the coffin lid. The resemblance is so striking that those who saw little Lillie think little Daisy looks just as she did. Her skin is just as fair—her hair just the same color—the same pretty blue eyes and sweet little mouth, but her forehead is not as broad and her expression is not just the same. Her little ways are just like Lillie at her age. O how often she reminds me of the precious one who sleeps in the South. I can imagine just how large little Lillie would be and just how she would look and act if she was with us now. * * *

Friday 22   I think I shall find it rather hard to write every day in my book—my thoughts will not flow as readily as they once did—like every thing else not much used they have grown rusty. During the war I had but little letter writing to do—all communication between our Northern friends was cut off. We were very anxious to return North and hastened home soon after the war closed. We some times regret that we were in such haste for we have been very homesick. If our lives are spared I think we shall eventually return South. For the present I am satisfied to be here. Southern people are having a great deal of trouble with the "freedmen" as the negroes are now called by their infatuated, deluded, *insane* deliverers. They fancy they have bestowed the boon of liberty upon an intelligent, enterprising, industrious & energetic but hitherto "down trodden and oppressed" people, and that the darkie will soon, if he is not already, be quite equal to the white race. I think a few years will prove to some at least that freedom is more of a curse than a blessing to the black race. Hundreds die every week in many a Southern city for they will not, of their own *free* will, work even for bread to eat. They seem to think freedom means idleness. I hear my husbands step upon the stairs and will stop for to night.

Saturday 23   Busy all day cleaning my rooms—in the evening Jane came and staid with baby while S and I went up town   Chapel Street was thronged with people. The stores were handsomely trimmed and brilliantly lighted: some of them were so crowded we could not easily crowd in. Every body seemed to be buying presents for somebody. We felt the inconvenience of a shallow purse. S. bought a handsome [?] to present to his sister, Jane, some pretty red stockings & candies for little pet, and a few necessary articles of clothing for ourselves. Little Daisy did not wake while we were gone.

Mon. 25   Christmas day. Have spent nearly the whole day at Janes. She gave her Irish girl the privilege of spending the day with her friends concequently the task of getting a Christmas dinner for all her boarders devolved solely upon herself. Miss Tucker Sylvanus and myself rendered all the assistance we could. She got up a most excellent dinner—her table was heavily laden with both substantials and delicacies. After the gentlemen had seated themselves at the table quite an interesting little ceremony took place. One of the gentlemen made a pretty little speech and in behalf of the boarders presented Mrs. Lane with a handsome set of silver ware—forks, spoons, both large and small, caster spoons butter knives &c. She received it gracefully and in thanking them expressed herself in a becoming lady like manner. The day passed off pleasantly and all seemed to enjoy themselves finely. Sylvanus went up town and bought our little daughter Daisy a beautiful little rocking chair for her Christmas present. I dont believe the negroes in the South have enjoyed this the first Christmas of freedom as they did in the days of bondage when they had masters and mistresses to make them presents and give them good Christmas dinners.

Tues 26   A letter from Mrs. Tuttle to-day. It is many years since I have received one from her. She write[s] such a warm, friendly letter—She is so glad I am North again and so anxious to see me. There has been many changes in her family—she writes in a sad tone. Since I saw her she has laid two sweet children in the grave. I know well what that sorrow is. The little Emma who was my pupil nine years ago is married. To hear such news makes me feel old. Hyram who was also my pupil is a cripple for life. I must write her a long letter soon   I have much to tell her.

Wed. 27 Two years to day since I stopped writing in my journal. I hope I may not neglect it so again. My husband wishes me to write and if little Daisy lives it may be a pleasure in after years to read what her mother wrote in her infancy. Nothing of note to day.

Thurs. 28 Weather rainy and disagreeable. Thus far it is no colder than we have it in the South. I want to see clear cold weather and good sleighing. I was introduced to Mrs. Brooks and Mrs. Leeds at Janes this afternoon. The first is the mother the second the sister of my husbands first wife. Jane, Sylvanus and myself are invited to take tea with them to-morrow afternoon. It is the first time that I have been invited out to tea in New Haven. S. has gone to the office as usual this evening; he will not be home in an hour. I believe I shall retire as I am dull and sleepy.

* * *

Sab 31 The last day of 1865. The snow is several inches deep. I have to-day for the first time in nine years heard the merry jingle of sleigh bells. I do not think the sleighing will last many hours; it is getting warmer and there is every appearance of rain. It seems to me the weather is more changeable here than in the South. S. attended church this morning. I am staying home for the want of a bonnet. That article is so expensive and I wear one so little that I feel hardly able to buy one, but I must not neglect church on that account—I must get one or wear my [jaccey?]

Monday 1st 1866 New Years day. Has not seemed like a holiday to me. Have spent it in my room with little Daisy. S. has been at the office all day. Jane got up a New Years dinner for her boarders. They showed their appreciation in a way that left no doubt of their enjoying it. Jane presented me with a pretty embroidered handkerchief. Poor Sylvanus has not received one dime worth from anyone. I told him if he would give me the monney I would go up town and buy something for him, but he seems to think if he had the monney to spare he could just as well by it himself. I do sometimes long for a little more of this worlds goods: but thanks to God we all have the rich blessing of health to commence the new year with

* * *

Mon 22 Weather cool again. Went to a place of amusement this evening and did not return until late. Sylvanus remained at home and took care of our little daughter.

Wed 24 Weather same as yesterday. I have much to be thankful for and to make me feel contented and cheerful, but without being able to define the cause I am feeling dissatisfied and depressed in spirits Sylvanus has a bad cough I do not think his lungs will bear the severity of this Northern climate.

* * *

Sab 28 Have been alone with little pet all day. Have just finished reading a very interesting book called "Onward."[2] I am not steadily pressing "onward" in the strait and narrow way which leads to heaven I often fear I am going backward instead of forward, downward instead of upward in the christian course. I do not constantly enjoy that sweet peace which my Saviors presence alone can give. O how much grace I need to keep these erring feet in the footsteps of my Redeemer! Thanks to my Heavenly Father He is ever ready to grant grace to those who ask in Jesus name. "My grace is sufficient for thee." I bless my God for that precious promise. May I ever cry unto Him for help when assailed by the tempter and I know I shall come off conqueror through Him Who shed His blood for me.

SYLVANUS TO JENNIE

Macon, Ga., Oct. 18, '68

Dear Jennie,—

To-day of all others since I came to this place do I feel the most lonely, having nothing in particular to interest me or take my attention, and my mind looks back to its home on Green St., with a yearning only equaled by those who inhabit that quiet place. How I should like to clasp you in my arms and take one kiss from the lips of our little ones.[3] How I miss you all, morning, noon and night, you—alone can imagine, and I know you can appreciate my feelings as day after day passes and I come not. It seems sometimes that it could not be thus, yet for the present I know it is best, but if fortune smiles upon me our separation will be of short duration; for wherever my lot is cast there must yours be also.

My health is excellent and my cough has nearly left me, and with a good appetite I fancy I do justice to the very bountiful table of my landlady Now I suppose you would like to know what I have to eat—well for breakfast we have very good coffee hot rolls, *warm biscuit* of course, beef steak, cold ham, hash, batter cakes, &c.; at noon not less than three kinds of meat & fowl, Irish & sweet potatoes, rice and hominy, light bread & biscuit, turnips & greens, and nearly every day dessert of pudding or pie with a glass of sweet milk or butter milk; and for supper we have the usual variety of meat & fowl with preserves and jellies and tea & coffee. On the whole I have concluded that I shall not starve. I pay $30 per month for board room & lights. Now if they can afford to board for that, I am satisfied we could live nearly as cheap here as in New Haven. House rent is high in this place. For such a house as we occupied here we should have to pay about $30 per month in a healthy locality. I took a stroll this morning with Mr. Baird and passed by our old residence, it looked quite natural only that it has been painted and improved. I called on Mrs. Wrigley the other day, found her in good health, her oldest daughter has been married about two years and lives on a plantation twenty miles from Griffin, Miss Lucie was not at home when I called. I was invited very cordially to call again. I have met but very few acquaintances as yet except among printers. The population has very much changed since we left but the place looks quite natural.

I wrote you immediatly on my arrival here and enclose in my letter $2. Did you receive it? I intended to have mailed a post office order to you today but the office was closed when I received my money last night. I shall however send you money order to-morrow for fifteen dollars and should more but for a misunderstanding of Mr. Halls in regard to the amount I was to receive, he only drew the rate of $25 a week but said he would rectify next Saturday. Greenbacks are rather scarce here and city money is mostly used, which will make it troublesome as the Post Office will not take it for orders   Mr. Hall says he will try to get as much greenbacks as I will want but for fear I should not get as much as you need in time for the rent, I do not think it best for you to pay any bills unless it is the $5 to Jane. When you write let me know what day you receive this; it will leave Macon at 8 o'clock Monday morning; Give my love to Mr. & Mrs Smith, Mr & Mrs Kelsey Jane, Kattie, and all who inquire about me. Now kiss my dear Daisy and Herbie & tell them to kiss you for papa.

> Affectionately
> Sylvanus

SYLVANUS TO JENNIE

> Macon, Ga., Oct. 25th [1868]

Dear Jennie,

* * * Until to-day I have been rather unpleasantly situated as far as my room was concerned, but I now have very comfortable quarters with a stove and my window overlooks a beautiful garden from which delightful odors are wafted on every breeze; the weather is still warm

and pleasant, and as yet we have had no frost; the nights are cool enough to keep the mosquitos quiet, so that one can enjoy his sleep. My health is excellent, and I cough but very little. Everything is quiet here, and the negros seem to be very civil and as a general thing polite; almost every negro I meet touches his hat the same as they use to; how they would be as servants I do not know. I shall send you a post office order to-morrow for as much as I can get, but I am troubled to get greenbacks in exchange for our city money, although that is good enough for local uses. Let me know how you stand for funds and whether you received the order I sent last week. I shall probably send you another next week and the week following I shall have to use for my board, which I pay monthly. When I send orders do not feel slighted if I do not write as I think it safer to mail them by themselves. Find out if you can Mr. Kelsey's address as I wish to write to him & have forgotten his name and No. I hope some time we may be established in business somewhere in this country for I am confident we could make money here.

Now Jennie, a sweet good night. with a kiss for my little cherubs Daisy & Herbie.

Sylvanus

Remember to direct,
    Key Box 41

SYLVANUS TO JENNIE

Macon, Ga., Nov. 8th 1868

My Dear Jennie,—

* * *

I received your letter in due time, (Friday,) and was very sorry to learn that you had not got mine. I write you *every Sunday* and mail it in time so that it will leave this place on the Monday morning train. This I done two weeks ago and on Monday, Oct. 26th procured money order for $34, which should have left on Tuesday morning. Last Sunday I wrote again and on following day Nov. 2 sent order for $23. I hope you have received all before this. Hereafter when you are expecting an order and do not receive it before the following Tuesday I think you had better telegraph me (to the care of J. W. Burke & co,) so that I may look after it; and when you do receive them before writing mention the fact in your letter, that I may feel easy about them. I shall be sure to write every week if well & if sick shall get some one to write for me, which I hope will not be the case, therefore if you do not get a letter when due you can feel easy about me, and lay the blame upon the miserable radical Post offices of the country. I shall not be able to send order this week on account of my board, but if nothing happens will send you one Nov. 16 My health is excellent—a blessing which I prize and *think* I can appreciate. The weather is still delightful and I am now sitting by an open window enjoying the warm and fragrant breeze from without, and the congeniality of your spirit which I imagine is before me while I write; would that my imagination were in truth a *reality*. It is a month to-day since I said good-bye, and it seems a year since we parted. Can it be that months must still elapse before I see you and our little ones? I hope not. I want you to come as soon as you can make arrangements to do so and as Horace Gardner often meets with acquaintances from the South they might secure you company through, by letting them know in time. When you come, I can get board until we can secure a suitable house. I wrote to Father last week; have also written to Mother and Mary, and Lyons & Graver, and received answers from each. I received your first letter last week after it had been advertized; it had been in this office nearly two weeks, and I inquiring for it every day; I gave the clerk my opinion of him (respectfully), to which he made apologies and promises to do better in future. Be sure to direct Key Box 41, and I shall have no trouble. I shall write to Mr. Kelsey this week and perhaps to Hattie or Mr. Kellogg, though I should be puzzled to know how to write an interesting letter to her. The Election passed off very quietly in this place also throughout the State with the exception of Savannah and Augusta. In the former place there were five or six white men killed and about fifteen niggers, who were the immediate cause of all the trouble. The Democrats carried this State by over forty thousand majority in spite of the "scalawags" and "carpet-baggers". You ask how many servants we have here—I think there are four "on the lot"; one of them is a boy who attends to me studiously—blacks my boots every morning, and if it is in any way cool, builds me a fire to get up by. As 7 o'clock is the hour to commence work, I am there at that time and go back to breakfast at 8,—this gives me an appetite, and I have but a short distance to walk. My washing is well done but they will shrink my flannel. I got one of the negros at the office to take it home to his wife. I pay $1 per dozen, which amounts to 5[0] cents a week.

Now one word to my little pets. Papa is so anxious to see them. With what pleasure would I meet my little Daisy could I see her tripping along the walk as I come to my meals. How often do I see her smiling face, in imagination, as she would run to meet me. Little Herbie I want to see *so* much,—now that his teeth are through I hope he will be better. Kiss them both for me.

May our Father in Heaven protect you and spare your lives and health and hasten the time when we may be again united in our own home.

Remember me to Mr. & Mrs Smith Jane, Hattie and all my acquaintances

Sylvanus

JENNIE TO SYLVANUS

New Haven Nov 20 1868

My Dear Husband—:
* * * Jane thinks it would be better for us to live this way until another Fall as you might in that time get clear of debt and have something ahead. *Pecuniarily* I presume it would be the best plan; but I do not think it is always best & wisest to sacrifice happiness to lucre. I am *very* anxious to have you clear of debt before I leave, but we can not do *more* than is possible   I think however we can stand clear of all except Tuttle Morehouse & Taylor, and perhaps diminish theirs. I wish you would send Mr. Ramsdell what you owe him, also that little to Mr. Taylor; cut short my allowance for a couple of weeks and settle those little bills wont you? * * *

Jennie.

SYLVANUS TO JENNIE

Macon, Ga., Nov. 29th, 1868

Ever Dear Jennie:—
* * * I shall send you an order to-morrow and I want you to do one thing for me and that is to call at the Palladium office on Union Street, just above Chapel, and ask for Mr. Tyrrel the foreman, and pay him my dues to the Union which I think is $3.56. This should have been paid before the last meeting but I forgot it. The next meeting takes place on Saturday night, Dec. 5. and I am afraid that if it is not paid by that time they will report me to this Union   Now please do this for me. Mr Tyrrel is President of the Union,—you will find him in generally in the afternoon and evening. I should like also for you to pay Mr. Taylor if you will,—I suppose I owe him $9. I have written to Mary, to know how to have a Money Order issued, and, when I hear from her shall send it. Mr. Ramsdell's I shall send soon. By all means get the furs for Daisy, and do not get them too cheap, but get good ones. How do you stand in the way of funds, or is that a secret? I believe I asked you once before but got no answer. Do you get all the papers? I send you two and Daisy one every week.

Now, my dear, I must write a few lines to my little Daisy, for she must not be disappointed. I met Mr. & Mrs. Tubers on the street the other day and they invited us to call on them when you come My love to all.

Yours affectionately
Sylvanus

* * *

SYLVANUS TO JENNIE

Macon, Ga. Dec. 13th, 1868

My Dear Jennie,—

I am shivering with cold although I have a good fire in my stove, but the wood is so poor that it does not throw out much heat. Yesterday and today it has been as cold as I ever knew it in the State. Night before last I suffered with cold, and slept but little, and how I *did* wish you were here that I might snug up and keep warm, so you see I miss you night and day. If I were destined to live in this way as long as I remained in the State, I assure you my stay would be short, even at the risk of my health, but I live in hope and this makes me in a measure contented. While I know that you are all well and getting along comfortably I feel easy, yet I fear that you will work too hard and make yourself sick, now do hear to me and take things as easy as you can, and if it should delay your coming a little longer it will be much better than to work so hard and get sick where I cannot be with you to assist you. Get some one to assist you in your sewing, for you have enough to do to take care of yourself and our little ones this cold winter. I asked you in one of my last letters how you stood in the way of funds, not because I was afraid that you were extravagant, by any means, but that I might know that you were supplied with every thing that you need, for I don't want you to get out of money or be in need of anything to make you comfortable and happy; my income is sufficient to support us comfortably and remember that my life is devoted to you. Do not feel anxious in regard to money for I know well enough your economy and discretion in using it. You have done better than I expected. I shall send you an order to-morrow for $25 and should more but I have had to pay wood and washing bills and buy tobacco, postage stamps &c I have concluded to have you pay Tuttle, Morehouse & Taylor 20 or 25 dollars as soon as you have it to spare, (if you will be so kind to do it for me), for you can tell better than I can when it can be done without cramping you; therefore I shall continue to send all money to you unless you should prefer otherwise.

I want you to try some other medicine besides the pills—you know the nervine helped you before and I think it will now. Do not put it off any longer. You wanted to know if I tell you *truly* in regard to my health,—which I assure I do. The slight cold which I had a few weeks since made me cough some but that has left me now; my bowels are in good condition and regular as a clock, once in twenty-four hours. *I am strong, hearty and well!* All this I attribute to the climate, and I am in hopes it will have as good an effect on you as I am confident it has on me. * * *

> Most lovingly I am your
> Sylvanus

SYLVANUS TO JENNIE

Macon, Ga., Dec. 27th, 1868

My Dear One,—

The Post Office being closed on Friday I failed to receive your letter, which would have been the most acceptable Christmas present that I could have received, but however it reached me on Saturday morning, and I assure you found a welcome reception. Christmas has come and gone, and never had I witnessed such a celebration; it commenced on Thursday night at dark and every body seemed determined to see which could make the most noise. You know in this country it is like the 4th of July at the North   Everything that would hold powder was brought into requisition, from a cannon down to a fire-cracker, and it was nothing but *pop, pop, bang*, until 11 o'clock last night when a copious rain dispersed the crowds and cooled their excitement. As for myself, I remained quiet and passed a lonely day, thinking of the loved ones far away, and how I longed to be with them on that happy morning! When I saw others around me giving and receiving their presents, and the little ones with their joyous faces and light hearts, it made me feel sad indeed, and I then felt that *I was alone!* My mind wandered back to your quiet home with our little ones around you but I know *you* missed me, dear. Our good landlady met us in the morning with an eggnog for each (you know it would not be Christmas *here* without that) and then we sat down to a nice breakfast—hot coffe, buckwheat cakes, sausage, &c. At 4 o'clock we were summoned to dinner or rather supper and the first sight of the table made me feel hungry, for it was litterally loaded with both substantials and luxuries, and for the next hour we gave a *practical* illustration of our appreciation of the good taste of our generous landlady. Wandering about and finding nothing to interest me I retired at an early hour, and thus passed my Christmas. The next I hope will be a more happy one to us all.

* * *

With much love and affection I am Yours Devotedly
Sylvanus.

SYLVANUS TO JENNIE

Macon, Ga., Jan 3d, 1869

Jennie Dear,—

Another week has passed—another year has gone—a new year has dawned upon us, with prospects for the future bright and promising; let us hope and trust that their effulgence may not be dimmed by the clouds of adversity. May our Heavenly Father, who has smiled upon us thus far, continue His blessings with us; and although separated many miles, we may trust in Him who doeth all things well, that ere long we shall again be united; it seems to me now that *that* day will be one of the happiest of my life—when I may look again upon the faces of *my loved and loving ones*—to enjoy the congenial society of you, *my Dear one*, and hear the sweet voices of *my little pets*. To live in this way is not life—it is a lonely existence—time hangs heavily upon me. While in the office I get along very well, but when unemployed, loneliness takes full possession of me; this may seem unmanly, but it is the cravings of an affectionate heart. Although it has been scarcely three months since we bid each other adieu, yet it seems years, and to think it must still be months before we meet again makes me feel dejected,—but then it may be for the best, and I must wait with patience.

Your letter reached me at the usual time together with the georgeous neck-tie for which you will accept many thanks; had it arrived one day sooner I might have made many conquests at the wedding which I attended on Thursday night. There were five couples who "stood up" with the happy pair—all of whom were dressed richly; the ladies dresses trailed from 1½ to 2 yards. The ceremony was performed by Rev. J. W. Burke, the senior proprietor of our office. The evening passed off sociably and pleasant, and it was near the "wee sma' hours" when the company dispersed. To read your last letter almost gives me a chill—not from its coldness, by any means, for it breathed *warm* words of *affection*, and *love*, but to imagine you sitting by a red-hot stove and cold at that, while I am basking in a summer's sun, *enjoying* every cool breeze and looking for a shady place. O, how I long to have you here to enjoy this delightful [climate?]   We have had a few cool days and four or five cold nights and the rest of the time it has been unusually warm and pleasant, making an overcoat a useless article in one's wardrobe. You can act your own pleasure in regard to the pictures, if you think they would prize them and choose to do so you can. I should like to have all your pictures taken over (Herbie's Daisy's and yourself,) large, for frames, for our own use, for they take them very poorly here and charge high,—also get one of those oval frames with dark rim and gilt, which I told you of for Charlie & Eddie's picture, and send on the money for Father & Mother's, and send enough to pay for it, as the old negative may have been destroyed and a new one would cost more— this you had better attend to soon, and not wait till you go on.

In getting your dresses do not economise too much but get nice ones, and have them made fashionable and stylish. Here, long trails are the rage. I have not determined as yet how we shall live when you come, whether to board or to keep house. I have a place in view (to board) in a very *nice* family, but I have not learned the price as the lady wished me to call and see her which I shall do when you determine when you are coming. It is not a regular boarding house and it is not expected that the income will support the family. At this place where I am the best rooms are occupied by families and I should have to pay $90 per month,—washing, lights and fuel extra.

* * *

Yours devotedly
Sylvanus

SYLVANUS TO JENNIE

Macon, Ga., Jan. 10th, 1869

My own Jennie,—

Your long, (not too long) interesting and *precious* letter came to hand one day sooner than is usual, and I assure you was gladly received. I find myself ever looking forward to their arrival with both pleasure and anxiety, fearing that they *may* bring me news that you or my little ones are sick, but I hope for the best, and feel thankful that thus far your lives and health has been spared. Do take the best care of your health possible and do not neglect to get more nervine if you have not got it already and hereafter do not feel that you cannot aford it, but when you get out by more. I intended to have sent you a little money in this letter but my watch got out of order and cost me $4 and then my boots need repairs so that I shall have little left after paying my board which is due on Tuesday. Business is very driving in the office and I have to work nearly every night. I made $38 last week and took things quite easy—I earn 50 cents an hour and can work as many hours as I please. In regards to your coming—I think with you that it will be impossible for you to come by 1st Feb. and get things which you want and must have, and shall therefore try to feel contented and patient— though it does seem hard that I cannot see you; I know, *dearest*, that it would not be thus if you could avoid it. While you are there it will certainly be best for you to remain until you are quite ready, and I have no doubt you will get through all right, if you are able to stand the fatigue of so long a trip. I know you can buy a ticket from New York to Macon, but I am not certain that they will check baggage through—if they do not it will be just as well,—for you could then stop over at the place where it has to be re-checked, get the conductor to direct you to the *first class hotel* of the place, and there stay long enough to rest, and they will see to re-checking your baggage when you come on; your *through ticket* will be perfectly good if you should stop over. In coming, I think the route through Philadelphia, Baltimore, Washington Richmond, Wilmington and Augusta will be the most pleasant and least trouble; from Augusta you come direct to Macon and do not pass through Atlanta; as that is 130 miles out of the way. Should you need any further directions let me know or inquire of Mrs. Gardner, as Horace or Gussie can post you fully. I want you to start with plenty of money for emergencies, and be able to pay the children's fare if it is required. I priced Chamber sets in this place and find them very high—one light painted set, very inferior to ours cost $80 and from that up to $400; a small rocker $5, quite ordinary carpets from $2 to $3 per yard, and I am told crockery is as high in proportion, so on the whole I think it will be best to keep as much as we can and get more if possible, provided you can get them boxed safely. If Mrs. Minor will ship the crockery, send toilet set and all,—the goblets & glass dish you had better ask their advice about—perhaps you could pack them in your trunk best, but remember trunks have hard usage—the jars it is immaterial about as they would be hard to pack, but you can do as you please about them. In regard to the expense you would only have to pay boxing and drayage in New Haven and the freight would all be payable here. If you should attempt to sell your things it would make you trouble and you would get little for them. *Let me caution you right here* that when you break up to hire a woman to help you and do not attempt to work or lift a thing—you will need *all* your strength before you get here, and I want to see you well when you arrive. Whenever you please you can call on Mr. Douglass 118 Orange St., and select the size trunk you want, with such arrangement inside as you like, and have him make one for you. Have him mark it on each end (J. A. Lines, Georgia,) He said when you wanted a trunk to call and tell him who you was and he would make a good one for you cheap. Tell him your husband published the Advertiser and directed you to him   My rocking chair would be most too clumsy to send, therefore I think you had better send it to Mother—should not want to sell it. Write to Mary & ask her what to do with the bed. & say nothing to any one else about it. I think you had better pay Dr. Park $20 and have him give you his address that I may send him the balance, for I want to pay T. M. & T. as close as I can, as that was borrowed money, and I cannot think of paying all up in full before I see you. I want you by all means to remember Father & Mother with as much as you can and not forget Charlie & Eddie. You will probably get a little something for such things as you had to sell, but I do not expect you will get much and it will not do to make calculations or depend upon it at all. I have tried to answer all your inquiries, and hope you will not let things worry you—but take it as easy as possible, and all will [?] but the sooner you attend to these things the better as they will [?] your mind and you can feel easy[?].

I have filled the first sheet with matters of business but as I have no other way of talking to you about such things, I must do it in my letters. I wish I could sit down with you and talk over these matters and also to be with you and assist in your arduous labors preparatory to leaving, and thus save you much anxiety. I have about made up my mind not to expect you before the fore part of March but it does seem that I could not bear this loneliness till then. Jennie, my love has been tested; and the ordeal of our separation has been severe indeed. It has proved to me what intensity of affection my heart was capable; and how often do I think how you have watched over me in sickness, kissed my fevered brow, performed the many kind offices while I was languishing in pain, and with tearful eyes and anxious heart watched over me day and night—O, can I ever reciprocate your kindness, love and devotion. How often do I think of and regret my many little acts of impatience, and would that they could be blotted from memories page; that I could recall those acts and in their place imprint upon your lips a kiss of affection.

I long to see my affectionate Little Daisy—the pride of my heart—and my Little Herbie, who you tell me talks so cunning. I cannot think of him but as he was when I left him,—only saying but a few words, and by the time I see him he will have changed a great deal. You must certainly get Daisy a nice doll to bring with her, and I want you to fix her up in good style. You will need to get yourself something warm to travel in as it will be quite cold until you get nearly here. The weather here is quite warm but for the past week has been rainy and unpleasant—and has helped to give me the "blues." My health, as usual, is good. * * *

> With true love and devotion I am
> Your affectionate husband
> Sylvanus

SYLVANUS TO JENNIE

Macon, Ga., Jan 17th, 1869

My Loving Jennie—

Were it not for the cheerful reception of your weekly letters and the gratifying and consoling influence which they have upon me in their perusal, I could not remain here thus *alone*; but each one affords me food for thought and mental reflection until its successor arrives and I am again communing in spirit with its writer. Your last letter, dear one, caused feelings of sadness, filled in part, as it was, with *undue* self-reproach; you have been too loving, kind, patient and enduring to merit the reproaches which you have taken to yourself. Think not that I cannot appreciate the trials and perplexities of a loving and devoted wife and mother and these coupled with ill health, which is enough of itself to discourage and embitter the feelings of the most patient. You have, dear Jennie, been above reproach and my heart's desire has been more than realized since it has been united with a congenial and reciprocal companion. We ought not to wish our precious time to fly away, yet it does seem to drag wearily along and the weeks seem months, and the months, years since we parted and the time when we shall be again united. I but be in constant fear lest something may happen especially to little Daisy, who you say is looking poorly; be sure and have plenty of food and that which is *substantial*. I have no doubt you will all improve in this climate, which makes me doubly anxious to have you here. In regard to our location when you come I have had that in view, and upon inquiry have found the upper part of the city to be the most healthy and free from chills, and acting upon the advice of a physician once given here, I have been looking for a house or board above second street. I think if I can find good board within my means that I should prefer it to housekeeping, for the present at least. If you can get the children's pictures taken together (large) I think I would do so, otherwise have them taken separately, and go to Hawley & Bro. and get suittable frames and for variety get them different from those we have. also have yours retaken. They do better work in that line in New Haven than here and at less price, consequently I want you to go as far as your means will allow while you are there. In selecting your dresses, I think it would be well to have an eye to the season here and buy accordingly, as you know the spring opens here quite early and by March it is quite warm. Do not put off your wardrobe till the last of next month if you can avoid it, for remember it will take you a week or two to visit after breaking up. I want you to visit Mary if possible and you will of course spend a short time with Mrs. Gardner. I should like very much to go to Atlanta to live but the wages they offer will not warrant it; and then I am very pleasantly situated here as far as the office is concerned, and if our health is good here it will be best to remain for the present. In regard to our furniture,—I am a little afraid *matting* would not protect it sufficiently, it might do for the chairs and table, and perhaps the bedstead,—if the bureau and wash stand were matted I should think it would be well to put a simple frame around the corners to protect them. The looking glass might be sent with the pictures with more safty. I want them to be packed safe even if it cost $20 and it will be cheaper in the end than to sell and buy new. I earned $37.50 last week and shall send you an order for $35 tomorrow, and if nothing happens as much more next week. It does seem good to receive the worth of one's labor, after having worked hard for a bare subsistence, and now that my health is good I feel encouraged that I may soon be free from debt, and do more for my family. If you have any surplus funds you can pay T. M. & T. more on account but I would not do so if it would prevent you from getting a carpet and other necessary things while you are there, for I can soon settle with them after you come on. I think I mentioned twenty-five yards of carpet so that we could cover a large room if I were fortunate to get one in boarding; let me know how carpets are selling in New Haven

Give my love to all acquaintances and accept a large share for yourself and pets.

Most truly yours in patience waiting
Sylvanus

JENNIE TO SYLVANUS

New Haven, Jan 26 1869

My Dear Kind Husband:—

I intended to have written last night so that I might not think and write so much on the subject of our temporal affairs on the Sabbath. Mrs. Grant and Mrs. Smith came in and prevented me so I fear I shall trespass again.

Your letter and order came on Friday—they always come together. As usual I was all excitement and emotion after its perusal. I lay awake thinking all night *nearly*: buying and selling, cutting and sewing, visiting and traveling and then the meeting with you; until at length exhausted Nature sought a few moments rest in the arms of her restorer; but still the mind worked on. I dreamed we were together again. I trust we shall be before many weeks: but with you I think it best to remain long enough to get such things as we need and I think too it is best to get them in prefference to canceling all the debts for as you say with health you can soon settle up all after we get there. I want to pay Dr. Park in part if not full also something—more on the debt to T. M. & T. I have not paid out any of this order for debt and do not think I had better any [?] I get such things in the line of dry goods as we want so that I can be making what is neccessary. I priced carpets yesterday   I can get a good ingrain two ply $1.25. the *best* two ply $1.50 probably that is what we shall want; but shall we need 25 yards? will not 20 cover any room we shall be likely to get? The difference in the cost would by something else. I went to see Mr. Bowditch again. He says he can put the washstand and bureau and I think he said table too in what they call *skeleton* boxes and mat the other things for about $12. He thinks they would go safely so. I bought Daisy a nice little rocking chair for $8. Mr. B. said he presumed it could be packed in with other things and not cost any thing to get it there in that case we should save $2. by getting it here. I also called on Mr. Douglass about trunks. He is not going to make one expressly for me as he keeps them on hand all the time. The largest size of those which are finished up so nicely with that iron finish to protect the corners is $14. the next in size is $13. the next $12. I think the $12. one will do very well dont you? I dont feel as if I could pay more. I can get the largest size *without* those corner fixings for $12 which do you think best to get? I think I will not buy it until I get your reply to this. I bought me a dress yesterday and each of us a pair of shoes also Herbie a pretty dress. I intended to get [ress?] for a dress but could not find any, so I bought empress cloth   it is a pretty green and a nice piece. I went to every store on Chappel St. and finally bought it at a Germans. saved $1.50 by doing so. he let me have eight yards for $6.50. Next week I shall have to pay rent and by coal. I economize all I can but we do not go *hungry* dont fear that. In regard to pictures I would like very much to have the children taken together and will try to do so.

*   *   *

Your Affectionate wife
Jennie

JENNIE TO SYLVANUS

New Haven, Jan. 31 1869

My Dear Sylvanus—:

Again I have put off my writing until Sabbath evening and until quite a late hour too as Mrs. Kelsey came in after tea and remained some time. I do not like to have any one come on Sunday night as it encroaches on time I wish to devote to you. And now to the first question in your letter, as to whether I can firm any idea when I will break up. I am anxious to do so the last week in February, and then it would be the second week in March before I could start for Georgia, provided I go to Worcester and Utica and I presume I should need to remain that long for more funds too. I do not see how we can decide about time yet. my sewing shall not keep me here longer than this month if I go with it undone. The order for money this week (which is more than I expected) I shall spend for cotton cloth, bedding table linen & towels, which as near as I can come at it will be about $25, then my rent $12.50, and the rest for necessary and incidental expenses so you see how that $45, goes. I dont know where you get so much money. After we get there we can surely lay up for if I get all I intend to you will not have much dry goods to buy in a long time. By the way you spoke of sacking for yourself. Mr Kelsey wears a brown sack which they like very much as they do not show the boot stain. Shall I get you some of those also some white ones? tell me what size. There are the childrens pictures, if I have them when both large and small, and frame will cost considerable. I have been counting up the orders I expect to receive before the first of March but I can not come to any definite idea as to how I shall stand for funds. I shall not give up the rent until I can decide so that if it is neccessary for me to remain a week or two longer I can do so. A gentleman came to look at the rent last week he says if he takes it he will take the oil cloth on sink room and back stairs also on hall. They have never kept house so I am in hopes they will want all I have to dispose of, but I have no idea what to charge for any thing—must take what I can get. How I do want you here dear. I feel as if a mountain rested upon my shoulders and they are not very strong at present. I can not tell you what I have suffered the past week with dyspepsia. Am taking "Hooflands German Bitters" now. Have felt a little better to-day. They contain no stimulant and I am so weak I need it, and think I shall get some gin although the directions say stimulating or acid drinks must not be used while taking the bitters. If my health does not improve I shall not be able to go to Worcester or Utica but save all my strength for my long trip. * * *

SYLVANUS TO JENNIE

Macon, Ga., Feb 14th, '69

Dearest One,—

After having a week of the most delightful weather I ever experienced, we have to-day a dark and rainy dreary and lonely, and to me anxious day. To be here alone and hearing of the sickness of my loved ones far away makes me sad indeed,—and this is why I would hasten the time for our little circle to be reunited. If I knew you all were well and getting along nicely I would try to wait with patience until you could complete your arrangements and accomplish your desires, and I think it would be better to wait until the weather was warmer to travel, but to bear the suspense and anxiety and this too in silence and loneliness is truly hard and yet I cannot see how it can be avoided. I know, dearest, you are having too much care and labor upon you even were you well, but I fear that you yourself need care and nursing. I received a letter from Mary on Thursday last and she writes me how miserable you are, which makes me fear that you are even worse than you are inclined to tell me; do let me know how you are so that when I receive such letters I may not be worried beyond reason. If I know you are telling me just as it is I shall know then how to act and shall not give undue weight to what I hear from others. As I have not heard anything further since your letter of last Sunday I hope and trust the children are better. When any of you are sick I wish you would try to drop me a line during the week that I may know just how you are, and if *very* sick I shall not stay here but come on immediately. Now that your stay in New Haven is to be so short and you need to consult me in regard to what you shall do, just send to me any time during the week not thinking you must write a long letter; but do not let them interfere with your regular Sunday letters, for I look forward to their reception next to seeing you. I have been suffering for two or three days with a severe cold but to-day I am feeling about well and should be quite so if the weather was clear

Business—Your calculations in regard to time and funds are about correct and you seem to have anticipated what I wrote in my last. I believe I then made calculations for four orders of $30 each,—the 4th one on the 8th of March thus taking my board money, which would be due on Friday the 12th, and paying it on Saturday, 13th,—giving you the advantage of that weekly and only leaving my board over one day, but on reflection I think you would not have funds enough to carry you through. I know you will have a great deal of expense in breaking up and want you to feel free to hire done what you have to do and not attempt to do it yourself, whatever *anyone* may say—save all your strength for you will need it. I made $40 last week which I shall send to-morrow, and if nothing happens shall send you at least $30 next week, probably more, but it would not be best to base your calculations upon anything more than my regular wages as I have to keep up with my incidental expenses, and I cannot tell how long I shall have extra work to do. As I told you last week I would not have you start with less than $75 or $80 from Utica and would rather you would have more. I do not think it would be best to be in a hurry to break up and then depend upon visiting until I send you money enough to start with; the best way would be to remain in your home until you could see your way clearly, making calculations to receive one order of $50 in Utica which I shall manage to send you while there;—and now for the almanac, and as we have to look at things in the prospective, we will take it for granted that all will be well and that I can send you

Feb	15th	$40
"	22—	30
Mar	1—	30
"	8—	30
"	22—	30
"	29—	50
		$210

This will correspond with your calculations in time and enable you to receive the last order about April 2d or 3d in Utica; the order of the 22nd of March I could send to Worcester, so that if you should start for that place during that week it would meet you about March 26 or 27 Now I am afraid that even this will not be sufficient to defray all your expenses and allow you to get all that you want to, leaving sufficient to travel with, for I know you will have heavy and unavoidable expenses. If the gentleman, Mr Wilson would take the crockery at a fair price perhaps it would be best to sell rather than to take the chances of having them broke coming, thus saving the expense of packing and freight. The whole cost in the neighborhood of $18. but as some of it has been broken and otherwise injured, perhaps it would not be worth over $10 or $12—use your own discretion in the matter and I shall be satisfied. In regard to the looking glass, you can ask Mr. Bowditch and if he thinks he can pack it safe let him do so. Do not think I would put anything in the drawers as it would strain the locks too much in moving about and perhaps burst them open. I do not know what became of the key—get Mr. Kellogg to fit a new one and also to put a new lock on the lower drawer, for if I remember rightly there was none on it. You might be able to pack the oval pictures or a part of them in your [?] weight I [?] too much for safety. The frames like the one with Mothers picture had better be sent to Mr. Hawley's; and if you choose you can find out his charges for gilding the large frame, also packing and shipping and let me know the amount and I will send it to him direct thus saving that much of your funds to yourself,—by the way I wish you would get about one dozen "Porcelain head picture nails with screws"—these you can get at Hawley's, or if he has not got them he can tell you where you can get them. T. M. & T.'s bil was $77 dollars if I remember rightly and perhaps you can make out $9.50 thus leaving $30 and I know they will be satisfied until I can do better. The $20 you pay Dr. P will be as much as you can spare and I think will satisfy him—get him to give you his address so that I can mail him the balance. I should prefer if possible to have the children's pictures taken in New Haven as it would be much cheaper and as yet I have not seen a good one taken here you will also want to get a frame for them there. Do not be afraid to use your funds as your own good judgment dictates, for I have no doubt you [?] and will do [?] than [?].

Now I believe I have answered all your inquiries and given you such instructions as occur to me at present. Do not try to do all your sewing before you start, but save your strength and this will lighten your burdened mind. And now anxiously awaiting your next and hoping to hear that you all well and happy   I will bid you good night and pleasant dreams.

Yours devotedly
Sylvanus

JENNIE TO SYLVANUS

New Haven Feb 27th, 1869

My Dear Devoted Husband—:
* * * I have been sitting here thinking and figuring until it is bed time so I do not think I shall write as long a letter as usual this time. I am out of both hard coal and charcoal,—have had the old bed stead cut up which I shall use for charcoal and must order ¼ ton of hard coal tomorrow. You sent me $35, I have $7 to put with it making $42,00   Tomorrow I shall go up town and order coal,

	order coal,	$3,00
	buy trunk	12,00
	pay rent	12,50
	Toward a carpet save	10,00
	buy lunch basket	1,25

wanted to buy three pair shoes but must save rest to live on.
I lay by ten of it for carpet because I do not count on but $30 before receiving it but am always glad of the *overplus* for besides the expense of living and incidental expenses there are so many many, things I want to get. The carpet you know will be about $40, that is a heavy item. Last week I bought waterproof cloaking for Daisy and myself, table cloth and napkins for Anna meterials for Herbie a cap, and several small articles. Paid Dr. Park $20, T. M. & T. $9,50   This with the expense of living swallowed over $45, butter has gone up to 60 cts coffee sugar 22cts   Order of March 1st with what I have on hand will be carpet [?] overplus for expenses of livings. Order of March 8th for pack-

ing and breaking up expenses. Orders of 22. & 29th I *must* keep for traveling expenses. so you see I shall have to depend on what I get for our things to buy me a Spring dress, our traveling hats & the childrens pictures, Should I get what I ought it will be sufficient and allow me to buy something for those at home. I *did* want to be able to give father a few dollars in money as it will in all probability be the last visit I shall ever make him, and shall do so if it does not draw on my traveling funds   I dare not cramp myself in that respect. There will be my expenses from Utica to New York and across the city and my fare from New York to Macon Mr. Baird tells me will be $40. I have written to Mrs Gardner and asked Horaces assistance. hope for a reply soon that I may be relieved on that point. I do not feel inclined to prolong my stay beyond the time I have already decided upon. My break up here the last of March spend the first week of April in Utica, start for Georgia 6 or 7th reaching Macon 9th or 10th. but should I see that I am going to be cramped I could visit a week longer, could go to Plantsville the first week in April and to Utica the 2nd and there receive another order but that would cramp you and I will not do it if I can only sell our things as I ought. * * *

[Jennie]

SYLVANUS TO JENNIE

Macon March 14th '69

Ever Dear Jennie:—

As I seat myself this beautiful day to write to you, how my longing spirit would have it otherwise, and instead of writing in lonliness, you should be with me with your loving smile and affectionate heart, and this would be happiness indeed. You say my letter seemed to breathe a spirit of lonliness & anxiety—this was but too true, for when I wrote to you I *was* lonely, & not receiving your letter, then past due, I could not but feel anxious. Your last two letters have served to cheer me up for they told me that you were well and this relieves me of much anxiety; and as I look forward to our speedy reunion I feel less lonely. When I wrote you last Sunday I was about sick and this continued till Wednesday and I was unable to straighten up without pain, but I am now well again, and happy as circumstances will allow. Friends & acquaintances I have here in abundance but what are they to me, one of your sweet smiles is worth more than all to me. This is not flattery but the feelings of a devöted heart which has met with reciprocal love from its congenial companion. I think I hear you say—"he's getting sentimental or love-sick"—well, perhaps I am, but this is not a fault nor in my case a misfortune. Time and separation has taught me how deeply I love, and to you I have the right of expressing my feelings. The weeks seem to drag lazily along, and as one after another passes by and I can count days instead of months before we shall meet, I look forward to the renewal of our "honey-moon," enhanced by the presence of our little pets, with the greatest pleasure.

Now for business—You speak of selling our set and buying another,—allowing the case to be as you state, it might be the best plan, but I am inclined to think the lady was mistaken in the price and when we come to order it we would be unable to find it for twice the amount and then it would be necessary to be there to select it & see it shipped or we should be imposed upon. On the whole, I think best to keep the set we have, and as soon as we are able we will get one to suit us, and dispose of it here or keep it for a spare room; I saw a very inferior set sold here for $50 and I have no doubt ours would bring $75 or $100 should we feel disposed to sell it. We could send on at any time to parties we know and have a set sent out; while you are in at Bowditch's look at his furniture and get his prices for such as would suit you and we can order from him and depend upon his word. In regard to shipping the glass with the furniture ask Mr. B. if he can pack it perfectly safe and if he thinks Mr. Hawley could do best with it take it to him. I intend to have the pictures here as soon as the furniture therefore there will be no trouble in that way and I think you had better get Mr. Hawley to send for the large picture right away that he may get the gilding done by the time you break up, he will then be prepared to ship them immediately, also to give you the exact amount of his charges that I may send it on in time to receive them before you get here. I wish to have our room prepared for you on your arrival; Let Mr. Hawley pack the nails with the pictures and charge it in the bill with the ballance.

You spoke of not visiting mother, but I cannot see how you can avoid it unless you should stop with Jane or Ma Smith, as you will have to remain somewhere while your things are being sold, if you have to put them in the auction room, and it will be best for you to call on an auctioneer and tell him you have a few things you wish sold and ask him what day you must send them and tell him you wish them disposed of immediately, he can probably tell you what day to call for the money—this you can do a week before you break up. There was a good Auction room two doors above Cannon's store on State street, and their sale days were Wednesdays & Saturdays. When you are ready get some one to send an Express waggon for the things. I should like to have you get the childrens pictures if you can; and also get a frame at Hawleys as you can make a better selection there than here—he can also put this in his bill. If you should have them taken, better attend to it soon, as it sometimes takes a week to finish them up. You ask if you can go from New Haven to Utica in a day. I think you can provided you started early and make connections in Springfield and Albany. I left New Haven at 6 and arrived in Springfield at 9, there I bought a through ticket and had baggage checked to Utica—arrived in Albany about 12 and Utica at 4 in the morning—thus you see I went through in ten hours. In all cases ask the Conductor to assist you in changing cars, checking your baggage and getting your ticket unless you meet up with some one on whom you can rely—*and look out for sharpers* who might offer to assist you; and I would here suggest the propriety of separating your money, keeping in your pocket-book only what you will need before you get to a stopping place and the balance well secured out of the reach of pickpockets. I think you will get along first rate everywhere with the exception of New York where you will be obliged to have some one assist you in getting from the boat or depot to the train you start South on and to get your ticket and checks. If you do not hear from Mrs. Gardner some one must go down from New Haven to meet you and get you started and you pay their passage;—this some one *must* do as you would not know which way to turn in New York or what train to take. If you get along well at this point. I have confidence you will have no other trouble on the way. You must appoint your day far enough ahead that you will be in New York that there may be no mistake and also whether you come down from Albany on the cars or boat. I think your best plan will be to take the cars from Utica (buying a through ticket by boat to New York) about noon and take the night boat arriving in N.Y. in the morning, you will then feel fresh and if you come right through you will have a whole day to be on the way and perhaps meet with some one to assist you. Mr. Baird thinks there is little or no choice in the routes therefore if you do not see Horace or Gussie you had better take the route leading through Washington, Baltimore, Richmond, Weldon, Wilmington & Augusta and from there to Macon. The other route would bring you through Tennessee & Atlanta but I am not posted in regard to that route. Mr. Baird came through from New York to Macon in 60 hours. If you see Horace or Gussie take their advice and directions I will tell you here that should I fail to meet you on your arrival, you can give your checks to the "Brown House" porter, which you will know by the sign on his cap, and he will direct you to the House directly opposite the depot, and then get the clerk to send for Me at Burke's Printing Office. I shall be at the train if I know what day to expect you and the route you will take. I believe I have neglected to answer your question in regard to what you shall do in Albany. As they do not sell through tickets in New Haven for Utica you will buy it for Springield; there you get through tickets and checks and change cars in the same depot, arriving at Albany you will only have to get out of one train into another close by and do not be afraid to ask any one in regard to which train if there is more than one. Now I believe I have answered all your questions and given you such directions as I think of.

I do wish I could be with you in these trying times, but I think you will get along far better in your travels than you are wont to imagine,—you will need money to meet emergencies, therefore I think you will be compelled to receive three orders before you start on your Southern trip. I shall endeavor to mail the last order I send on Saturday instead of Monday that you may have as much time as possible to make your arrangements.

Now I will close and write a few lines to little Daisy and then go to church so good night Darling

Your affectionate husband
Sylvanus

P.S. If it should not be necessary to send you $50 in the last order, provided I send three more, you can let me know as I shall need a considerable to pay freight, but do not cramp yourself, for you must have at least $80 to start with, and if it is left when you get here we can use it to good advantage.

Sylvanus

The missing letter has not reached me yet and probably will not

DIARY

Plantsville[4] Aug. 28 1871: More than five years have passed since I wrote the above. Five years fraught with changes, hopes & fears, joys and sorrows, sickness and health, life and death. Our family circle numbers now just what it did when I last wrote. For a little more than two years we counted one more. Another life mingled with ours for a few brief months and then our Father transplanted the rose and precious flower to bloom and shed a richer fragrance in a more genial clime. O! the pang it cost our hearts to give up our only son—our darling boy none but those who have themselves tasted the bitter cup can tell. Such a loving and lovely child,—so affectionate, gentle, sweet tempered, and so bright, intelligent and beautiful too. Such a child as rarely graces the home circle. It is more than two years since he died but how sadly we still miss him our darling Herbie. Our little daughter Forrest Daisy, our second child is still spared to us. She is now seven years old—a bright, intelligent child, very active and fond of fun and frolic. I feel the great responsibility of training this child right, and my own inability not only to guide her aright but to live right before her; but I try to teach her from whence my own and her help must come. O! how anxious I feel and how earnestly do I try to pray that this little lamb may in early life become one of the good Shepherds flock. Our little son, Herbert Akehurst was born in New Haven. We had a pleasant home there, but both Sylvanus and I had to struggle with bad health and than our income was hardly sufficient for the out go, that kept us anxious and worried. Finally Sylvanus completely failed and he was obliged to return South. He soon regained his health and got along much better pecuniarily; Our prospects for a short time seemed much brighter. Then came sickness; both of our children were taken down with dysentery, that terrible foe to childrens life and health; Daisy recovered but our dear little Herbie died after only six days illness. Sylvanus took the dear remains to Atlanta and had them laid by the side of little Lillie. Daisy lay very sick at the time so that I could not leave her to see my little boy laid away, and I have never seen that little mound. We have lived in Macon since our return South. A few days after little Herbie died I was taken down with a disease which had long been preying upon me. I was confined to my bed many weeks, and have not been well since. Have been confined to my bed and room months at a time. I was confined to my bed all last winter and to the house until June. My physician recommended and urged my coming North to spend the Summer. So here I am with my little daughter. We have been visiting about among our friends and are now at Sylvanus' mothers. I expected him on this Fall but he has concluded he can not afford it this Fall. Our Friends are all very much disappointed in not seeing him and I am more than disappointed in not having his company and protection on our homeward journey. My health has not improved as much as we wished but I am much better than when I left home. We are in the country now and the air is delightfully cool and pure and the scenery rich and romantic. I think the country air and the rest and quiet I enjoy here has helped me much.

Tues. 29   Received a letter from Sylvanus last night. He is well. He has concluded to buy the journal office in company with Mr. Smith and Mr. Wing. I do most earnestly hope and pray that they may prosper in business. I have always been very anxious to have my husband in business for himself, but in my view of the case, he is not going in under very favorable auspices now. and then it cuts off the prospect of our having a home of our own very soon, and I had been flattering myself that we should before many months find ourselves under a roof of our

own. I have so long yearned for a home. I do not see how we can economize any closer than we have done; and I do not want to be obliged to:
we always *are* cramped, and always more or less in debt. I must confess
the conclusion of this business matter has given me a discouraged
weary feeling. I fear we shall not be as comfortable as we have been
either, and all those debts feel so heavy on my *back*. Perhaps he will
succeed and prosper—then I shall feel as if I do not deserve the prosperity for feeling so hopeless now. I will try to write him a cheerful letter, for he will have discouragement enough without my despondency.
If was strong and well I should feel more nerve and energy to battle
with toil, care, anxiety, privations, and even poverty itself would loose
some of its dread. I have had to battle with these things to a greater or
less degree all my life, and of late affliction and ill health have been
added. I sometimes feel as if I have lived a very great many years and
am bowed down with age and care and am longing for a quiet rest the
remainder of my pilgrimage; but here I am at lifes meridian when I
should be full of hope and vigor, and if I ever regain my health I shall
be for I am not naturally such a gloomy hopeless mortal. But it is true
that life to the most favored is a longer or shorter struggle; but what
does it matter if we at last gain the victory over all the sins the frailties
and the many cares of which as mortals we are the heirs; and find that
when we have crossed the last river we are also "heirs to that inheri-
tance which is incorruptable undefiled and that passeth not away"
Evening   I suppose this is the last night we shall spend at mother
Beechers. I have enjoyed the quiet and the freedom from city customs,
not having to dress see company &c: have not visited much for mother
never gets time when she is at home to sit down until night then she is
too tired and sleepy to talk. She is one of those who seem to think the
great end and aim of womans mission is to do all the hard work and
drudgery she can and she who can do the most in a day is the smartest
woman.

*   *   *

Frid. Sept 1   Have had a long ride to-day and enjoyed it much. Mr.
Beech took his wife Daisy and myself in his carriage to the light house:
I can not describe the beautiful scenery that captivated my sight; we
rode in sight of the waving billows for seven miles: we got out at the
Light House and sat on the rocks by the Sea a long time, or I did the
rest walked about. Jane and Mr. Beech were picking muscles and my
little Daisy was picking up little shells and pebles to carry to Georgia
she said. I am very tired and must retire.

*   *   *

Tues. 5   Did not sleep until three o'clock; do not feel able to sit up but must as I am away from home—have been to the drug store and bought a bottle of . . . elixir of opium a dose of it has some what relieved the pain in my back and limbs I feel a little more cheerful too   Mary went home   I doubt if we ever meet again. I regret that my last and parting recollections are not pleasant and kindly so that friendship may strengthen by separation. I am thankful that I have nothing to reproach myself for. I neither did nor said anything that I would now fain recall. O how thankful I am that it is not my lot to live near those who would continually criticise my every action and condemn what I regard virtues as gross faults. But perhaps this is the very fire through which I need to pass to put down my self love and teach me humility and to help me to do right for the sake of *right entirely* and not for the applause of poor fallen mortals like myself. I feel sometimes like shouting for joy when I remember that *God* is my judge and not man.—*He* knows my *inner* life—tis true he knows all my sins but He knows my sorrows too—He knows how I loathe this sinful nature how I long for holiness.

Thurs. 7   Down town again this morning. Received a letter from Sylvanus he is well has not got his new office to running yet. I am afraid we shall feel the need of monney before he gets to making much.

* * *

Friday 15   Cool and cloudy. I wish I was at home that I could be in bed and doctor my cold. I do not feel able to sit up. Received a letter from Sylvanus yesterday also monney order for $50. I went to the post office & drew the monney. There are many things I want to buy, some which I *need badly*, but I am afraid to spend any monney lest I do not have enough to travel in safety with. Sylvanus is so cramped now that he is just starting in business that I fear we shall have to economize in a manner which is uncomfortable and unpleasant. Hope to hear from the Kelseys to-day so that I can go to Clinton to-morrow—must write a letter to Sylvanus now.

Sab. 17   Well here we are at Hatties yet. Heard from Mr. Kelsey yesterday afternoon, but it was too late to make preparations to go last night and I postponed it until Monday night. The weather is charming again. My cold is better—feel some return of my old trouble this morning—did not rise until nine o'clock. O how I long to be at home and settle down in home ways especially on the Sabbath, so that I can observe it more in accordance with my own ideas of right. My little Daisy is needing quiet, home influence. She is so sprightly and intelligent that she receives a good deal of attention, perhaps more than is good for her. I have just finished a letter to Sylvanus, and now as I am tired of writing will read a while.

Mon. 18   Came to Clinton. Found all well and received a hearty welcome. They have a pleasant home and two beautiful children to brighten it. Seeing little Lena reminds me so much of my precious little Herbie.

Wed 20   Nothing of note to-day. It is very quiet here in the country. Have felt rather gloomy on account of not feeling well and then the weather is cold and cloudy. Daisy is not very well. I am in continual fear of her getting sick before we get home. It will not be long now before we turn our faces homeward, but I feel as if I can hardly wait.

Thurs 21   two letters to-day. One from my beloved, the other from Mrs. Gardner asking me to defer my return home and spend the second week in October there. As much as I would like to see her I can not think of remaining North any longer than this month. The days pass wearily now that the time for us to start on our homeward journey draws near. Sylvanus is well and thinks he is going to do well in his business. He tells me he thinks it is doubtful about our getting back our old cook. I fear I shall have some trouble with a new one—they are all so untruthful and dishonest. If I were only well and strong I would not ask much of them. Poor little Daisy suffered a good deal of pain in the night; she is looking pale but seems to feel quite well and happy. We all took a little walk this afternoon. The sun has shone brightly all day but still it is cold and dismal in the house I have hardly been warm to-day.

Frid. 22   Nothing of note to-day. Called with Mrs. Kelsey at her mothers: she is one of the largest women I ever saw; she says her last weight was 199. it is probably considerably more than 200 now. She has had 14 children all but one living to man and womanhood but one: she is now hale and hearty   She must have had a stronger back than I have.

Sat 23   Mr. Kelsey got a carriage this afternoon and we all took a pleasant ride. We rode down to waterside where his father lives he has a pleasant residence overlooking the water. The mistress of the house—

the wife and mother has recently died—the place must have a deserted desolate air to the family and friends. We had a long ride and my poor weak back feels it very much. I find I can not take long walks without suffering severely for it. My walk from Hatties to Janes on Monday is causing me a great deal of suffering this week. O! what would I give to be well & strong.

Mon. 25   Monday has come again, how the days and weeks fly past   If all goes well Daisy and I will soon be at home again and I shall once more take upon me the duties and cares of housekeeping. how light and pleasant they would seem if I was only armed with good health. I fear that is an armor I shall never find myself girt with again. I have tried to pray with ernestness and faith for good health, but thus far, for some reason, probably a wise one, God has denied me the priceless boon.

Wed 27   Felt better—bid adieu to the Kelseys and came to New Haven. Found a letter and money order from Sylvanus.

Thurs 28   Did not sleep until three o'clock this morning. Suffered agony from neuralgia in my head face and breast. This morning took a long ride with Jane in the horse cars,—this afternoon went up town made a few purchases, but did not buy near all I wanted for the want of funds. My back is very lame and weak—walking hurts me sorely. Received another letter from my husband this morning. He tells me Mrs. Fox will meet me in New York and assist me in getting started South. I must write him what time to look for me. My face is nearly free from pain and I must retire early hoping to get a good nights rest.

Frid 29   Wrote a letter to Mr. Fox the first thing this morning telling him to look for me Wednesday morning—shall take the Tuesday night boat. Have just written to Sylvanus. I do not know what route I shall take until I get to New York. I dread the journey and shall fell very thankful to get through in safety   My dear little daughter—my pleasant little companion in all my travels and visits is well and very happy in the prospect of soon seeing papa and home.

Sat 30   Mother Beecher came down this morning and returned home this evening. I felt sad at parting with her—in all probability we shall

never meet again; she is very old, and I am very feeble, which will receive the final summons first our Father alone knows. I received another letter from Sylvanus this morning; probably the last before I
start for home. This evenings mail brought a note from Mr. Fox, he
promises to meet me on Wednesday morning in New York.

Sab. Oct. 1   I am feeling worse than usual to-day; but I must bear all
my sufferings in silence, for any complaints would be treated with indifference and contempt rather than sympathy and kindness. I wish
Jane could feel for one half hour the pain which racks my poor back
and the trembling weakness which almost prostrates me. I only want
her to feel it long enough to satisfy her that *I suffer* and am not able to
do or endure what those in full health and strength can. It is hard
enough to suffer all the time and then to have no sympathy is rather
more than I can bear with womanly grace and dignity—it makes a
great crying baby of me. It is a beautiful day, clear and cool—quite too
cool for my comfort as there is no fire except in the kitchen range and
no warmth from that reaches my room. I feel chilled through all the
time my blood is so poor & thin. How little those in perfect health know
the wants of the weak and suffering. Neither Daisy nor I have been to
church. I think I shall go and spend an hour or two with ma Smith this
evening if I feel better.

Tues. Oct. 18   Home again after an absence of more than three months.
I left New Haven just two weeks ago to-night Oct 3 and arrived in
Macon Frid. 6. Nothing unusual occurred during our trip the journey
was as pleasant as dust and fatigue would allow. I met with Mrs. Michell, an Athens lady, in Washington I traveled with her six years ago,
and was happy to renew the acquaintance and have her company in
traveling again. She is an acquaintance of my dear old friend Jona-
than, alias Miss Atkisson. * * * My little Daisy enjoyed the trip with
all its discomforts; the thought of home and papa kept her buoyant and
happy. We found Sylvanus at the depot awaiting our arrival; he *looked*
very glad to see us and had a carriage waiting to take us to our new
home. It is a nice little cottage just large enough and none too large for
our little family. Sylvanus had engaged a cook; she met us at the gate
with a broad grin of welcome saying she was mighty glad we all had
come as she was lonesome staying by herself. I like her so far and hope
she will prove to be a faithful efficient and willing servant and I will
try to be a kind, patient and reasonable mistress. Sylvanus had had
our house white washed and cleaned and one room settled enough to be
comfortable over night. We have all been quite busy but are not en-

tirely settled yet as the house has to be newly painted besides many
little. repairs which Sylvanus is trying to make himself besides discharging all his office duties, which are heavy as they are crowded with
work. The prospects for success in his business are very promising at
present. I can not get over rejoicing that our little circle is once more
permitted to gather around our own table and fireside (though we have
not needed any fire yet)   For several days after my arrival, I was constantly saying to myself O I am so glad I have got a husband child and
home. Yes indeed I *am* glad—what would this world be without these
sweet home ties?

Wed. 19   Sylvanus has gone to the office this evening; little Daisy has
read herself sleepy and retired; she is so proud to have a room to herself
that she enjoys going to bed and getting up; she says it makes her feel
as if she was a young lady to have a room alone, concequently she tries
to act like one and wants to dress and undress herself, and tries to take
charge of her room; she is an active, busy little puss—this childish activity is, I think, the germ of mature energy and industry; I shall try to
encourage and cultivate the desire for "something to do" for I would not
have her a drone in this great human hive. I have just finished a letter
to mother Beecher and do not feel like writing any more as I am very
tired. Caroline has been ironing all day and as she is not well versed in
that domestic art, it has taken a good deal of talking showing and some
ironing on my part. She is a very good washer, and cook and seems willing to do as I direct, so I will try to be patient and bear with her short
comings hoping she will improve. The weather is cooler and I am feeling better. It is so pleasant to be at home again—to have "a place
for every thing and every thing in its place." I like having the whole
house to ourselves too; it is a long time since we have enjoyed that
satisfaction. * * *

Thurs. 20   House cleaning day. Our rooms were all swept & dusted,
windows, oil cloths and lamps washed by nine o'clock. I like Caroline so
far, better than any servant I have ever had, but still she needs a great
deal of watching and directing to do work as I want it done. I think
when we get entirely settled and she becomes accustomed to doing
work *my way* (which is very different from what she has been used to)
she will be able to go through the regular routine of duties without
quite so much vigilance on my part. I always systematize my household arrangements so that a servant knows what work is to be done
each day. I have been painting window and door casings to-day. Mr.

Bronson, our landlord, agreed to furnish paint if we would have it put on; Sylvanus thought he would save the expense of hireing, by painting himself, but he is so hurried in the office he only has time to eat and sleep at home, hardly that this week as he works every night until ten o'clock. I do not have any calls yet—I thought I had a good many friends in Macon but perhaps I am mistaken, but then I am in a new neighborhood now and I suppose ladies are waiting for me to get rested and settled. I do not get lonely, for I always have enough to occupy both hands and brain   I could not well be lonely with my little Daisy in the house for she is a "chatter box and busy body too" as sweet Lillie used to say of herself. Daisy has resumed her studies which occupies some of her time and mine too. Have written a whole page now will retire.

Sat. 22   After all was quiet last night I got my journal pen and ink & seated myself for a little talk with you my book, when behold a very important article in an old lady's work basket was missing—my spectacles; yes dear journal *my* spectacles! were thy pages animate I should expect a fluttering of astonishment, for when I commenced writing this book my eyes were still bright with youth, and there were no silver gleamings amid my auburn locks; true the years that have passed have not been so many that I can justly censure the cold touch of time for all these premonitory symptoms of lifes decline—the scathing fires in the furnace of affliction and the wasting hand of ill health have done their part. I find many who have numbered more years than I whose vision is yet unclouded and whose step has still the buoyancy of health, and the elasticity of youth. I received a letter from a friend of my girlhood last night—one who has not written to me for many years; she writes as if time was telling tales on her too. She is not married, and I think the venerable father should hold his withering breath when passing her. She writes like Miss Atkisson of Covington days I trust she is the same warm hearted whole souled friend; I only wish I could be favored with her congenial companionship. I must & will write *soon*. A serious accident occurred in Sylvanus office last night. Mr. Wing, one of the Proprietors, had his hand mashed in a press so badly as to necessitate the amputation of the three fingers. Mr. Wing is young—just married, and just starting in business—this is a great misfortune to him.

Sab 23. Very warm again. We did not rise very early this morning, and then did not feel like going to church. Sylvanus slept all the morning and has now gone to see Mr. Wing. Daisy has just returned from Sabbath school, and is allready absorbed in the contents of her sabbath school book. I feel too dull to write and might as well lay aside my book and go out on the porch where I can get a breath of cool air if it is too be had.

Mon 24   Oppressively warm to-day. A thunder shower is coming up. Caroline has hung our clothes out to day, but I fear she will have to take them all down wet; she has worked very moderately to-day or they would all be dry before now. I think she has done her work well that is some satisfaction, but I do like to have clothes dryed the same day they are washed, and with our small family it is an easy matter if the washer would only take interest enough to make an effort to get them out in season. It is very comfortable and pleasant to have a home and home comforts but to keep house thoroughly and have every thing done in a propper manner and in propper time requires a great deal of energy patience and vigilance. Ladies at the North think Southern ladies have nothing to do because they keep servants to do their work, but if we perform less labor we have more care and anxiety, so our lot is not so much easier after all. * * *

Wed. 26   Clothes all ironed, aired mended and laid away in their respective places. Caroline has done very well to-day. I dampened the clothes and starched the shirts and collars, and saw that every piece was just right to iron nicely. Sylvanus remained at home last eve— hung the pictures in the parlor and mended some broken places in the plastering: we are not settled yet so the poor man does not get much rest when he is at home. We always find so many little improvements and repairs to make every time we change our residence that it is some time before we can feel at home. I have *dreamed* of a neat little home of which my liege lord (*hope* I shall succeed in finishing this sentence have jumped up three times since I commenced writing it; once to give a suitable reception to Captain, Daisy's dog, which she has just brought home, and again to drive a cow out of the front yard, and then to find my spectacles) was master and landlord and my humble little self the mistress and our little ones the sunshine thereof. Lo these many years it has been a cherished petted dream and I begin to fear a dream that will not be realized, but, good book, you need not repeat that fear to my better & hopeful half.

*   *   *

Frid. 28   Little Daisy went to the fair to-day with Miss Julia Stubbs. She came home about five o'clock looking pale and tired but delighted with all she had seen, and very anxious mama should go and see the beautiful things; mama is not very anxious as she does not enjoy crowds and excitement as her little daughter does. Perhaps I may go and ride around the grounds some day next week if Sylvanus can go with me. Am suffering a great deal from my old trouble can not stand or walk without great pain.

Sat 29   Do not feel able to sit up, yet I *have* been on my feet a good deal, and have had to run to the kitchen several times; Caroline either can not or will not manage the stove so that oven will bake. I have showed her and told her so much too. I lost my patience with her to-day perhaps that will improve her will or memory which ever is at fault. O how hard it is to always "let patience have its perfect work" Miss Stubbs & Miss Lunday called on me this afternoon enjoyed the call very much.

Nov 1st   Have not written in my journal for several days and do not feel much like it now. Am feeling very much annoyed with my cook; she has been slow and careless about the work for several days, not best by any means, and to-day she adds sullenness to her list of misdemeanors. I think I shall discharge her to-night although I do not yet know where I shall get another, and am not able to be without one. The weather is still very warm and I am feeling its debilitating effects.

Thurs 3. Last evening Mrs. Stubbs Mrs. Flurnoy & Miss Julia Stubbs called on me. I told them how I was troubled with Caroline. Mrs. Stubbs says aunt [?] will take us to board and she will give me her room if we want to come. the way I feel now it would not take much to per-suade me to break up and board but I do not think Sylvanus would con-sent—men little know what housekeepers have to contend with they either have to become kitchen drudges themselves or be annoyed with filthy, indolent impertinent servants; all the negroes possess these qualities, and the Irish servants at the North are not much better. I discharged Caroline last night as I intended and now all the burden of the work as well as care rest on me; but my little Daisy's nimble feet and willing hands save me many a step and many a light task such as her little strength can perform. My Dr. called to see me this morning; he did not stay long and I did not trouble him with a rehearsal of my many ailings. I am very unhappy to-day. Am hard at work too, making a carpet—new work for me.

PART SIX

DENOUEMENT

1871-1886

SYLVANUS TO JENNIE AND DAISY

Indian Springs[1] Aug 5th 1874

Dear Jennie and Daisy

Here I am safe and sound and if you will excuse my pencil I will give you a few lines. Leaving Macon nothing occurred of interest till I reached Forsyth where I found the stage waiting to carry us to our destination; I say us as we had a goodly number of passengers to wit: Col. Tom Hardeman, two ladies and three men besides myself. After starting I commenced getting hungry & had recourse to the basket which I found opened to a charm only that like Alexander, the Great, who wept when he had no more worlds to conquer, I sighed when I had no more of "Grey-loss" bones to pick; yet it answered very well. Arrived at 3 o'clock, dusty and hungry; took a bath and then dinner, which was in good style & I think I done justice to it for me. Did not go about much yesterday for I was too much fatigued. Being on a strange bed did not sleep first rate but yet I rested very well. To-day I have strolled about some and felt tolerable well and had a good appetite, and I cannot but think this trip will do me good. I did not find this place at all as I had pictured it, still it is pleasant, romantic and delightful, with running water in every direction and cool breezes. We have no use for nets as musquitoes are unknown here. My room is not very inviting but then as I am by myself I can get along very well. If you were here perhaps I should fare better in this respect as the ladies have better apartments, but then I shan't grumble; the proprietors are perfect gentlemen and the servants polite and attentive. I am sorry you are not with me as I cannot enjoy these things without you and then I know it would do you both good. There are a great many Maconites here, but most of them stop at the other house, yet I see them every day. I have met commenced on the Cod Liver Oil, for I do not want to spoil my appetite and keep nauseated, therefore I am taking the other medicine and I think it will do me the most good. at least while I remain here.

Now, my precious Dears, how do you get along?—lonely? well cheer up, and I shall soon be with you; and if I dont weigh twenty pounds more than I did when I left I will come as near as I can to it. Cannot tell you now when I shall come home but will write you again on Friday or Saturday. Hope to get a letter from you both soon.

I will enclose this with one to Mr. Wing as you will get it sooner than any other ways, as he will send it directly on receipt.

Now good-by for this time with love and kisses for both Mama and Darling

Sylvanus

Direct your letter thus
  S De F Lines
  Care of Elder & Son
  Indian Springs
  Ga

SYLVANUS TO JENNIE

Indian Springs
Saturday, Aug 8th, 1874

Dear Jennie

I have just received your letter and feel very much troubled about you. Sorry that I left you or rather that I did not bring you both with me. I was afraid you would overdo yourself. Hope, however, you are better before this, if I did not think so, should come home to-morrow. I had intended to come on Tuesday, but shall come sooner if necessary, which will be determined when I receive Daisy's letter, if it should reach me to-morrow. I do not now know whether we get a mail on Sunday or not. Do not worry yourself about me, for I am doing first rate—feel much better notwithstanding what people tell you. I know that the Spring water is not good for me and therefore I let it alone, but the air is delightful and bracing. I have taken some cold since I came, but that is better now and I can generally devour full rations; but how can I eat if you are so sick and need me there, yet as I cannot get to you I will try to think you are better. I hope you will get a cook before I get home, but if you do not, pray, dearest, do not do too much yourself but let it go undone. I think the Misses McIntosh were very unkind and I do not think I shall soon forget it,—"A friend in need is a friend indeed"!—but away with such friendship as theirs; I have had too much of it in my day.

But I won't write more this time as I am not certain that you will receive it as I am obliged to send this by private conveyance to Forsyth to be mailed on the train. If I do not come before, tell Lewis to be sure to meet me at the Depot on Tuesday night a 10 minutes past 7; as I think that is the time the train is due. If I should fail to come, don't be alarmed as I may get left here, for the stage leaves here a 6 o'clock in the morning and I might oversleep myself.

Hope I shall get that dear letter from Daisy to-morrow, for I am so anxious to hear from you.

Much love & many kisses for you both.

Good-bye Darlings
Sylvanus

DAISY TO JENNIE

Mobile Ala.[2] Jan. 11th 1882

My Dearest Darling

Your *precious* letter came Monday morning together with the Christmas cards. They are *perfectly lovely* and have been very much admired. I had not the slightest idea who the picture was until I read the letter. Aunt Jane does not look at all as I thought she did; much younger. She is *real nice looking* isn't she? It was so kind in them to remember us. I am so anxious to see your handkerchiefs. My gloves are beautiful and she couldn't have selected *anything* which would have been more acceptable; for really my brown are getting so shabby, they will not do to wear to church many more Sundays. And I was wondering how I would get some more. It rained last Sunday so we could not go to church. I wish you could have eaten dinner with us. We had a *splendid dinner*.

Roast beef, oyster pie, baked sweet potatoes, mashed Irish potatoes, turnips, lettuce; bread, butter, rice, maccaroni, split peas, stewed tomatoes, and pickles, sweet, sour and chow-chow. For desert, mince pie, cake and gelatin with milk on it. Eddie has taught me to open oysters, and he and I opened all of them for the pie. I hope you don't starve your poor little self. I want you to half live on *cheese*, unless you have got over wanting it. And *don't* stay at home & get lonely & gloomy; but go out a great deal. The paper has just arrived. Am *so much obliged*. I appreciate reading it more now that I am away than when at home. Whenever you get hold of one and have a spare stamp please send it to me; I like to know what is going on there. So *Georgia* and "*Chick*" received! And *Sallie* was *left out*! What does that mean? Wasn't Sallie offended? I wonder if Georgia would have asked me to receive with her, if I had been there. Do you know whether they had many callers?

Last Thursday night there were three young ladies and four young gentlemen here. Misses Carrie & Fannie Bligh, their cousin Miss Grace Myers, and Mr. Jim Bligh, Mr. Denny, Mr. McNeal, and Mr. Denver, a young gentleman from Canada. The latter quite took possession of my heart. We are to go to Mrs. Blighs next Friday night; the same crowd will be there, with perhaps one or two additions. Mr. McNeal is going to bring his banjo, so I guess we will have a gay time. Last Friday night we went to one of the neighbors to spend the evening.—Mrs. Robertson's. There are two young ladies in the family—Misses Lola and Annie, and a young gentleman Mr. Willie. The oldest daughter was married about two weeks ago. We had a *very* pleasant evening. Miss Lola plays beautifully. They passed round cake and wine. Last night a young gentleman called to see us, and staid until 11 oclock. Mr. Dowe; he was very pleasant company. Your letter will have to wait until I get a stamp or some money from you. I owe Fannie two, now: I should not have borrowed them, but I had to pay 3 cents on the package containing the gloves. And she *insisted* that I should take one to mail my letter to Mr. Waite, which was already written. It was mailed yesterday. I did not write but four pages. Auntie has commenced a letter to you in poetry. She says she will finish it when the "spirit moves" again. What are you reading now? I have read The Planter's Northern bride by Mrs. Hentz,[3] Leslie Goldthwaite by Mrs. Whitney since I have been here, and am now reading Lena Rivers. I am *so sorry* Minnie Paton has moved away; hope you will get the money; but *don't* worry your little self sick over it. I would not count on Paul at all, for I don't believe they mean to send him at all; what is the reason *now*? Give Sallie my love and tell her *please* send me one of those pictures she promised me; try to get her to send it; I would like it so much. A propos of pictures I wish I could have mine taken while I am here. They do them *beautifully*, and for just *half* what they charge in Macon. Cabinet size which there are from *$12* to *$16* per dozen, you can have taken here for $6 per doz. Cards are only $3. and in Macon they are $6.

Sunday 15th 1882

I was in hopes that I would get a letter from you yesterday, but it failed to arrive. I fear this will be rather stale before it reaches you. It rained Friday night so that we could not go to Mrs. Bligh's; I was quite disappointed; we shall go some time next week. Fannie and I went to church this morning. A Mr. Mitchell preached a splendid sermon. Mr. McNeal will probably be around tonight; he comes regularly every other Sunday night. Macbeth is to be playing here Tuesday night. I wish I could be so fortunate as to secure a beau to take me. Oranges are 20 cts. a dozen here now, and bananas *10 cts*. A boat has just come up loaded with oranges & bananas. When I come home I want to get a bunch and bring with me; I could get a *large* bunch for 30 cts; wish I could send them but it would cost so much, and then they might spoil before they reached Macon. Mama if we could get positions in the public school here would you not be willing to live here? We could get $60 per month each of us; and on that we could live and save up enough to leave the place in summer, the only time when it is unhealthy, & then not unless the yellow fever happens to get here, which they say is not often. The superintendent of the Public School is also superintendent of the Presbyterian Sunday School; Auntie and Mr. Barham know him well; and auntie says that she thinks we would have no trouble in getting positions here as they are changing teachers constantly; to think of making *$120* a month. The regular tuition in private schools here and in Montgomery is 4 dollars per month; never less. My gloves are rather large for me, I am so sorry; they are such fine kid; that they are very elastic; I shall make them do; but they are so pretty, I am sorry they do not fit me better. How do your black ones do? Have you been to church since I left? It has been raining nearly every day the past week, and is clouding up again. * * * Oh, I *hope* not, and does it look just the same. If it were not for that, I should be very well contented but that worries me so I can not enjoy anything.

Now *my darling mama*, I shall mail this as soon as I get hold of a stamp. *Oh so much love* to you, and so *many* kisses, and *such* a *squeeze.* Are my letters too long?

Give my love to all your pupils. Think I shall write them a letter soon.

Your loving
Daisy

DAISY TO JENNIE

Irwinton Ga.⁴ Feb 6th 1882

Darling Mama,

Though late I will fulfill my promise to write you, though I've but little to write about. Found Tom waiting for me at the station. We could not bring the trunk with us so I paid a dime yesterday to have it brought up. I forgot the scissors after all; Mary has been making us a pin cushion tonight, it looks real pretty. Sunday evening M. and I went to ride; had a delightful drive through the "piney-woods." Just as we reached the hilltop the sun was setting over the dark woods that bounded the horizon, the fragrant breath of the pines borne on the evening breeze, the twitter of the birds in the trees, and the stillness over all, was sufficient to inspire a poetess had I only been one. We went to church Sunday night, had a real, ranting Methodist sermon. Last night Mr. C. came round and brought with him Colonel Ocklington, one of the Irwinton Lawyers an old bachelor of about 50. Received an invitation today to a "Grand Soiree" to be given in Toombsboro on Friday night. All the Irwinton boys and girls are going in a large wagon and I guess will have a gay time. I do not know yet whether we will go or not; I should be crazy to go if I could dance, but as I can't I shall not enjoy it much. Don't you think being out of Irwinton I could dance? "I'ants to." All have retired but myself so goodnight my darling little mother.

Wednesday. After a hard mornings work and a good dinner, consisting of boiled ham, turnip greens, sweet potatoes, biscuit, coffee and potato custard, I have a half hour to myself. Mr. Chapman has said nothing to me about the money, but I suppose he will before the week is past. You shall have it as soon as I get it. I am almost out of soap, if can not get Castile here, I will send you money to get me some there if you will, please. Mrs. F. asked me if you said anything about coming down to see me; you *must* come soon. One of the young gentlemen said he wanted to drive me up from the station, but had to go away. Wasn't it a pity. I haven't written that note to Mr. Fitzgerald yet, do you think its worthwhile. Couldn't you fix it up and send it? I am afraid Mrs. Russell will ask me about it.

They have all fallen in love with my blue dress; have not had my black one on yet.

Well I guess "Romeo" is not going to write again; I was certain I would get one today.

The school-bell is ringing so must run. Write soon and a long letter, my darling.

Lovingly,
Daisy

DAISY TO JENNIE

Irwinton, Ga. Feb 10th [1882]

Darling Mama,

How I wish I was where I was *last* Saturday night in my *dear* home, with *you*, my *precious*. I don't believe I shall *ever* get over being home sick here. I wish the term was over; how *can* I stay here *five long months*. And I *know* I can never please them; Mr. Chapman came round yesterday and paid me ten dollars ($10.00). I will send you a money order for that, if I can get money orders here, if not will send a registered letter. Am sorry it is not more. He said (with *apologies*, but *still said* it) that one of the gentlemen had told him, his little girl had

had the same lesson for a *week*. He was mistaken and I told him so. He advised me to never give them the *same* lesson *twice*; but whether they know it or not, *push* them on. The people here are like the old negro, think you can "take a hickory and make them spell *clean* through the book," and Mr. C. humors them in their belief. They use these miserable "Blue-back" Spelling books with words that no one ever heard of before in them and the children *can not* say perfect lessons, and then if they don't I must call them out and "*half-kill* them" to use Mr. C's words. I can't teach them the way *they* want me too, and make them *learn* anything. However there are *some* who are pleased and say their children are doing better than ever before, and that encourages me. It seems quite lonely here tonight. Mamie F. and Lula Balkcom went to Griswoldville[5] Friday night, and Minnie Carswell is spending the night next door. I shall have my bed to myself tonight which I shall enjoy. Got about five minutes to myself today to take a *bath*, in the bowl. But just as I got half through the girls came to the door; I kept them waiting though. They took their Saturday *wash* to night of *neck* and *feet* and then "*padded*" round barefoot on the dirty floor. *How can* people be *so nasty*. We did not go to the [?] last night, as we heard it was to be a public affair, to which *everybody* was invited. Many thanks for forwarding the papers and postal. They were descriptions of the Mardi-Gras, from Johnnie and Fannie; soon as I get a two cent stamp I will send you one of them. *Why don't* you write to Auntie? *please* do. Wish you could be to breakfast with us tomorrow. Mr. F. and Ruf. went hunting today and killed thirteen partridges. Our bill of fare does not often vary from biscuit, ham, rice and coffee. With the addition of greens and peas for dinner, but I enjoy the eating for it is *splendidly cooked*, and I have an excellent appetite. Today we had only boiled pork, *lye hominy* and biscuit for dinner with potatoe custard for desert. Mrs. F. makes delicious potato custards. The girls in the next room are chattering and laughing so I can scarcely write, so excuse mistakes. I wish my room had a *door* that could be shut. I *wish* you could have seen me *fall* the other night; we had a hearty laugh over it. Minnie and I were dancing the Racquet, which, by the way I can dance real nicely now—when my feet slipped from under me and *down* I went as flat as could be. I've been rather *lame* since, you may imagine. I cannot get any white Castile soap in town, so I will send 10 cents and please get me some; that will leave me just $1.15 for washing; *don't* know what I'll do about the other ten, but I must have some soap; I wanted to get something and make me an apron, but can't now. Put the lace in my black dress today. It looks *beautifully*. I have a *splendid* washer, I suppose you have Rose. My dearest, I will bid you goodnight and add more on Monday. o o o

The above are good night kisses. Am sorry you cannot arrange it to come sooner. Wanted you to spend Sunday Feb, 25th with me, as they are to have a "big meeting at the church."

Monday 12th. On coming home to day, was greeted by your precious letter, my darling. Haveing just finished a good dinner of boiled beef, turnip greens, cornbread, biscuit, butter, coffee, and pie, will finish my letter to you. On reading over what I wrote Saturday night, I find it is such a blue letter, it ought to be torn up, but haven't time to write another now, so will send it. I find I can not get a money order here, so will send a registered letter; will have to do without the soap as I cannot send silver money in a letter, and besides will have to pay cts. 13 on the letter; Had three new pupils today, every minute of my time is occupied, but don't fear I shall work too hard. Am so sorry, darling that I have but $10 to send you; you shall have every cent as fast as I get it. Before very long I shall ask Mr. C. for "*more*." I am devoured by curiosity concerning the young gentleman on whom I made a "smash" (to use your expression). I *can't* guess, be sure and tell me, who he is and where he saw me. Let Miss C. know the next time I am coming home and she might contrive an introduction then. Thank her for me for finding out about Willie Mason. Am *so* sorry to hear of Mrs. Pratt's misfortune. Thanks for the cards, they will do for the present. I wish you could send me my sunbonnet; I need it; if you should, send it without the pasteboards. If you could fix up a note or go and see Mrs. F. I should be very much obliged. I believe I told you what the old lady said. Wish I could write more but it is almost time for the bell to ring. Always write so your letter will reach me.

Lovingly,
Daisy

DAISY TO JENNIE

Irwinton, Ga. Feb 26th 1883

My sweet Mother

The mail to day brought quite a budget for me, your letter, containing Aunt Mary's and a *long*, interesting one from Fannie. Am so sorry, darling, that you are without wood, but Hope that you succeeded in getting some today. Saturday was a miserable day here; cold and *pouring* rain all day. Yesterday how ever it partially cleared off, and we all went to church. Dr. Key of Macon preached a splendid sermon. Dinner consisted of chicken-pie, sweet potatoes, rice, biscuit, coffee, fried ham and cake for desert. Soon after dinner the boys began to drop in, as usual; there were eight here in the afternoon; and last night we all had a beau apiece to church. My medical friend was not here, but the boys told me he had been "writing poetry" about me all week. By the way an invitation has been extended to me to visit his mother, in her country home this summer; she is to have a crowd of young people staying with her; among them some of my old classmates from Forsyth.

But in spite of the company and all, I 'ants to see *you*, my darling little mother. *When will* you come? You must have your [?] to fit you, and bring that with you; can't you get fur *anywhere*; I want you to have it for the other day I said something about your having a cloth jacket trimmed with fur, and they'll think I've told a fib about it. They are all prepared to fall in love with you, and I know they will. Let me know when you are coming, and I will ask Mr. Chapman for some money, and send you. For since I'm so rich, I don't want you to pay your fare down here. Am sorry I have not the dollar to send you. The girl to whom I sold the book cannot bring me the money until Friday, but I will certainly get it. They sold it for 65¢.—Fannie said she saw Mr. Reneau during Mardi Gras; that he enquired after me and sent his kindest regards. Isn't he sly, not to tell her he was corresponding with me? Am so sorry to hear of Ruthie's affliction; do write to Aunt Mary right away, and I will do the same; I think her address is 88 Chandler St. but am not certain. Find her last letter, to make sure, & let me know. Am glad Tillie liked my letter; wish she would answer it. Leila has never replied to my letter. Don't be discouraged about your school, precious, the Measles and Whooping-cough can't last *forever*. My children have been very troublesome to-day; I have a class in Addition of Fractions in the Intermediate Arithmetic that give me more trouble than all the rest put together. I *can not* make them understand it; and I don't know how to explain it to them so that they will; the thought of the examination worrys me, for I don't believe they will ever learn it well enough to work examples before a crowd, as they will be expected to do. Ten oclock has just struck, and as the rest of the girls have retired, I suppose I must, for fear the light will trouble them, or rather Mary; I wish I had a room to myself; that is the greatest objection I have to my surroundings. Deliver me from ever rooming with school-girls again; they are so *dirty* and *careless*. Everything that I do not lock up becomes common property. Toothpowder, soap, wash-cloth, but as papa said, I can get along until they begin to use my *tooth-brush* and then I'm going to say something. But mind I'm not complaining; they don't mean anything by it. Its only their way of being sociable. Goodnight my precious.

Tuesday. Dinner just over, bill of fare boiled ham, sweet potatoes, peas, cornbread, biscuit, coffee & custard pie. I enclose 30¢. Will you kindly get me two Sterling Copy-books, the number containing all

Capitals. I think it is 4. I suppose you can make 10¢ on the two, keep that for your discount.

* * *

Love to all, and plenty for your dear, sweet, self.

From Your Flower.

JENNIE TO DAISY

Macon Sept. 1883

My Own Treasure

How I want to see you this day my own heart alone knows. I was so glad to get your letter—had imagined innumerable ills that might have befallen my darling; but thank God not one of them had. I dislike to write Daisy, for have not yet got any new pens. I am so glad you are enjoying your visit, but is it not time to think of drawing it to a close? dont wear out your welcome. There is nothing to hasten your return except the fear of doing that. Although I am anxious to see you yet I shall be glad to get a start before your return. You said nothing about *money*; you must let me know in time if you need it to come home with; have not a cent now—have only taught three weeks you know, will send you three stamps—we can soon use two cent stamps. I saw, and answered an advertisement for a teacher, wanted in Eastman Ga. all that I heard of the place and people seemed favorable and I really thought you might secure the position, but more than a week has passed and box 4E has not responded, so I suppose *that* is not the place. I sent your present address, so if you hear from them you will know what it means.

Let me suggest that you make the present trip one of business as well as pleasure by being on the look-out for positions to *teach* not *settle*. O my darling if I could only make sufficient how gladly would I keep you with me, it would be selfish I know, for you are not happy at home—indeed you have very little to make you content, save a mother's love, that love craves your dear presence, and is, I think, pardonable in its selfishness, for you are all that is left me, and I wish we need not be separated while I live. Mrs. Brown has moved it looks lonely over there. Tillie has had a hitching post put in front of her home, for the convenience of her "country fellows" I suppose. Walter Stubbs has gone back to Florida. Georgia Lundy is married and gone on her bridal tour. Mrs. Stubbs is in very poor health, as I cant mail this to-day I think I will go up and see her. Lu has run away, so the [?] of your hat is spoiled in that quarter. Adieu for this time.

Tuesday night. Mrs. Clisby came to see me this evening. She tells me

Mr. C. wrote not only to Dr. Cook but also the minister in Millegeville, and has never heard a word from either. I think from what she said he wrote *very complimentary* of you. Am glad to tell you dear, that my school has increased to twelve in number, shall be glad when I can begin to collect, the sight of money will do me good. By the way I have a little girl from Florida Hattie Harris. Stay just as long as you can feel happy yourself and make others so. As I said before tell me what money you need and in time to raise it. Have had quite a severe attack of cholera-morbus—fortunately it attacked me on Sunday—, by Tues. was able to go to school, and now feel all the better for the cleansing. Tillie sends love also Lillie.

Now my precious one good night, write soon to mama.

JENNIE TO DAISY

Macon Ga. Wednesday 27, 1884

Well Dearest

I will write to-day as you wish although I have nothing of much interest to tell you. You have doubtless received Tillie's letter before this. I expect Lillie feels neglected as I have not been to see her and she sick too, but I can-*not* go out, that is when I have to dress, until the weather is a little more bearable. Have not got your things yet but will get them on Saturday if not before so you will get the package in Tuesday's mail. I saw Caroline to-day—she says Lillie is better. I am lonely indeed to-night. Mrs. G. and baby have gone after [?]—will be absent two nights. Mrs. A. suggested my staying over there if I felt afraid—I am not at all afraid, but dislike the idea of being alone in the house at night with Mr. G. or any other man, but as Mrs. A. says he would protect me in cas[e] of any alarm instead of being the one to cause fear, she did not urge my coming so I shall stay at home.

We were speaking about you and this old house last evening. Mrs. A. proposed your going to stay with them if Mr. Reneau comes. I think they love my little one sincerely; dear Miss Eliza say "O how I do miss Daisy." Mrs. A. told Mrs. G. that if you should lose me she would gladly give you a home, but she is older than I am and her general health is not as good but she must have more strength by the way she carries water for her flowers.

Mr. Beggs is going to live in Mrs. Ann Freeman's house. I went up to the drug store this evening.

Mr. Stallins was *extremely* pleasant. I had no money as usual—and asked him if he would trust me he said "*Why certainly*" with *such* a smile as made even my old heart palpitate. I wish you could have met him and believe you would eventually have done so. Mrs. Carrie is improving but suffers terribly from rheumatism she seemed *so pleased* that you remembered her & sent love with all the rest of our neighbors. Remember me to Mr. & Mrs. Lanier (if you think best) and tell after what you have written I feel quite content and happy about you while with them. Met Lizzie Demming—she has been at home three weeks—returns to her field of labor on Sat.; says she can only hope you will be as well pleased as she is with her home. I can-not feel satisfied to have you debarred from all society—have you met no young people? received no calls? And not [sic] my precious one let me caution you *never* take walks *alone never*, even to & from your school-room. Never stay in the house or school-house alone—no matter how much you may want to be alone; promise me darling that you will not go before the children or remain after them.

Now me thinks I hear you say what is all this & caution about. Did you hear of the negro man being hung in [Dawson?] last Monday? He committed a rape on a young married woman—took advantage of her being alone in the house—got her to go into the pantry on some made up errand then shut the door and had his satanic will. I have been frightfully nervous about you since I heard of it. I hear, Mrs. A. & Miss E., have just come in so I will stop. I must tell you first that I am not suffering as much with my arm, it seems less numb my medicine is out but expect every [day] more will be sent.

Good night love
Mama

JENNIE TO DAISY

Sunday Aug. 31, 1884

My Dearest Child

Your eagerly expected letter did not come on Friday nor Sat. and I am feeling worried; but I will write all the same so you may not feel troubled at the non-arrival of mine. I will not write a long letter however as I wish to inclose a part of aunties received yesterday. Dined at Mrs. Audoins yesterday: went downtown in the morning & invested your dollar. Bought a nice little hoop could not get the one you mentioned, think however you will like this. I do and am going to get me one like it as soon as possible. got ¾ yard of mull; Mrs. Anzeworth said that would be enough to line & trim and she thought it pretty & suitable. I searched Macon for a belt & this is the best I could do—cost 50 cts could get a narrow white one for 25 cts but did not think best—hope you will like it, I had to have it made smaller as you will see.

Will send the string as soon as I get some money which I hope will be so you can get them on Friday. Have paid Mrs. G. the $2.50 I owed her when you left, also $1.50 to drug store $1, for milk and $2.25 for three weeks washing to Ida besides living and paying for my medicine every week: but to morrow is the 1st and I have not one cent for rent. If the children I have now continue two weeks longer I shall have nearly enough, so I am not going to worry much. Mrs. G. knows I do the best I can so she must & will wait. I am feeling pretty well & cheerful or should if I could know my darling is well & happy but let me hope so until I hear. Mrs. Audoin is going up the country to-morrow for a weeks absence. Tillie offered to stay with Miss Eliza. This is not a long letter my own love but if I continued writing all night I could not finish.

Love from all,
Mama

JENNIE TO DAISY

Macon Ga. Sunday September 14, 1884

My Own Darling,

How I want to see you this day! I did not go to church to-day—have not been feeling quite as well as usual the past week—rather dull and feverish—the cause *constipation* I think; and so concluded to take a couple of pills last night—shall be all right now. Your letter came on Fri. and your money Sat. gave $3. of it to Mrs. G. tomorrow shall collect three more then the rent for Aug. will be paid. I went right up to Mrs. Stubbs and paid her—she seemed much surprised to get it so soon, sends much love to you. Lillie is well—have not seen her. My precious, genorous, thoughtful loving darling to send mama all your hard earnings. If there were any other way it *should not* go for rent or debt; but if I *do* get pupils and do even as well as I did last year you shall have it back. Shall I not get you one of those indigo blue calicoes—like Georgia Browns you know? Tillie has one ready to make up. I should have sent you ten yards before now but have had no means to get it, you will need it for fall. I have not cloth for my gowns yet, but have used up all the scraps of cloth and have two yokes ready—one of straight ricrac and one of wheel ricrac. Mrs. Audoin wants me to make her one with wheel ricrac. Shall do so with pleasure as soon as can get materials.

I hunted up Maria and "*scared*" her into bringing me one dollar. put ten cents with it and got my gray goods and gray hose—both had been put back in stock but fortunately not sold. Maria still owes me and I went to her house again yesterday and left a threatening message; if that money comes shall take it for cloth for gowns—shall soon need them. My shoes are out at both sides.

How I do need money. I want to be sending you things from time to time. I think I shall have to write you journal letters for I forget so much that I want to say. Be *sure* you let Mr. Hughey know you want a more lucrative position and *not* in the country. You are good girl to try and content yourself, but I am not to have your sweetness and brightness wasted on loneliness and solitude. It does not seem right for youth to lead so secluded a life—how are you to have an opportunity to settle in life. Daisy darling I fear Mr. R. is *not* the one to make your life happy. One so changable could never amass enough to make you the home you are fitted for. You could never be happy my precious, to be so situated that you would be out of the pale of good society.

But I must not murmur while your health is good. I try to take care of myself for your dear sake and I beg that you will be very careful not to expose yourself to the night air—do not let it blow on you when asleep. I think and dream of my treasure night & day.

There is much more I would like to write, but it is getting dark and must mail it. Mrs. A. has company from Warrenton. Tillie does not visit me at all. Her mother and self dropt in a few moments twice.

Daisy did'nt you visit Mrs. T. when Tillie was in the country? She Mrs. T. denies it *emphatically*.

Lovingly
Mama

DAISY TO JENNIE

Altamaha Ga.[6] Nov. 27th 1884

Sweetest Mother,

No letter from you on Teusday [sic] received one from Mrs. Audoin though and she said you were well. I suppose you wrote and it is somewhere on the road. Well I went to the party Teusday night, and had a "splendiferous" time. Did not get home until five oclock Wednesday morning. Danced until *half-past four*! Miss Missouri Phillips and I went with Mr. Swain. The drive was about five miles. We danced until twelve oclock, and were then invited out to supper. The table was loaded with everything nice. Turkey, chicken, ham, breads, pickles, pies, cakes of various kinds, candies, raisins, and coffee. The cakes were beautifully frosted. After supper dancing was resumed, and no one seemed to tire, but the musicians finally gave out. I danced fifteen sets and *how* I *did* enjoy it. It was styled a Cleveland party in honor of the success of the Democratic nominee. There were between fifty and sixty in attendance. I formed several new acquaintances. Had only two hours of sleep after reaching home, as I had to be better ready for school by nine. Have felt no bad effects from it; except lameness from the unusual exercise. And I'd stand that and more too, for just such another good time.

I wished this morning that I was at home with you today, my precious. I hope you had a nice Thanksgiving dinner from somewhere. It is not observed at all in the country, so every thing has gone just as usual, with me.

The weather is real cold; I am glad I do not have to go out to school. If it is cold when I come home, I don't know what I shall do for a wrap on the ears. Two weeks from Saturday I shall leave. Will get to Lumber City Saturday night, and home Sunday morning for breakfast. Or possibly there is a train that I can take and get to Macon some time Saturday night but I would prefer getting there in the morning.

How is Carrie Westcolt now? I feel as if I had not heard from you in a month; why don't you mail a letter or postal on Wednesday now? Stamps are scarce, perhaps. It quite gives me the night-mare to think of all I want to do when I get home before Christmas. And I know my money will come short of my wants.

Have not taken any horse-back rides lately; it has been too cold.

You have been having grand times in Macon I hear over the election, Fire-works, processions, etc.

Mrs. Audoin said she had mailed me some papers; I guess I will get them Friday.

Have not heard from you in so long have nothing to answer; so you will have to get along with a short letter this time.

With bushels of love from

Forest.

DAISY TO ANNA MARIA AKEHURST BARHAM

Macon Ga. May 17th 1886

Darling Auntie,

Your loving sympathetic letters are both received, one yesterday after I had come back to the lonely room, which seems *so empty, so desolate*; the second came this morning. After the change for the worse of which I wrote you on Wednesday, mama grew rapidly worse, and Friday afternoon and night it was as she said, "a continual fight for breath." She feared that the end would be painful, that she would suffocate, and prayed that she might pass away easily, and God mercifully granted that prayer. I think she was partially conscious until the last, though we kept her under the influence of an anodyne as much as possible. She never lay down, but sat in her chair until she left it forever. She asked for water, and took the glass in her own hand and drank; as I took it from her, her head drooped a little, as it always did when she slept, her breathing grew perfectly easy, but fainter and fainter, and while I pressed a last kiss on her forehead, she fell asleep.

Two of her best loved friends were with her, and dressed her for the last time. She was dressed in her black dress that she wore the last time she went out, her hair lay in waves on her forehead as it always did. Every line of suffering had passed from her face, and as I looked at her lying so peacefully, I could not think of my own utter loneliness. I could only think how sweetly she was resting after so many weary months of unrest and almost ceaseless pain. Nor can I realize it yet; I feel in a dream, I can only think it all over and over, until my brain refuses to think, and I sleep; only to wake and go over it again. I can not realize that she will not come back that never again will she kiss me Goodbye when I go out, or be here to welcome me when I come in, with such a loving glance; that *never* will I hear her tender voice call me her "baby" again. Oh Auntie I have so much to tell you of her, of her sweet patience, and cheerfulness, but I will wait until I can talk to you. You know we have no cemetery lot here; we have one in Oakland Cemetery in Atlanta, where Papa, Herbie and Lillie are resting; but of course it is utterly neglected for we have never been there since papa was laid there, and I could not bear the idea of taking mama there, and I knew she did not wish it, but I did not know what we should do. But everything was made straight a dear friend of ours Mrs. Audouin who has been kindness itself to us, offered a part of her lot, and know. . . .

MACON TELEGRAPH

Sunday, May 16, 1886.

Friends of Mrs. J. A. Lines and Miss Forest Daisy Lines are invited to attend the funeral of the former this (Sunday) morning at 9 o'clock at the residence of Mr. Hines, corner of Walnut and Spring Streets.[7]

Notes

INTRODUCTION

1. The information concerning Jennie's childhood and her family is gleaned from a lengthy, introspective meditation that she wrote in 1851. This essay dwells extensively and somewhat darkly upon her understanding of death.
2. Institutes were the primary vehicle for educational improvement in ante-bellum America. Henry Barnard, later first commissioner of education of the United States, began classes for teachers in Connecticut in the 1830s, well in advance of the normal school movement that would become the major instrument for teacher training after the Civil War. Jennie probably obtained most of her professional training in institutes of several weeks duration. For a full discussion of the importance of the institute in American educational history, see Paul H. Mattingly, "Educational Revivals in Ante-Bellum New England," *History of Education Quarterly* 11 (1971): 39–71.
3. For an explanation of the set of ideas defining woman's role in nineteenth-century America, see Barbara Welter, "The Cult of True Womanhood, 1820–1860," *American Quarterly* 18 (1966): 151–74.
4. Historians have increasingly turned from examination of the lives of individual women in the context of the frequently male-produced prescriptive literature to the more difficult examination of the actual circumstances of individual lives. For an exploration of this approach, see Mary Beth Norton, "The Paradox of Women's Sphere," in Carol Ruth Berkin and Mary Beth Norton, *Women of America: A History* (Boston: Houghton Mifflin Company, 1979), pp. 139–49. For an account of prevailing trends in the historiography of American women, see the introductory essay to the same volume, Norton and Berkin, "Women and American History," pp. 3–15.
5. Three recent articles on women's health in the nineteenth century are Ann Douglas Wood, "'The Fashionable Diseases': Women's Complaints and Their Treatment in Nineteenth-Century America," in Mary S. Hartman and Lois Banner, eds., *Clio's Consciousness Raised: New Perspectives on the History of Women* (New York: Harper and Row, 1974), pp. 1–22; Carroll Smith-Rosenberg, "Puberty to Menopause: The Cycle of Femininity in Nineteenth-Century America," in ibid., pp. 23–37; and Regina Morantz, "The Lady and Her Physician," in ibid., pp. 38–53.

6. For an exploration of the complexity and social significance of female friendships in nineteenth-century America, see Carroll Smith-Rosenberg's excellent article, "The Female World of Love and Ritual: Relations between Women in Nineteenth-Century America," in Nancy F. Cott and Elizabeth H. Pleck, eds., *A Heritage of Her Own: Toward a New Social History of American Women* (New York: Touchstone Books, 1979), pp. 311–42.

7. Jennie's experience was by no means unique. For a superb treatment of the individual experiences of some of Jennie's teaching contemporaries, see Geraldine J. Clifford, "Home and School in 19th Century America: Some Personal-History Reports from the United States," *History of Education Quarterly* 18 (1978): 3–34.

PART I. TEACHER IN NEW YORK, 1851–1856

1. Anna Maria Lines Akehurst, widow of Joseph Akehurst, Jennie's brother.

2. Oneida County, New York. Jennie spent most of her childhood in this town of 4,847 people (1850 census).

3. Chenango County, New York.

4. Chenango County, New York.

5. Jennie referred to her father, James Akehurst (b. 1798), and her stepmother, Mary Akehurst (b. 1810).

6. Probably the name of the plantation upon which Maria was teaching.

7. Ezra Akehurst, Jennie's brother, was confined to a mental asylum as a youth, possibly a victim of epilepsy.

8. Martha Stone Hubbell, *The Shady Side or Life in a Country Parsonage* (Boston: John P. Jewett, 1854).

9. Possibly from the nearby Hamilton Literary and Theological Institute, later Colgate University.

10. Edward Akehurst (b. 1849), Jennie's brother.

11. Ontario County, New York.

12. Martin Tupper (1810–89), poet-essayist.

13. Johann Peter Eckermann, *Conversations with Goethe in the Last Years of His Life*, translated by S. M. Fuller (Boston: Hillard Gray and Co., 1839).

14. Thomas Babington Macaulay (1800–1859), English historian.

15. American spiritualism with its emphasis upon the phenomena of the spirit world enjoyed substantial popularity in antebellum America. For a brief analysis, see Alice Felt Tyler, *Freedom's Ferment: Phases of American Social History from the Colonial Period to the Outbreak of the Civil War* (New York: Harper, 1962), pp. 78–85.

16. Probably Hannah O. C. Conant, *The Earnest Man: A Sketch of the Character and Labors of Adoniram Judson, First Missionary to Burmah* (Boston: Phillips, Sampson and Co., 1856).

17. Chenango County, New York.

18. Chenango County, New York.

19. Maria Susanna Cummins, *The Lamplighter, or An Orphan Girl's Struggles and Triumphs* (Cleveland: Jewett, Proctor and Worthington, 1854).

20. Hebrews 1:14.

PART II. TEACHER IN GEORGIA, 1857–1858

1. Preston Brooks (1819–57), South Carolina congressman, severely beat Charles Sumner (1811–74) on the floor of the Senate in 1856 during debate over the extension of slavery into the Kansas Territory.
2. William H. Seward (1801–72), United States senator, secretary of state.
3. Andrew Pickens Butler (1796–1857), United States senator from South Carolina, 1846–57.
4. James Buchanan (1791–1868), fifteenth president of the United States, 1857–61.
5. County seat of Bartow County, Georgia, approximately forty miles north of present-day Atlanta.
6. Bartow County, Georgia, approximately fifteen miles west of Cartersville.
7. Bartow County, Georgia, two miles south of Euharlee.
8. Sylvanus DeForrest Lines (1829–75?), cousin of Anna Maria Lines Akehurst.
9. Augustus Baldwin Longstreet, *Georgia Scenes* (Augusta: S. R. Sentinel Office, 1835).
10. Bartow County, Georgia, approximately ten miles north of Euharlee.
11. Cassville Female College.
12. Alexander Pope (1688–1744), English poet-essayist.
13. Probably in neighboring Chattooga County.
14. Georgia law permitted the public support of a few students in each county.
15. A nationwide financial panic in 1857 caused the failure of many banks that had issued negotiable currency.
16. Mrs. H. B. Welton, New York-born wife of a local architect.
17. John L. Rogers, first pastor of the Central Presbyterian Church.
18. G. P. Campbell, Atlanta dentist.
19. John E. DuBose, pastor of the First Presbyterian Church.
20. Theban general and statesman (418?–362 B.C.).
21. Jennie had applied for a position in the Atlanta Female College.
22. The Shelman plantation.
23. Sylvanus was staying with his mother and sister in New Haven.
24. Emory College, Oxford, Georgia, a Methodist institution, founded as the Georgia Conference Manual Labor School in 1834, chartered as a college in 1836.
25. The Southern Masonic Female College, founded in 1852.
26. Jennie had moved to the Sardis Church community in Walton County, twelve miles from Oxford.
27. Clarkesville, county seat of Habersham County, Georgia.
28. M. Creed Fulton, vice-president, 1854–59, president, 1859–60.
29. Psalms 146:4.
30. Jennie doubtless referred to Arminianism.
31. Morrisville, Madison County, New York.
32. In Fayette County, southwest of Atlanta.
33. Cyrus Field's transatlantic cable broke in 1858 and was not repaired until 1866.

34. Donati's Comet appeared over the United States in 1858, causing widespread fear and alarm.

PART III. TEACHING, COURTING, & MARRYING, 1859–1860

1. One of numerous travel volumes written by Taylor (1825–78), U.S. ambassador to Germany.
2. Octavia W. LeVert, *Souvenirs of Travel* (New York and Mobile: S. H. Goetzel and Co., 1857).
3. "Miss Muleck" [Dinah Marie Craik], *John Halifax, Gentleman* (New York: Harper Bros., 1856).
4. Edward George Bulwer-Lytton, *The Last Days of Pompeii* (1834).
5. County seat of Coweta County, Georgia, near the Alabama border.
6. Southwest of Atlanta in present-day Fulton County.
7. Probably Mrs. Caroline R. Gardener.
8. David Young, pharmacist, minister, furniture dealer, and staunch Unionist during the Civil War.
9. Possibly *Lena Leslie, or the History of an Orphan. Written for the board of Publication, by a Lady of Kentucky* (Philadelphia, 1857).
10. Atlanta's population was approximately 11,500.
11. Jennie's friend from Oxford, Mrs. Jennings.
12. Luther T. Glenn.
13. Thomas Reade Rootes Cobb (1823–62), politician, Civil War general.
14. Joseph E. Brown, governor, 1857–65.
15. Probably the Greenville Female Academy, in Meriwether County.
16. Sylvanus belonged to the Atlanta Typographical Union.
17. McNaught and Ormond, wholesale grocers and commission merchants in Atlanta.
18. Dimick, Wilson and Co., dealers in boots, leather, and shoes, Atlanta.
19. Alexander H. Stephens (1812–83), Georgia politician and vice-president of the Confederacy.
20. Honora Corbit, another New Yorker whom Jennie sought out.

PART IV. WARTIME, 1861–1865

1. Meriwether County, in western Georgia.
2. Coweta County, Georgia.
3. Like most of the transitory newspapers with which Sylvanus was associated, few copies have survived.
4. Maria was now matron of the Female Orphan Asylum in Columbus.
5. Anna Maria Akehurst Cady, Journal, October 24, 1864. Akehurst–Lines Collection, University of Georgia Libraries, Special Collections.
6. Forrest Daisy Lines, born August 7, 1864.

PART V. READJUSTMENT, 1865–1871

1. Sylvanus's mother, Amarilla Lines Beecher, who had remarried.
2. Possibly the periodical *Onward: The Woman's Home Journal.*

3. Herbert Lines was probably born in 1866. He died at about age three.
4. Near Hartford, Connecticut.

PART VI. DENOUEMENT, 1871–1886

1. A fashionable spa in Butts County, known widely for its sulfur springs.
2. Daisy was a visitor in Maria's Mobile home. Recently remarried after being widowed for a second time, she now signed her name M. L. Barham.
3. Caroline L. Hentz, *The Planter's Northern Bride* (Philadelphia: T. B. Peterson, 1851).
4. Daisy was now teaching in this Wilkinson County community.
5. Unincorporated "dead town," located in Jones County, about ten miles southeast of Gray.
6. In Tattnall County, ten miles southwest of Reidsville.
7. Jennie is buried in Macon, Georgia, apparently in an unmarked grave. Neither I nor the staff at the Macon Public Library were able to locate the grave or "Mrs. Audoin's Lot," in which Jennie was buried. No record exists at Oakland Cemetery, Atlanta, of Sylvanus's, Herbert's, and Lillie's graves, but they are probably buried on the same lot with Daisy, who died in 1912.

Index

INDEX